(Un)Certain

(Un)Certain

A collective memoir of deconstructing faith

Olivia Jackson

scm press

© Olivia Jackson 2023

Published in 2023 by SCM Press
Editorial office
3rd Floor, Invicta House,
108–114 Golden Lane,
London EC1Y 0TG, UK

www.scmpress.co.uk

SCM Press is an imprint of Hymns Ancient & Modern Ltd
(a registered charity)

Hymns Ancient & Modern® is a registered trademark of
Hymns Ancient & Modern Ltd
13A Hellesdon Park Road, Norwich,
Norfolk NR6 5DR, UK

Scripture extracts are taken from the New King James Version®.
Copyright © 1982 by Thomas Nelson. Used by permission.
All rights reserved.

British Library Cataloguing in Publication data
A catalogue record for this book is available
from the British Library

978-0-33-406363-6

Typeset by Regent Typesetting
Printed and bound in Great Britain by
CPI Group (UK) Ltd

Contents

Part 2: Stumbling Blocks

Part 3: Slippery Slope

To Annie: thank you for teaching me that the nice girls don't get the pearls.

Acknowledgements

The contents of this book are primarily based on the results of an in-depth online survey and follow-up interviews: this book could not have happened without the contribution of everyone who filled in the survey and was interviewed. I am grateful to each one of you, whether or not your name appears in the text. Additionally, the support of the Beloved Listeners and the Nomad Podcast hosts, in particular Tim and Joy, has been invaluable. Jojo and Penny spent many hours helping me to create the survey. MJ: thank you for allowing me to use the healing space you have created online to push this project forward.

The Dissident Daughter book group has been a life-giving place of connection and solace, and the Waterebels have provided sanity and distraction at much-needed moments. Tracey, Linzi and Caroline have listened to hours of my rants.

A huge thank you to my cousin, Richard, who believed in this from the start and has provided so much advice and encouragement. Also to Joanna, Annie F. and Naomi, who have been so supportive in the last few years. And to Wendy, Rose and Inky: thank you for being with me every step of the way, for listening, for providing so much input and inspiration and for making me laugh.

On Fire

I am a late-blooming 14-year-old on a week-long Christian summer camp. I am deeply shy, and this is my first introduction to the evangelical world. We're by the beach, and everyone includes me in the fun. The leaders are charismatic and sure of their faith. I've never sung modern worship songs before, never seen people cry or raise their arms as they sing. No one else seems bothered by this, so I go along with it all, swept up. By the end of the week, I have learned three things:

1 Jesus loves me and will fix my life.
2 But I'll go to hell if I don't get saved.
3 If I have sex before marriage, I will be impure and no one will marry me.

I am 18, working in Australia after leaving school. I spend a few days with a veterinarian as he travels from one farm to another. As we drive through miles of parched, brown earth I look at the dried-up trees beside the road. Yesterday I had cut branches so the sheep could eat leaves, because there is so little grass left. The vet tells me that the land is getting drier as the climate grows hotter.

'What d'you reckon?' he asks. 'When's it going to rain?'

I take a deep breath and send up an 'arrow prayer'. This is my chance to be bold for the Lord: 'I think this is God's judgement on Australia. If Australia would turn to Jesus, then God would send rain again.'

There is silence from the veterinarian. I spend the rest of the afternoon helping pregnancy test cows, which involves armpit-length gloves.

I am 23 when, out of nowhere, I am convinced God wants me to go to South Africa and join an international youth mission organization. It's only meant to be for six months, but it becomes ten years and defines my career and my life for far longer than that.

I am 40, and too many things I've been taught are not working in the real world. Reading outside the narrow field of approved evangelical writers has made me reassess gender roles, hell, and whether same-sex relationships really are sinful. I have been told that I am a liberal and a heretic.

I study New Testament Greek, and 'the Bible clearly says' crumbles irrevocably.

When you start dipping your toe into deconstruction, you're not just deconstructing one aspect of your life. You are deconstructing the core values of who you are as a person, and that's a very profound and significant thing. (Ed, UK)

For me, deconstruction fits in a larger spectrum: we're deconstructing history. We're deconstructing what truth is and how truth gets made. We're deconstructing authority. Faith deconstruction fits into that context. A lot of people are noticing that there's not a simple right and wrong: there's a spectrum. There are no easy binaries in anything that's meaningful. Complexity is not an easy message, and conservative churches love an easy message because that works. (Vivian, Netherlands)

I think of deconstruction not as loss or even as evolution of belief, but as a shedding of extra baggage. All these non-negotiable add-ons – evangelicalism, reading the Bible in a particular way, conservative politics – all those had been made as part of the package deal. I grew up on C. S. Lewis, and I often think about Eustace trying to scrape off the dragon skin. (Traynor, USA)

This book is a blend of many voices. While it is made up of courageous individuals who have told their stories, it is not only about individuals or isolated incidences. It's about patterns, a movement, a reach toward solidarity and community. Through an anonymous online questionnaire, completed nearly 400 times, and 140 follow-up interviews, I have tried to bring together the stories of ordinary, committed people whose Christian faith has undergone a profound shift, an unravelling, an expansion. Where they have landed – for now – is a reflection of the diversity of their stories. A few have stayed, many have found a freer expression of spirituality in or out of church, some have walked away from faith completely. Some have become ministers or pagans or atheists or theologians. While the road is often hard, we are overwhelmingly enjoying the freedom of uncertainty, of living with authenticity and curiosity.

We range in age from 18 to 77, with the majority between 25 and 50. 59% are women, 39% men and 2% non-binary or gender-fluid. We are spread across the globe: while just over half are from the UK and 30% from the USA, 6% are Australian, 4% Canadian, with others from or in Bosnia and Herzegovina, China, Costa Rica, Denmark, Finland, India, Ireland, Mexico, Netherlands, New Zealand, Nigeria, Norway, Puerto

Rico, Sweden and Thailand. Over 70% have spent more than 25 years in church, and 80% have either left altogether or moved to a very different kind of church. One pattern was clear: we are overwhelmingly, although not entirely, white, and of those who are not, all had experienced racism and ethnocentrism in majority-white faith contexts.

Like all those I interviewed and surveyed, I was utterly committed to a very particular form of Christian faith. The majority of us fell into some category of evangelical, be that charismatic or conservative, with a scattering of others, such as a couple of Seventh Day Adventists and a former Catholic nun, as wildcards. This demographic pattern of white evangelicalism in decline is reflected in deconstruction spaces online and in (USA-based) research by the Public Religion Research Institute (Blake, 2021). Many of the same reasons for deconstruction also applied to those who did not identify as evangelical. For most of this book, then, I shall refer to evangelicals, and use the term in a broad sense, while I am aware that not all of us are or were evangelicals, and not all evangelicals recognize some of the paradigms or experiences described.

Evangelicalism is described in various ways, depending on who you ask, and the evangelical churches have become, as a group, defined by far more than theology or denomination: evangelicalism is a culture with its own language, music and celebrities; an industry with its own merch; an all-encompassing way of life. Amanda (USA), a pastor, puts it this way:

> Evangelicalism within the historic Church is so young, and it's not necessarily a theology. It's just a cultural iteration of the Church. When you actually start digging in and thinking about 'what do I think about God, what do I think about deeper questions?', you realize there's this major disconnect between the culture which is evangelicalism and deep theology, thoughtful theology. So those who are deconstructing are people who take our faith very seriously, not because we don't take our faith seriously.

When I asked in the survey about the impact faith had had on people's lives prior to deconstruction, the answers were consistently things like, 'It was everything'; 'Strong sense of personal identity as a born-again Christian'; 'A daily cycle of either feeling wonderful and close to God or guilty that I didn't feel that way'; 'Everything was ordained to happen by God, everything mattered on a spiritual level, everything was about doing right by God.' The permeation of faith into all areas of life is clear when people described their life patterns: 'Quiet times every morning, home-schooling my kids, it was the reason I lived, the reason I stayed married to an abusive man. It was my everything'; 'My faith dictated everything about the way I lived: the clothing I wore, the people I associated with, the media I consumed, the language I did or didn't use' and, 'Huge impact in the way I understood myself, my body, the role I should play, the way I should act and interact with others. The faith I was embedded in influenced everything.'

The numbers bear it out too: 60% grew up in Christian families; 46% previously worked for a church, Christian organization or mission agency and 18% still do, including several ministers/pastors; 61% participated in short-term missions and 15% long-term overseas missions. People spoke of experiencing close community and happy memories of church, but also of shame and ostracism and an ongoing fear of hell and rapture; a space in which no questions or deviations from a narrow theology were permitted.

> I remember the pastor using the word 'deconstruct': 'You can't just deconstruct truth or the Bible or tradition.' It sent a very hostile message towards anyone who was trying to think critically or ask those kinds of questions about things, so that was the point where I was like, 'I don't feel welcome here anymore.' It feels like they're very hunkered down in their beliefs, and that's why a lot of people are ready to shift out of that, I think. (Elena, USA)

Contrary to the accusations thrown at us, none of us deconstructed our faith because we just wanted to sin (usually sexually) or because it's cool (Butler, 2021). We are accused of being bitter and reminded that no church is perfect, dismissing the fact that many people have been badly mistreated. Or we are told that we – the ones who sacrificed relationships, health, careers, financial security and bodily autonomy to serve God; the ones who were ordained or spent years in overseas mission; the ones who risked belonging, community and identity when we left our church – were 'never really saved'. We were the good church kids who prayed and read our Bibles: the ones 'on fire for the Lord'. We stayed sexually 'pure' or denied our sexuality altogether. We submitted to leadership (and sometimes spouses too). We evangelized our friends, even when it was awkward, and had nightmares about them going to hell. Perhaps because of that very sincerity, eventually our questions just couldn't go unasked anymore, or harm done by churches became unbearable. The unreachable standards, cognitive dissonance or performative faith were no longer viable.

The negativity of many churches and evangelical organizations towards deconstruction seems to come from a place of feeling threatened as much as a concern for our salvation. It's as though to change our minds is automatically heretical, and what we first believed can be the only truth; as though no learning or human development were permissible and are certainly not a sign of faith or authenticity. Elise (UK) is an Anglican priest:

> The Church is really worried about how it's going to sustain itself into the future, so there is an anxious institutional dynamic. There's an 'institution that isn't safe and can't be trusted' dynamic. There's the complete public change in opinion around Black Lives Matter and sexuality and everything relating to that, and I feel like that is a God-shaking. I'm really comfortable with a God who progressively develops theology as human experience and understanding grows. I think that's what scripture shows, I think that's what culture shows. What the dickens was the Reformation, if not something along those lines?

Elise, who remains in ministry, is also an example of how deconstruction doesn't necessarily lead to the 'slippery slope' and complete loss of faith. Many reported a more vibrant faith now than before. Others cling on by their fingernails, like Harry (UK), who experienced such church abuse it led to a breakdown:

> My life would be so much easier and less complicated if I just packed up the Christian box and gave it back to Jesus and was like, 'There you go mate. Didn't work out, you know, stay in touch, but whatever, bye.' But I don't want to, because I feel like I have seen too much of the way, the truth and the life, so to speak.

Still others do go in different directions. Ellen (USA) is exploring Christian witchcraft, and Gordon (UK) has his own YouTube channel, *Bible Reading Atheist*: 'Since I retired, I've done over 140 atheist videos.' Most people fall somewhere in the vast space between.

The reasons we deconstruct are expressed in individual ways, but form broad patterns, regardless of geographical location. Some begin by deconstructing church, and others with theology that excludes, doesn't add up or doesn't reflect the loving, just God they thought they followed. Either way, most of us eventually deconstruct both church and theology to some extent, and share a sense that faith has expanded well beyond what we would once have recognized:

> Such a teeny-weeny God we worshipped. And when you come out, you go, 'Oh no, there's so much, there's so much!' I think everyone should

leave church and find God. I think we would all be a bunch better if we stopped putting rules on God and find out who this divine entity is. (Veneda, USA)

When you remove the rules, the edges of faith get fuzzier and old certainties crumble. I remember talking to a group of people who were discussing how completely certain they were of what they believed, and it struck me that that isn't faith: in fact, certainty might be the antithesis of faith. Steve A. (UK) feels the same: 'I've gradually moved from certainty to uncertain, which feels more like faith, actually. I wouldn't have said before I had any faith. It was all certain belief.' Greg (USA) takes it a step further: 'It almost becomes an idol, the certainty: I don't need God, I need my certainty.'

Alan Watts, the late writer and 'philosophical entertainer' as he called himself (and one-time Episcopalian priest), distinguished between the two:

The believer will open his mind to the truth on the condition that it fits in with his preconceived ideas and wishes. Faith, on the other hand, is an unreserved opening of the mind to the truth, whatever it may turn out to be. Faith has no preconceptions; it is a plunge into the unknown. Belief clings, but faith lets go. (Watts, 2012, p. 24)

That speaks not of certainty, blind acceptance or ignoring critical thinking, but of agency and engagement. While deconstruction is a buzzword, for those of us going through it, it is an overturning of decades of identity, belief, belonging, language, culture, meta-narrative. Some find it a gentle, natural process, but most have tangles and trauma to work through while simultaneously finding freedom and authenticity. You can't go back but you don't necessarily know how to be in the new place.

'Deconstruction' isn't everyone's chosen word to use about their own process or experience. However, it is the word most used at the moment, so, much as I also dislike it at times, it is the word I will use for this book. I define faith deconstruction as an intentional examination of one's core faith and beliefs, leading to a profound change in, or even loss of, that faith. I see it as a gradient colour wheel, with those deconstructing represented in every shade, and no right or wrong place to be on the wheel, no right or wrong way to deconstruct or place to land. It's too easy to replicate a fundamentalist mindset (having had one for far too long) and to claim that someone is not deconstructed enough or has gone too far, but most of us have had enough of black and white, in and out, them and us, and, if nothing else, our deconstruction has brought us to a broader place of inclusion and respect for others' journeys. So, regardless of terminology, this is a book about what happens when the certainties – about church, about leaders, about faith – start to crumble, and what happens when the crumbled pieces end up in unexpected places.

* * *

The earliest record I can find of my house is from a census in the 1790s. It's an old farmhouse on the side of a hill, exposed to frequent high wind, snow, rain. It was built directly onto the rock beneath, with no deep foundations. Over the centuries, people have changed it to fit their needs – bits added, the staircase moved. The cow barn and hayloft were changed into a garage and bedroom, and the garden is a section of field which someone put some fencing around, although wild rabbits, and sometimes sheep, appear not to notice the division. When my neighbour's grandparents lived here, they pulled off some brickwork to discover a huge fireplace. The outside of the house was once painted, but that was removed 30 years ago, changing the appearance of the house completely. Its name reflects the original colour but is left meaningless since the house was stripped back to the stone.

Since I moved in, renovations have been necessary, and once you start in a house like this, you never know what you'll find. There were patches of damp, and the 20-year-old boiler was inefficient. The roof leaked and changed angles halfway down, where someone had started tiling, realized they weren't in line to meet the ridge, and altered their course. The chimney was sitting on plyboard – a miracle it hadn't come off in a high wind. The builders found that what was supposed to be lead flashing was, in fact, the side of an old washing machine. The foreman gave his verdict: 'It's a fucking mess.'

It's like faith, though. Over time, the use has changed entirely, several times. Different 'owners' have added or moved things to suit their own purpose. Toxic substances were seen as harmless and useful when installed. Some parts have stood firm over time, others have deteriorated or are no longer relevant to today, despite our attempts to make them work. When you start chipping off one patch of flaky theology, a whole lot more crumbles too. Occasionally something amazing from the past is uncovered. Many years from now, perhaps only a few foundation stones will remain.

Saying something is just done to suit modern sensitivities or cultural norms doesn't really work: we now know that living in a damp home is bad for our health and that asbestos is toxic. We can't use our homes or our spirituality as our ancestors did.

Allowing unqualified people to fix things according to their own ideas results in more damage and expense further down the line. Even qualified people can get it wrong: a workman recently tried drilling through the thick, stone walls, bending the metre-long drill bit and cracking a window. But he told me immediately and had the damage repaired, rather than blaming someone else, denying that anything was wrong or trying to cover it up.

And so with the Church and the faith we unpack: it's a fucking mess.[1]

* * *

A note on names: I have given contributors' full names only if I quote their academic or professional work. Where two people from the same country have the same first name, I have labelled them alphabetically – Tom A., Tom B. – rather than use their real last name. The questionnaire was anonymous unless participants voluntarily left names. For those I interviewed I offered pseudonyms. Some were keen to take this up, like Louisa (UK), who told me, 'Yes, please, I would definitely like to be anonymous, which shows how you feel there's the possibility of being shamed, doesn't it?'

Others, such as Jude (Australia), wanted their real names used: 'There's the redemptive power of being allowed to use our voices, and where I am in my story right now, I'd like to stand alongside my own story. There's been a silencing.'

The italicized words at the start of chapters and sections are my own experiences. Other people's experiences and reflections are attributed by name and country. Where contributors are bi-national, I have stated this to give cultural context. As far as possible, I have left people's words as they said or wrote them, only amending for clarity or brevity. I hope I have done justice to each brave contribution.

This book is intended to raise the voices of those of us who deconstruct and find ourselves isolated, anxious, dismissed or silenced, and to be a source of solidarity for those who question or walk down this path. We deconstruct one by one, often feeling profoundly alone. But we are finding one another and building new communities, creating new ways to flourish.

---

1 With thanks to Emily John Garcés for the house analogy inspiration.

PART I

Money, Sex and Power

It's Not a Religion: It's a Relationship

I am 24, standing in the auditorium of a large church. The music is loud and the preacher louder. He shouts down the microphone, exhorting God to pour the Spirit upon us. People are crying and falling and jumping. Stories have been circulating for weeks about healings, about gold dust and feathers falling from the sky, about teeth turning to gold. I feel uncomfortable, like it's all getting a little or a lot hyped up, and anyway what is God doing sprinkling feathers when there are hungry, suffering people in the world and in this church? I tell myself to have more faith. Suddenly, my friend holds her hands out: 'I have gold dust on my hands!' Sure enough, her palms are sparkling. We stare, astonished, for a few moments.

Something nudges at the back of my mind. 'Didn't you … put on bronzing powder before we came out this evening?' It dawns on us what her 'gold dust' is, and we begin to cry with laughter every bit as hard as those Spirit-filled folk around us.

I am around 30, living overseas while working for a missions organiza-tion. Things are not good, and what would later be diagnosed as PTSD is making them worse. I speak to someone in senior leadership about it. She looks at me intensely before asking, 'Is there sin in your life?'

I am in my early 40s when I read through a checklist for coercive control: love-bombing; gaslighting; isolation and monitoring; financial abuse; increasing rules; threats; erosion of the victim's sense of self and their autonomy. The article says a high percentage of victims do not realize that they are being manipulated and controlled. It reads like a checklist of some of the evangelical spaces I have spent the past few decades within.

The church gave me huge meaning: we were trying to transform the world. What a huge thing that is. (Hanna, Germany/UK)

When I was in my sophomore year, my mother died very unexpectedly, and I was an only child. So, the church really became my emotional

3

support. 500 miles away from home, and they were my family. (Crystal, USA/Ireland)

I don't think there was any malice in anyone I ever met. But it's just not what it promises to be, and it's hard to see that while you're trying to make it be that thing. (Scott, UK)

If only it were as simple as 'I believe Jesus died on the cross and rose again and he loves me.' If it were that simple, I could just say, 'OK, fine, go believe that, it's all good.' But no. It has tentacles that go far-reaching. (Kirsten, USA)

You're looking for family: you've found the family business. (George, Australia/UK)

Church can be so many things: structure, stability and belonging alongside restriction, control and fear. Often it is a place of happy childhoods until you start asking awkward questions or act with a little autonomy, the way we do as we become healthy adults. If I could create a word cloud of people's church experiences, the largest words would be things like 'community', 'purpose' and 'friendship' nestled right in with 'pressure', 'shame' and 'believe the right things'. On the survey, participants could check multiple options for what attracted them to church: 70% stated the sense of belonging and community; 59% the friendliness and kindness of members.[1] Yet 24% reported leaving because they or others were abused or exploited, and an anonymous participant spoke for others when they wrote, 'The first trigger to deconstruction was when I realized that the most judgemental people I knew were all at church, and I was having to modify so much of my behaviour around them as a result.' Like untangling a ball of wool, every time you pull at one string more start to unravel.

Church and missions were where I found lasting friendships. Church provided a cohesive social world when I first moved to London at 18, and it exposed me to a broader social group than I was used to. It was where I first engaged with social activism. Churches can make a real difference to the communities around them, and many people I interviewed spoke of a genuine desire to serve not just their church but those less privileged than them (and not just for the purposes of evangelism). In emergency

---

1 Other reasons included: 43% style of worship; 35% church beliefs and teaching; 33% search for faith and meaning; 23% religious experience at the church; 21% personal qualities of the leader.

situations, churches are embedded in civil society and can organize quickly: as I am writing this, a friend texts to let me know of churches in Ukraine which have converted themselves into housing units for those fleeing their homes, and I am aware of churches in this country which have spent years finding housing for refugees from all over the world.

As a framework for life, church is a positive experience for many people:

> There was so much stability that I found, so many answers to the questions of what am I doing and why am I here, how can I make a difference? It provided me with people who I was told and believed would love me and support me unconditionally, and it did sincerely feel like that for a while. (Austin, USA)

Katya (UK) has experienced the harmful aspects of church intrusion into family life, but also tells me,

> When I had my babies, I got really ill with postnatal depression. At the time, the community was very helpful and there were some amazing things that happened because of the values that the community espoused. There was a lot of really positive, practical things that people did which derive from those Christian values, which I'm enormously grateful for, and some genuine friendships were forged there.

As with so much in this book, there's the caveat of 'not all churches, not all Christians, not all pastors'. A few people I interviewed had not experienced hurt from churches and had felt very little pressure to believe or behave in particular ways. Their deconstruction tended to be a gentler experience, and mostly theological rather than church-triggered. But people don't deconstruct church because it's been overwhelmingly positive for them, and as this book follows deconstruction stories, I will necessarily focus on the negative aspects, while acknowledging that there are positives mixed in.

Plenty of people, upon expressing problems with church, hear the 'no church is perfect' line. Well, no, but some are so far from perfect as to be toxic, while demanding total commitment and near-perfection from members, immersion in church activities, rigid adherence to belief and behaviour at the expense of individual exploration, authoritarian leadership which ultimately puts doctrine above compassion and diversity. 86% of survey respondents said they had experienced pressure to conform to certain beliefs or activities; 63% to codes of dress or behaviour and over 34% to participate in prescribed accountability practices. The boundaries of evangelicalism are strictly enforced, each adherent trained to be a gatekeeper. Anyone who doesn't quite measure up – other Christians, for instance – is deemed 'not a real Christian', and anyone who intentionally steps outside the boundaries is backslidden, liberal, on the slippery slope. Those who go so far as to leave are beyond the pale. I have been on the giving and receiving end of those accusations, and I remember the genuine concern I had for people when they got a bit sinful or a bit liberal (often conflated), as though their 'sin' was my business.

Much of it is well-intentioned people, misguided or acting well beyond their competence, training or responsibility, or simply acting within the framework that church culture and teaching has given them. Underlying that culture and teaching, however, are too often shame, fear and dynamics of power and control. There is a constant policing of sin and adherence to a narrow, 'correct' theology combined with exhortations to be 'all-out for Jesus' and be part of what God is doing in the world; the othering and the insistence that you can only trust people who believe the same as you, and that they want the best for you more than others do (even if those others are your own, 'unsaved' family). For all the talk about freedom in Christ, it can be easy to feel like the opposite is true in evangelical spaces.

Then there are the claims of unconditional love, community and church family, but also constant reminders that acceptance is, in fact, conditional upon correct beliefs and behaviours: the invitation to 'come as you are' includes the caveat of 'but leave parts of yourself behind'. Many people spoke about facing pressure or even ostracism when they began to ask questions. Some said that as soon as they left, church members they had been close to for years or decades never spoke to them again.

Evangelicalism wouldn't be evangelicalism without the added extras that make up the behemoth of evangelical culture. There are the books, the music and its megastars, the homewares, wristbands and t-shirts. There's the jargon and coded phrases: you'll have your own favourites. Mine are things like 'I'm only telling you this so you can pray about it' ('here's some juicy gossip'); 'speaking the truth in love' (often a cover for cruelty or judgement) and 'he's very anointed' ('he claims God works through him – it is usually a "him" – and therefore cannot be questioned').

There are the weird practices: the foot washing in cultures where it isn't necessary or appropriate, and when there would have been more useful and less performative ways to help someone or model humility. The cultural appropriations: someone would pull out a shofar and start blasting it in the middle of a worship service, far removed from its purpose and meaning in Jewish tradition (and usually used as a display of Christian Zionist sentiments). Why God would act because of that always baffled me, although I can see why demons might flee: I used to take earplugs to worship. I think it was in the same category as the 'prophetic acts' (symbolic actions taken to release the power of God into a situation) such as 'crossing the Jordan', where the same tired piece of blue fabric would be laid out on the floor again, while we each stepped or jumped over it to claim whatever it was that time in the name of Jesus.

Breakthrough

Amber (UK) did a church gap year project when she was 18 and continued working there during university and beyond. Her story illustrates the damage that can be done by multiple Christian institutions and workplaces combining toxic theology, high-demand systems and leadership out of their depth. It is told more fully here as it touches on so much of what Part 1 covers.

The teaching was frightening, and I just internalized all of it. I went with my heart wide open, like, 'I need God', and so I gave everything I had to it. I'm very gifted, I'm a natural leader and high intelligence, all the things that they like, so I was hugely invested in as a leader and given a lot of responsibility as an 18-year-old who was actually just trying to recover from something quite traumatic and find God. But there was no healing, even though they said a lot about healing. There was just a lot of expectation of the kind of person that pleases God, and so my real self just got buried, and a false self emerged as super-Christian Amber, so I was running an inner-city youth project by 19 and facing really tough situations like dealing with gangs, with no pastoral support whatsoever.

I had no time for socializing, no friends outside of the church and got engaged at 20, kind of because we weren't able to live together or have sex before we were married. My husband started to get into all this charismatic and prophetic stuff. He's the most wonderful man I've ever met, but he's very black and white. So, everything was either 'God says' or 'God doesn't say', right down to what we had for lunch. He was like, 'God says we need to get married', and I was like, 'But I don't feel safe.' In the end I submitted and we got married.

We were so young, and we had no support in our marriage. All our leaders were like, 'Oh yeah, you two should definitely get married. You're such a gifted ministry couple, God's going to use you greatly for the kingdom, whatever.'

We went to Africa on a mission trip and it was terrifying, a terribly run organization. We were surrounded by missionaries in absolute burnout. I was 19 and holding dying babies and being given no grid except worship to deal with it. Then I got amoebic dysentery and the organization refused to take me to hospital for days. It took me a long time to bounce back, and I started to get such high anxiety that I couldn't keep food down, and I developed a life-controlling eating disorder.

I went to three of my leaders during this time. I told them, 'I'm not well, I don't know what's going on, I'm really scared.' And they were like, 'Amber, your ministry's doing amazing, you're such a great leader, you're doing fine. Let's pray for you, you're just having a bit of a wobble.' I'd lost two and a half stone in six months. So there I was, married and running the youth project, aced my degree and won a prize for my dissertation, you know, classic overachiever.

It was getting scary in my marriage as well. My husband was freaking out because he thought he'd lost me. He felt like it was his responsibility to fix everything. It saddens him greatly to look back now, but at the time, he was just scared of displeasing God. Combine that with this belief of God saying stuff was right and wrong, and it was toxic. I wanted to do a master's, he said God didn't think that was right: 'No master's, God wants us to go to Bethel [Church, in California].' I didn't want to take his name, but he said, 'There's spiritual stuff in your family we need to leave behind. You need to take my name.'

Then we went to Bethel. I was eating disordered, completely disconnected from my own sense of self and clinging on to this idea of God with all I knew how. I saw it as my fault I wasn't healed: to be ill at Bethel is one of the worst things you can go through.

At Bethel, there is a huge emphasis verbally on vulnerability. Three weeks in we all went away on this weekend. We were going to 'smash shame in the face'. And so all of us, one by one, are going to stand up and say the thing that we think would disqualify us from God's love. In a group of 70 people it took 13 hours.

There was lots of confession. It was frightening. Not only were you watching people get up and be completely re-traumatized by saying stuff like, 'I was sexually abused as a child and I never told anyone', or 'I think I might be gay', and then getting it prayed off them and people cheering and praying in tongues. Because that's the healthy way to deal with vulnerability, right? The worst part was they said, 'Tomorrow you're going to experience what's called a vulnerability hangover and the devil's going to come to you and he's going to try and lie to you and say what you did wasn't safe. But you need to remember that we love you and you are safe here, we're your tribe, so you just resist those lies of the devil. He wants to isolate you and draw you away.' So, you'd just bared your soul and then you think that your core intuitive bit that was telling you that that wasn't safe, is, of course, demonic.

I struggled with how we were all expected to think and believe the same. On a very deep level that contradicted a big part of who I am. It was fascinating to watch. At the beginning, everybody came with their own clothes from all over the world. By the end of the year everyone was wearing the same thing: black, grey, keys around their necks, slouchy beanies.

We had these hour-long slots of worship every day in a dark room with 1,200 people and it was deafening and scary. I would just leave; I couldn't stay, I would go and walk, and that was where I found God. There was this river trail that ran along the Sacramento, it was stunningly beautiful, and there are mountains in the distance.

The couple who used to lead our church had planted a new church. We came back from Bethel and immediately became their student workers, unpaid, and I got a zero-hour contract job to try and keep us afloat. I eventually got a slightly better job at a Christian company. I should have smelled the whatever right at the beginning when they said, 'We'd love to have a woman's touch around the office.' I signed the contract and then they phoned me retrospectively and were like, 'We're taking two grand off the salary and adding some things to your job description.' They added emptying the bins, doing cup of tea runs, keeping the place clean. It was really misogynist. It was as cultish as the church.

We were expected by the church to take annual leave from the job that was paying me to do stuff at church. We were working all evenings, and we didn't have a car either, so I'd regularly walk four miles to work then four miles to church and four miles home. It was just exhausting. That carried on for years.

In 2018, finally, I said enough was enough and I kicked the eating disorder. Something rose up from within me, something of myself, and I found the strength to start eating and fighting for my life in a way that I never had before. Recovering from an eating disorder is brutal. All the physical pain of everything you've done to your body hits you at that point, as well as all the emotions you've numbed for however long. But the church were like, 'Oh wow, Amber's been healed', and had me up on stage doing testimony of my healing. I tried to say, 'But I'm not actually healed yet. This is just the beginning of my journey.' But I was cut off, on stage, as I'm vulnerably sharing. I wasn't allowed to call it an eating disorder.

I began to get PTSD during the final year at church. I didn't know what was happening to me. I had already had a lot of very damaging prayer ministry by this point, but this was another level. All the trauma started to surface, but the woman praying for me has her own history of sexual abuse and was like, 'You were definitely sexually abused as a child.' I was like, 'I don't remember anything', and she was like, 'No, you've repressed the memories.' So I was doubting my own memories. She was like, 'It could have been your own father.' My dad was the one vaguely stable person in my childhood.

Of course, I believed them, but then I became completely unstable. I couldn't do my job, so the minister's wife was like, 'Amber, we need to take authority over this in Jesus' name and we need to bind it and then we'll deal with it at a better time.' She prayed over me, bound it in Jesus name, and then was like, 'OK, you can go and do your work now.' I was having panic attacks and running into the toilet, dissociating, having a meltdown, beginning to tear at my skin, and then putting myself together and going back on stage, running morning prayers. Underneath, I was just disintegrating but I had nowhere to go. In the end, lockdown happened and that was incredible because everything went online and I didn't have to be in the building.

Amber left the church during lockdown. After hitting rock bottom in their marriage and spending time apart, she and her husband both entered therapy and were able to start rebuilding their lives together, without the church, and with healthier models of healing and support. She describes breakthrough theology as a 'product' sold by churches:

When I started to get my mind back, that was when questions started to crystallize about all the healing doctrine.

One of the women I worked with, for example, had had her hand nailed to the wall by one of her boyfriends, so she couldn't do Jesus or the cross. So what does that mean for her salvation? Does it mean she can't be saved? I encountered so much of God and the divine in the eyes of these women and I've seen so much beauty there, but there's no grid for what I'm seeing. This just feels too narrow. I began to question all of the theology around healing, transformation, breakthrough, and the thing that got me out was this rejection of breakthrough theology that had caused my own huge level of shame because I didn't have that breakthrough in my own life.

I've seen dysfunction in my leaders. I've seen the misogyny, I've seen all of it, and yet I was so divided from my sense of self that I just buried all of that and kept myself safe by playing by the rules and doubting myself. It was easier to doubt myself than to doubt God. Everything I saw, I just brushed aside and ignored and then developed an eating disorder to cope, basically.

I wish I could say that Amber's story is an isolated extreme, but it isn't. There were plenty of people who had received similar teaching and treatment from Christian organizations and churches. I certainly remember hours-long sessions of 'openness and brokenness' on mission training courses, with people 'confessing' not just their own perceived sin, but also abuses against them in the same broad category. High-demand systems are standard in much of evangelicalism.

All or Nothing

It was just all hands on deck, super-intense: church growth, evangelizing, doing events. It felt like church was the most important thing in life that came before everything. (Nina, UK)

People talk about grace, but it never won. Grace would never win above all the things that you were meant to do. (Sue, UK)

This cohesive world that evangelicalism creates skirts very close to what sociologists refer to as a 'total institution' (even more so for those who work for their church or go into mission). Your whole life and worldview centres on church (or mission), with outside influences sometimes actively discouraged, or limited by sheer lack of time or energy: services, Bible studies, prayer groups, courses, friendships and volunteering all take place at church. It is inevitable, then, that this ends up influencing where you put your money, who you take advice from, who you date and marry, how you raise and educate your children and, particularly in the USA, how you vote. Holly (UK) explains, 'It's not just that you went to church on Sundays and save sex for marriage. It's literally building blocks, every aspect of life.' Her experience is mirrored by Andrew (Australia), who grew up Seventh Day Adventist:

My whole upbringing, I was very much immersed in an Adventist subculture. It was pretty much a wraparound Adventist experience. The end result is that, without really meaning to, a lot of Adventists exist within their own little bubble. It's pretty much self-sufficient for identity and meaning and worldview.

Over 74% of survey respondents reported feeling pressure from churches to give more time, money or skills than they felt comfortable giving. Scott (UK) talks about other groups he's joined since:

We realized just how accepting those groups were, and it was very clear to us the contrast between them and our experience with churches, which was that churches suck you in more and more all the time.

It doesn't necessarily work for the best for those involved, especially if they grew up in church. Kay (UK) describes her education:

> The church I went to didn't really allow us to have any contact with anyone outside of the church. So we had our own school, but they were limited to the people within the church who were teachers, so some of the basic subjects weren't taught. I've done alright, I've gone on and managed to get a master's degree, but I still struggle with basics like maths and spelling because I just didn't have the education.

Ruth (USA) recently looked back over her home school curriculum and assignments:

> Some of them said, 'Read this book about evolution so that you can refute it with a Christian point of view.' Most of the curriculum teaches from a Christian perspective of white people: I didn't learn about indigenous or African American history.

I spoke to a number of people who had parents or a spouse in ministry. Katya (UK) tells me what it feels like to marry into the church:

> The whole parish ministry is deeply rooted in sacrificing the wife and family to the needs of a very needy, vulnerable and anxious community, and setting them up as figures that people can project their fantasies onto so that they can then destroy them and scapegoat them, frankly. I've seen it over and over again in my own life and with other clergy families. Part of my resistance is to say, 'You will not see me, you will not see my children. We are not here for your entertainment or for your speculation.' But then you're living in a house that is paid for and decorated by the parish. It's very, very stressful. There's a limit to how much we can tolerate in terms of the living in the goldfish bowl.

Even for ordinary church members, the pressure on parents to raise 'good Christian children' is there, alongside questionable parenting theories. I have heard more than one person say that a small child is crying because of their 'sin nature' and both misquoting and misinterpreting Proverbs 13.24 by saying 'spare the rod and spoil the child' (hint: a shepherd uses a 'rod' to guide sheep, not hit them). Abi (USA) recalls: 'Some of the literature was like, "trick your kids into disobeying so that you can train them not to". It's some real dark shit.' She and others mention *To Train up a Child* by Michael and Debi Pearl. The book recommends withholding food as punishment; pulling a baby's hair; using a willow switch or weed eater (garden strimmer) cord on the bare skin of children as young as four months. A mother is to hit her child if he 'whines' for her (quoted in Linda, 2010). The book is implicated in the deaths of three children (Lewis, 2013).

Within the evangelical bubble, everything needs to be run past God (or at least leadership, which sometimes amounts to the same thing). From what you eat:

When I joined the church, I was 19 and a vegetarian. Some people in church were like, 'have you prayed about that?' (Isabel, UK)

to who you love:

Then my wife: was I going to marry her? I basically just wanted God to tell me what to do, because that's what God is for, isn't he, that you just obey? (Lucas, UK)

to what you create:

I look back and think, 'Oh, you sad puppy.' I wrote all these really intense evangelistic songs. We set up a band and I only ever allowed us to play if it was an evangelistic event. Literally, we didn't practise. (Aidan, UK)

Pressed Down and Shaken Together

They wanted people to do this tithe test card, which was linked to physical healing. There was a guy who'd been diagnosed with MS in his 20s, and the leaders stood up in the front of church and said, 'People aren't getting healed because people are withholding their generosity from the body.' I just remember being enraged. (Elise, UK)

While there was a low-key offering in the Church of England church I first attended, one of my biggest shocks when I started going to other churches was the constant emphasis on money. I'm all for generosity, but the regular sermonettes that insisted that 'God loves a cheerful giver' (snatched from 2 Corinthians 9.7, NKJV) began to grate, and I was often not cheerful, even when told that God blesses the giver more than the receiver. The fact that the tithe – baseline 10% of earnings – always had to go to the church or other Christians, and always had to be paid, regardless of the giver's own need, just felt wrong. If only I'd discovered Deuteronomy 14.26: 'spend that money for whatever your heart desires: for oxen or sheep, for wine or similar drink' (NKJV), I'd have a herd of oxen by now.

Lynn (Canada/Ireland) recalls, 'the culture around tithing, the pressure in that. There was status in how much you tithed, and then above and beyond in the freewill offering.'

As someone who lived on 'mission support' for ten years, I experienced the sacrificial generosity of those who supported me, for which I remain grateful (and awkward). But I saw too many people in missions get into debt, often with a hefty dose of magical thinking about how they would get out of it. The assumption that God will provide without me doing anything, or even if I am completely irresponsible with money, was not uncommon in the first mission organization I worked for. In some cases, future planning was seen as a lack of faith: who needs savings when Jesus is coming back soon? There were a few sessions where we were supposed to 'wait on God' for money for some project or other, which meant sitting in a room waiting until the tension grew so high that people gave up to the target amount.

These teachings have had a heavy toll on the lives of Anne (USA) and her family. Her church also instructed her not to use her college degree to find work, but to be a stay-at-home mother:

> I tithed a great percentage of money even though we were in poverty with five young kids and in debt and lacking food and basics. They told me to keep sowing money because the harder our poverty got, the more God would pour out double what we sowed, and that if I felt doubtful about this, he would allow the devil to steal all our money.

Working in low-income countries, I saw countless people give more than they could afford to the church (pastor), generally after being told that God would make them wealthy if they did so. The thought of one pastor, decked out in an expensive watch with matching crocodile-skin shoes and jacket as his congregation struggled to feed their kids, still turns my stomach.

Called

I thought I was going to convert people. I thought God had chosen me and I was going to be the vessel for his power to revitalize this rundown church. The congregation would grow and it would be wonderful. Of course, nothing happened. We had a few prayer meetings, half a dozen of us got together, but the power of the Holy Spirit was not there.

I remember once getting really tired, which is not surprising because I was working in a new job and running the Sunday school and the Bible class and so many things. I thought if God was there, I shouldn't be tired, his power should be holding me up and his direction should show me what to do. (Gordon, UK)

It's this whole thing about revival is round the corner. Flippin' hell, how big is this ruddy corner? (Aidan, UK)

Charismatic churches and organizations, in particular, are fuelled by frequent talk of revival or victory, a 'shaking' on its way (never worked out what this actually meant, except it didn't sound fun), of God doing unspecified 'great things' through you, and variations on the theme of 'this generation' being raised up. It's enough to give someone a sense of the epic about their own life, and who doesn't want that, especially as a teenager? The drama! It's also an effective way of silencing complaint or perceived lack of commitment: anything is justifiable if there's a greater thing promised.

It goes quiet when nothing changes, when 'revival' is downgraded to 'renewal'. Or maybe the problem is you, as Amber (UK) experienced, in the 'Breakthrough' chapter above. Christine (UK) concurs:

I was in a church that was interested in the Bethel movement. There was a core group of us who were believing, 'we want to see miracles and revival'. It was a real shift in faith for me, being told, 'God has a plan for your life and you can have prophetic words and you can be an evangelist.' I felt so inspired and wanted to pursue that more.

Bethel culture revolves around this idea of heaven invading Earth and God is good all the time, raising expectations of what God is going to do in supernatural intervention. If I don't allow any room for God to be deficient but I'm not seeing what I am told that I should be, well, I must be the problem. It may be to do with faith, I'm not believing enough, but also maybe God can't use me because of sexual impurity or any other deficiency. Part of the impact on me of purity culture was that sense of blaming myself, just looking for a reason that God wasn't intervening in my life. It must be impure thoughts, you know, I'm not meeting the standards.

Laura (UK) and I compare notes about the sense of setting everything aside for ministry, including self-care and independent thought:

We had some very troubled people staying in our home who my parents were looking after. I remember standing up for my parents going, 'They're doing a really good thing', and at the same time, being 14 and somebody shared my room for a year.

I'm coming to a place of being able to accept that this is my parents doing what they thought was right, naively, no boundaries in place. Those are the kind of experiences that were typical of people who are immersed in that world. It was just all-out for God, you've got to save everyone, do whatever it takes to reach them.

Years later, Laura spent time on a mission ship:

It was a real mixed bag. It was an amazing experience in many ways, interacting with people from so many different countries and travelling. I always had questions about evangelism and found a lot of it really cringey. I was told to just go out and talk to people on the streets of Cameroon: 'Go and convert those people over there and tell them about Jesus and then pray with them. Well done, they're a Christian now.' I came away from there with a lot of questions and a lot of great experiences and a husband.

I went into it thinking this would be my life, so there was a big sense of failure at the end. You're primed to think, 'I'm giving my life to God', and then you get to three and a half years burnt out, disillusioned and you think, 'Was it me?'

There's that pressure to be involved and committed and that focus on doing rather than being. I ended up with hypothyroidism, fibromyalgia and sciatica costochondritis: all things that are set off by stress and not listening to your body saying, 'Stop.' That's been the only way that I've finally gone, 'Oh right, self-care. Good plan.'

I remember this mentality: it led me to burnout. In my 20s I worked on a community project in South Africa. Alcohol and drug addiction was endemic in the community, and there were high levels of HIV/AIDS and TB. Many of the young people I worked with did not have safe homes. Working hard and paying no attention to the toll the context and unfamiliar culture was taking, my health went downhill over a few months, resulting in glandular fever/mono and three years of ME/CFS. I was told that my exhaustion was because I was doing things in my own strength, not God's. What does that mean? All it does is cause shame and risk a further erosion of boundaries. Far more helpful were the friends who simply told me to slow down.

Churches and mission agencies often push missions or ministry as the highest thing you can do, exploiting people's compassion and commitment, and not necessarily in the interests of those the individual ends up 'serving'. And if God has sent me to you, well, obviously I know what's best for you (we'll look more at missions in the White Jesus chapter).

Wendy (USA) went on her first mission trip in her late teens, leading to long-term involvement:

It felt like being a missionary was the 2.0 of being a Christian, like you're serious about it: 'No, I mean it, I'll be a martyr.' Within my Christian college I found the missions people, and even among them, I had a tier system of the hardcore missions people and the vacation missionary type. I wasn't at all a judgemental person, as you can tell!

I would call myself radical and sold out for God and willing to do anything. In hindsight, really what I wanted was the feeling I had when I was in Guatemala the very first time. It was like a high, I felt special and called and like I was part of something bigger than myself. It almost felt like us missionaries were too good for the local church. I felt like I was flying at 30,000 feet for a living.

Anselm (USA) was inspired by Spike Lee's films and wanted to become a filmmaker:

I received a lot of messaging in college about the best way to serve God is to sacrifice what career you could have had and go into the ministry and change people's lives. For a 21-year-old that was so inspiring to me.

Once he went into ministry, reality kicked in:

It was like, 'OK, how many people are you studying the Bible with? Only five people, you need to bump that up. So, it's been two months that you haven't had a baptism yet. What's going on? If this is going to be the role for you, you're going to need to show it.' It lost the feeling of, 'I'm doing something great' and it felt more like, 'I'm just a cog in this machine.'

There's a lot to dissect because as a human being, I wanted to feel important, I wanted to feel loved. So now the love I thought I was receiving was jeopardized because I wasn't doing enough. I felt all this pressure to convince people to come to this belief and join this church so that they can keep giving their money and continue to support the salaries of the people on top. That also flowed into how I felt God must have seen me, that God was upset at me because I wasn't doing enough, I wasn't praying enough, I wasn't reading my Bible enough, I didn't have enough faith. Years and years of never feeling like I was enough. It's the line in the sand that keeps getting erased and drawn further back. It's been three and a half years since I left my ministry job and about a year since I left the organization, and I'm still dealing with a lot of that.

The way that evangelical Christianity works, there's this scarcity mindset as well, that I think limits people to thinking, 'I was put on the Earth for one purpose, and every day that I'm not living in this purpose, I am losing out or something or someone else is given the opportunity to do what was meant for me to do.'

Anselm is now following his original career plan as a filmmaker, but his experience highlights the continual growth mindset in churches, more akin to a corporate structure.

I ran into this 'highest calling/total commitment' thinking when I started working in mission. My mother was seriously ill back in the UK, but whenever I expressed ambivalence about being overseas, my leadership told me that to go home would be disobedience to God (which is unanswerable, because there's nothing objective to measure 'obedience' against, but the consequences of disobedience are potentially eternal). The various verses about those who do not hate father and mother not being Jesus' disciple (Luke 14.26 and others) were trotted out each time, more threat than guidance. I was a young adult with decision-making capacity, but I was also in a closed system where serving God was everything, the Bible was the ultimate answer and leaders were to be obeyed. So I stayed, and eventually stopped wondering if I should go home. Subsequent leaders were not so hardcore (although there was plenty of messaging around commitment), but by then I'd internalized the message.

If you believe God has a plan for your life, you are far more likely to accept unhealthy or abusive situations because you are in God's will and 'God will never give you something you can't handle' (again, it is your fault if you can't). That sense of being part of something significant, of one clear calling on my life, of black and white obedience to God is certainly something I have had to deconstruct. Parting with it was briefly a loss, then a huge relief.

Read your Bible, Pray Every Day

I was so zealous as a teenager. I remember going camping with all my friends to Pevensey Bay, and we decided to take communion in our tent. We were such weird 17-year-olds! We did this very solemn communion with chocolate biscuits and this drink, and I remember the moon was really clear and it had a halo around it, and at the end of the communion saying, 'That's God saying how pleased he is with us!' (Julie, UK).

'It's never about works' and all of that, but there was still a kind of, 'Well, if you're not reading your Bible and praying every day you're failing and you haven't believed properly, because if you believed properly, you'd look just like Jesus and you'd read your Bible every day.' (Rachel, UK)

Anyone who has spent time in evangelical circles, perhaps especially as a teen and young adult, knows the daily requirements of devotion, appearance and behaviour are ever-present. The resulting sense of inadequacy when you don't do enough Bible study or prayer undermines the comfort that can be found in these things.

Some do better at this than others. As a rule-keeping introverted teen, I was not bad at it back then. As Anne (USA) says, 'It made me a stellar goody-two-shoes Christian as a teenager. The better you are at being a Christian, it doesn't mean the better you are at being actually Christlike.'

The same cannot be said for Penny (UK):

As an extroverted dyslexic, literally the worst thing you can tell me is to sit quiet, and I'm not a morning person: 'If you love Jesus, you will sit quietly for 20 minutes on your own reading in the morning.' No, I won't. I just can't do it, and every time I tried and failed, it was just another shaming experience.

So many of us remember that feeling of shame, of never quite meeting an invisible standard, of making fresh promises and recommitting over and again:

I remember being 14, 15, in small group Bible study and being like, 'I'm worried about this test', and they were like, 'Just give all your cares to the Lord', and I remember stopping and being like, 'What does that mean? What is the step-by-step process for giving it up to God?' That always pissed me off, this emotional bypassing, because that was the answer to every question or every discomfort or anything that you brought to a group of Christians: 'Just pray about it, just meditate on the Lord, just read the Bible.'

I've done what you say it takes and I'm not getting the same comfort from giving up my cares to the Lord as you do, so obviously the problem is me. (Mara, USA)

My most intense spiritual experiences happened in summer camps like Spring Harvest, New Wine. I would have an emotional experience and vow to really commit and read my Bible every day, pray, be a better Christian. When I was 17, I was like, 'This is ridiculous. I can't get converted every year.' (Nina, UK)

A large part of those emotional experiences is the giving of testimonies: 85% of survey respondents had participated in this. Even here, a sense of inadequacy can creep in if your testimony isn't dramatic, as mine wasn't. David B. (UK) saw through it:

At that age in our town there wasn't a great deal of trouble you could get into, but I think people liked the idea of saying how terrible they'd been and then everyone could clap.

In hindsight, it can feel like the Church feeds off trauma in the form of these simplistic 'sinner saved' stories, without looking too closely at underlying pain or ongoing issues. The dramatic conversion story belies the fact that those who really do come from backgrounds of trauma often have a long road to recovery, and that healing is not a linear journey. This only adds to the shame when reality kicks in.

It isn't helped by attitudes to suffering: we must bear our burdens joyfully, Christians are never anxious, depressed or bored and suffering produces holiness (or my favourite, which I heard numerous times in the youth missions organization I worked for: if it isn't on a level with what Jesus endured for your sake, you shouldn't complain). You are supposed to have abundant life and freedom in Christ, to be an ambassador for Christ at all times. Modelling all this leaves no real space for messy things like ongoing grief, trauma or, perhaps worst of all, anger (particularly from women or people of colour). In my mid-30s I took part in a 'healing inner wounds' course. In our small group, I spoke about the impact of losing my father in early childhood. Our leader smiled perkily and told me, 'Well, he's with Jesus now, so there's no need to grieve!'

Instead, Christians are encouraged to find redemption in pain, and almost glorify suffering. (Although there are often double standards here, depending on whether it is you or me who is angry or suffering. These function a little like irregular verbs: I have righteous anger; you are just bitter. I am being refined by God to become more Christlike; you have sin in your life and are being punished.)

Sally's (UK) parents were missionaries when she was a child, and she was left at boarding school, with a far more severe theology than she had experienced in her family:

In my letters, I never told my parents how desperately homesick and unhappy I was. I just wrote good news because I was worried that if I told them what was going on, I would be responsible for them having to leave their posting and come back to England, and I would stop the Lord's work from happening. That sense of responsibility I carried heavily on my shoulders from a very young age, with a suppression of anger because there was a big cultural thing of having to be cheerful because the Lord was in control and all the military language, the victory of God in the end.

Sin Management

It's one slippery slide to a crazily hedonistic lifestyle. (Josh, Netherlands/New Zealand)

There's a lot of pressure within Southern Baptist life to be dressed right, look right, vote properly, portraying this conservative image. It sent a message about expectations, about what it means to be a man and what it means to be a woman, what family is supposed to look like. It's a control thing. There's just so much management of people's behaviours, of people's thoughts. (Ronnie, USA)

I am inherently evil and deserve death and hell. Every time I sin, I put another nail through Jesus' hands. That's a lot to grow up believing. While the 'God loves you just as you are' message is also there, 73% of survey respondents reported that they had seriously worried about their sin, and 72% that they were being disobedient to God or were outside of God's will or calling on their life. Emilia (Sweden) remembers the anxiety it caused her from childhood:

I was really scared of thoughts popping into my mind that weren't approved of by God because that could be a demon. When I left, it was like the weight lifted that I didn't have to control my thoughts. I just had my thoughts for myself. They were mine.

There are so many ways to sin; so many ways the devil is just waiting to trip you up. Liz (UK) told me about the party culture at her university: 'It was all dangerous, so the further you can stay from that, the more you can just be at a Bible study with your friends, that's the best. Safe.' On the other hand, there are the glorious results of doing it right: another face of prosperity gospel. Anne (USA) sums it up:

I'm completely vulnerable and powerless and weak, and my whole life is terrible in ways that I can't control. But oh, I can follow these rules and then come out to have a better marriage and better adult life. OK, well, I'll follow any number of hard rules if I can control my future that way.

In a culture where sin is routinely policed and peer accountability encouraged, it can feel like everyone is in everyone else's business, and pushback on this is not allowed, because they're just keeping you accountable. Confidentiality cannot be taken for granted, and the gossip chain exists in publicly praying about someone in such a way to make their sins quite clear to others.

On several mission training courses I did we were required to list areas we were 'struggling' with on application forms, and to hand in our journals each week to the staff member assigned to us, regardless of our trust in them, which normalized the sharing of our 'struggles' with those in authority, as Abi (USA) also found:

> I went to a Baptist high school where we had Bible class. We were supposed to turn in our devotions. I was almost a conscientious objector because I was like, 'You don't deserve access to this.' There's an expected vulnerability that you share your stuff indiscriminately with everyone.

Being told who to trust, based largely upon someone's position (regardless of whether they had earned that trust or if I felt safe) is something I found really problematic, which meant I was labelled as having 'trust issues'. It negates true trust and trustworthiness, and hands our emotional and spiritual safety over to others. Yet the constant sin management and policing and dress codes show a lack of trust in those lower in the hierarchy.

Elisabeth (UK) also did a training course with the same organization I worked for, although in a different place and decade to me. We both had the same experience of public confession:

> Everyone was aged 18 to 25. Looking back, it's like coercive control, very vulnerable people. People had to stand at the front and name people that they slept with and basically try to conjure up things that they were sorry for.

Josh (USA) had an even harsher theology to go with his own confessions:

> The Bible college I was a part of had this intense sin focus where on a weekly basis you were going to go up to the altar in deep regret over even the things that you were unaware of that might have put you at

odds with God. Their theology was that you could lose your state of salvation, so it perpetuated this constant sense of paranoia where at any moment I could totally unknowingly think the wrong thing, and then if something happens, if I get in a car wreck on the way home from church, I made a really good effort but now I'm going to be in eternal conscious torment.

Even if you don't confess your sins directly, generic repentance is right there in so many worship songs, with the frequent theme of, 'I am not worthy, I am nothing compared to you, less of me and more of you.' When you repeat lines like these over and over for years (and often over and over in the same worship session), they are going to sink in. It is supposed to be 'humility' but instead teaches us we are worthless. Nina (UK) reflects on the impact of this:

> I guess it's a really good way of controlling people, if you keep people feeling terrible and you've got the answer for them. I feel sad for my younger self to have gone through so much of life feeling bad about myself, the message that, 'Isn't it amazing that Jesus saved us because we're so awful?'

Sophie (UK) found it put pressure on friendships:

> You automatically try to box everyone into your understanding of what it means to live a godly lifestyle. I felt limited in how much I could truly accept people, love people, by these boxes of how people should act. Especially when it comes to sexuality or gender there's very much boxes of expectations of how people should be. Anything out of that was, 'The heart's deceitful. It's the flesh.'

It took me a long time to realize that what was classed as 'sin' was often trauma-response behaviour, or not wrong at all. Something sinful in one church might be fine in another. 'But why is that sin?' was met with either, 'Because the Bible says so' or, if said sin wasn't mentioned in the Bible, tangled and convoluted explanations involving 'not God's highest'. As Gary (Canada) puts it: 'You realized they had a belief system that was so black and white that they didn't have a morality anymore, didn't have a conscience anymore. They had rules that they follow.'

Spirit of Rebellion

I'm almost 60. I'm a critical thinker. But you were expected to dogmatically do what you were told and believe what you were told to believe. I had lots of people tell me that I wasn't safe because I was asking questions, and any time I asked questions of people that I thought I respected, they would come back with phrases like, 'Oh, you're thinking as the world thinks.' I dealt with a lot of shame for not being able to have this idealized version of what it's like to be a good Christian in this happy bubble where you feel the presence of God all the time and all your doubts and questions go away and there's this wonderful, rapturous smile on your face and the flow of the Spirit always. (Kathy, USA)

I was in a community that would say that anything is welcome, anything is on the table, but there were so many topics that it's like, 'Oh, but we can't question the inerrancy of scripture, we can't question eternal conscious torment.' There's definitely a pressure to conform which pits you against following your inner knowing. You're trained for so long to not just know the right answers but defend the right answers. The pressures of believing very specific doctrine, with the stake being your belonging within the community, creates so much fear. You can't have authentic conversations with anyone because you're just concerned about being right. (Hope, USA)

A major theme for those who deconstruct is the lack of space to disagree with or even question what is taught in church. Less than 24% of survey respondents said that they had been able to discuss their questions and doubts with their leaders when their faith started to change and only 41% could discuss them with other members, whereas 70% reported some version of 'I tried to resolve them myself/with one or two trusted friends.' The arrogance of any denomination or organization to claim that, after 2,000 years and tens of thousands of denominations, they are the only ones to have it right is extraordinary.

This lack of ability to question or disagree leads to cognitive dissonance for plenty of people: perhaps confused or even shocked at what is being said or done but also primed to believe what they are being told. Phoebe (USA) tells me:

Particularly with the pastor and the associate pastor, there was not a chance that they could be wrong with their particular interpretation of what scripture meant. I used to think that was the way it was supposed to be, that they learnt the one and only right way to interpret scripture.

I remember struggling to figure out how something made sense in the real world and being told to, 'just believe that you believe'. We are told to have faith like a little child – but children are always asking questions. Awkward ones which often expose the heart of a matter. In my early days with the organization I worked for, when I asked honest questions about why we were doing something, I was repeatedly told I had a 'spirit of rebellion' (I thought this was a joke, so I laughed, which didn't help). The word 'rebellion' – which I rarely hear used outside of church – came up frequently. Tim (Canada) says, 'Asking questions or challenging things or pushing back was labelled as rebellion or countering a system of authority that God had put in place.'

Even those in ordained ministry are not safe. Michael (UK) is a deconstructed minister:

The fear for me is the continual pushback from the power structure in the Church. I'm a university chaplain, but I'm barred from speaking at the university Christian Union because they don't like the questions I'm going to ask the students. I find that bonkers because those students are in a university where they have a safe place to ask questions. This is the place to discover your faith.

Why can't we disagree safely? For plenty of people, like Sarah (Canada), narrow theologies and lack of space for discussion is what keeps them from church:

I love my understanding of God and Jesus, but I hate everything to do with modern church. There's no autonomy. There's no respect for dignity. They have just weaponized the Bible. They make no room for community within the churches; everything is a curriculum. Everything is, 'You have to listen to this and discuss this within these confines so that it doesn't get too out there. We wouldn't want people actually having big questions.'

If there were opportunities to honestly and openly journey with people and to hold a range of opinions but still to do life with one another, that side of church is something that we would be happy with and committed to. (Ben, UK)

The Heart is Deceitful

It is hard to stop people from disagreeing if they still fundamentally trust their own judgement. But there's a verse for that. Two, in fact, neatly snipped from Proverbs 3.5 and Jeremiah 17.9: 'Trust in the Lord with all your heart, and lean not on your own understanding', and 'The heart is deceitful above all things.' 65% of survey respondents had consistently been taught this and found it harmful (only 7% had found it helpful). Combine these verses and you can't trust yourself at all, only external authorities, making people far easier to control and more likely to ignore their intuition, including about unkind or controlling behaviour. This is perhaps one of the most sinister effects of evangelical teaching. Joy (USA) realized how insidious this is:

> That verse about the heart being deceitful beyond cure was a very strong message: don't trust yourself, don't listen to yourself. I never knew that my body had instincts that would tell me before I was going to get sick or pass out because I had a medical condition. I had to learn these basic things of listening to your own body signals, because it was so attacked and so separated.
>
> There's a hierarchy in everything in religion. There's never not something that's placed above another thing, but especially things like the mind over the body. If you deny some of the most intrinsic parts of your physical and sexual self, why wouldn't you believe in all this stuff, because you've already denied yourself everything?

Laura (USA) was one of several people who couldn't even admit doubt or questions to themselves:

> I could only understand safety within the church family, and I couldn't do anything to put that perceived safety in danger, so I couldn't voice those doubts. I couldn't even hold them within myself as valid true things. It created huge levels of dissociation from my own experience of life. Which is a big deal, not being able to trust my own experience spiritually, physically, emotionally, mentally. Probably the biggest thing was the dissociative patterns that it caused that I'm now actively enduring.

She is also one of several women who told me that they still have trouble making decisions or even knowing their own preferences, right down to favourite colours. Emilia (Sweden) is another:

> I get deathly anxiety when I have to make a big decision because I can't trust myself. After a lot of hours in therapy, I've come to the realization that it's because if I make the wrong choice, then what will happen? I will die. So making choices is awful, even picking out this colour on the sofa, it took me two weeks of crying to be able to say, 'I like this colour, I want this colour.'

Combined with messages that we must 'die to self' and repeated pleas to God of 'less of me and more of you', it is no wonder that people are left not knowing themselves. Holly (UK) is slowly rebuilding confidence in herself, and reflects:

> It's a bad thing to have a strong sense of self in the Church. There's just so much focus on your identity in Christ, because God loves you, therefore … It's presented as such a beautiful thing and it is all so controlling.

It seems from the survey and interviews that these verses were pushed on women more than men, although not exclusively. Traynor (USA) tells me of the ongoing difficulty he has with his emotions:

> I remember talking with my father about all the grief that I was feeling, especially in those early months of the pandemic. I remember him saying, 'Well, you need to be careful about listening to your emotions too much.' I said, 'Dad, God also created our capacity to feel emotions.' And he said 'No, but the heart is deceitful above all things.' I feel so deeply and yet I have such difficulty in expressing that feeling because it goes into a shame spiral for me.

The other side of this lack of self-awareness and sense of self is that it allows people to act from a doctrinal framework, or do what their leaders tell them to, and ignore the cruel, controlling or manipulative nature of their actions, even if well intentioned.

Part of deconstruction is developing self-awareness, sense of self, trust in self. For decades, I assumed that if I wanted to do something, it must be wrong because it came from me, not God, so I would do the opposite. Learning to trust myself and not having to make 'perfect' decisions is something that still takes me conscious effort to do. It starts with little decisions and learning not to always refer to external sources.

Unoffendable

I was ten years old. My brother, who is eight years my junior, was very ill in an intensive care unit. The pastor came in and looked at my folks, and I was standing right there, and he said, 'Someone in this family has committed some awful sin for God to visit this sort of judgement.' I can remember it and take you to that spot today. I haven't said that in years and it takes my breath away just to say it. (Ronnie, USA)

What happens when authority must be obeyed and overtly honoured, when criticism of leadership is met with, 'Do not touch the Lord's anointed' and you are not allowed to trust yourself? It is a set-up for control, manipulation and abuse. The last few years have seen one evangelical abuse scandal after another on various continents, with survivors having been historically silenced, dismissed, disbelieved and blamed, further isolating them. Accusations are deemed Satan's attack on anointed leaders or on 'God's work'. It's as though if you just slap a 'holiness' sticker on it, you never actually have to investigate it, and leaders must always be trusted above those claiming abuse. Anything is justifiable if you are doing God's work.

At the core of much of this lies people's choice and ability to trust those they feel have earned it, rather than who they are told to trust. Not trusting the 'right' people can be seen as sinful, or at least that you 'need healing'. But trusting the 'right' people without ever asking questions can lead to disastrous naivety. On the basis of verbal repentance (or not) and a claim to have been forgiven by God (regardless of the impact on human victims, a perpetrator's efforts to make amends or a church's willingness to really look at the problem), perpetrators are put back in authority and deemed safe around the very people they harmed. Real damage is compared to far more minor 'sins' (known as 'sin-levelling'): 'Well, we all fall short of God's standards', or, more directly, the rapist compared equally to their victim who 'had sex outside marriage'.

Controlling or emotionally and spiritually abusive behaviour may not even be seen as such when it is just normal or committed by those in authority: it is hard to see a problem when this is the water you've swum in since you were a child, or when it is mixed in with talk of

33

unconditional love and perhaps genuine kindness (we're back to coercive control). When our narrative culture centres on how much good we are doing, it becomes hard to believe that there is abuse.

Mike B. (UK) is a minister who was shocked when he was first ordained:

> On the whole, nice, welcoming people, but so many power struggles in the church, and what I see now as religiosity. I was a social worker and counsellor, so I know how complicated we all are, but seeing the unhealthiness in church and a lot of healthiness outside of church and Christianity, and very little transformation of people in church, and such low levels of self-awareness. Maybe it's the lack of training, but also the soft theology allows for those very charismatic figures to lead and often to abuse.

This mirrors my own experience: most often, people were simply lacking self-awareness, putting doctrine above all else, with a genuine fear of people going astray. Anne (USA) explains how this adherence to doctrine worked its way out in her church:

> The more that we saw the actual lives of these leaders at the church that always looked so impeccable, so glorious, we wanted so badly to be like them, but we just saw it's heartless: you're so committed to saying and doing these right magical things that there is no compassion for anyone that it's not working for. So as our medical problems got worse and our finances were still bad, it always felt like there was an undercurrent of anger. Like if I came to church and said, 'I'm so tired. I've been up at the hospital all night with my kid again', as time went on, people would just kind of snap, 'Well, did you take communion? And did you have worship music playing? If there wasn't worship music playing in the ER room, then all the people who died there, they were influencing. And were you taking that room for the kingdom? Obviously you weren't because you were there all night and you didn't get healed.'

At another point in our conversation, she says:

> We started seeing the fallout where me or other people in the church would get the full brunt of people's anger and being screamed at and trashed and lied about, and the pastors would watch it happen but nobody was ever held to any standard of maturity or spiritual or emotional health. It was all, 'Well, but they did have this prophetic word. Remember that the man who just screamed at you said he had a dream about this and we can't go against God.' So people losing their temper or lying or hurting people was all written off as spiritual warfare.

George (Australia/UK) spent time in the same mission organization as me, and had a slippery blend of good and bad:

> It was complex for me. It was a high and a low point. When I went to university for my first year, I had a real crash. I broke up with a girl-friend, strange city, all that stuff. The leaders at that stage caught me and rescued me in a good way.

Sometime later, new leadership was in place: 'That was two years of trying to get out, and it was only because I got tapped by a bishop to go and get ordained I had a way out.' I remark to George that it is worrying when people feel like they can't leave. It's something that I felt too at times, and something others have remarked on in some churches.

My own memories are also mixed. Great friendships, deep kindness and a chance to do things I wouldn't otherwise have been able to (some of which I regret). But also: no written contract because 'it's all based on relationship', which is lovely until it isn't. When I pointed out that something wasn't legal or tried to get figures to put a budget together, I was met with the claim that we aren't bound by 'worldly' laws and ways of doing things. Accountability for everyone except, it seemed, leadership, whose ability to hear from God trumped anyone else's ability, experience or common sense. Then there were things like the times we were all instructed to fast for a week, without thought given to who might have issues around food; the coerced public confessions; the adults who had to ask leadership for permission to date. The instruction to 'be unoffendable' was often given if there was a complaint about damaging or hurtful behaviour. When I searched online for 'spiritual abuse' recently, up came a video from a senior leader saying that supposed spiritual abuse is just people telling the truth about things you don't want to hear (we're back to 'speaking the truth in love'), or people who feel bad about themselves but blame someone else. Sometimes it's a conspiracy against a leader.

Emma's (UK) experience rings all too true of the kind of not-always-obvious behaviour that allows those in power to manipulate and dodge responsibility:

> There was definitely a lot of pressure to serve, serve, serve, and they dangled leadership positions over people like a carrot: 'If you're good, you'll get to be X, you get to do Y.'
>
> There was a culture that if you're in leadership and you do something wrong, you don't say sorry because it shows weakness. It's not that there was anything criminal offence standard happening. It was all far more subtle spiritual and emotional abuse and a lot of gaslighting, like

if you had a problem, it would be, 'Oh, it's in your head. That's your sin.' And if you dared to ask a question, you're a threat to the kingdom work of God. There was no room to even approach any grievances, let alone hash it out, you know? 'The Bible says we have to forgive.' That was used a lot to get people off the hook, for sure.

When those who claim to be acting on God's authority behave like this, it is unsurprising that it leads to questions about God. Over the long term, it can lead to mental and physical health breakdowns, especially when church is also your employer. Harry (UK) had worked at church for several years, during which time the power dynamics from the father–daughter leadership became unbearable:

I felt like God was speaking to me throughout 2015 saying that it was time to move on. I was petrified, because generally if you leave to do something that's not ordination then it's frowned upon massively, like, 'You're betraying me, what are you doing?' Kind of like it's the mafia or something.

The minister called me into his office one day and said, 'I can see you're struggling. I don't want to lose you, but I think we need to have a plan to wind you down. We want to bless you and help you move on.' And I thought, 'Oh, my prayers have been answered. Praise the Lord.'

A short time later, things changed:

He pulled me into his office and it was like the conversation where he was blessing me didn't exist and he absolutely tore me to shreds. It was proper savage. I was told to repent and get to the foot of the cross on account of my feelings, this isn't what we discussed, and so on. I said, 'Look, you know I'm feeling depressed' and he went, 'That's not open for discussion.'

If I look back over my journals now, I can see how bad it was for a long time, but that was really where the shit hit the fan, and that has done untold damage to my faith even now, because I was seeing these people who have nothing to do with Jesus embody more Christlikeness in the way that they dealt with people than I was seeing played out in church. Sometimes we'd encounter the minister in the street and on the school run and he'd just blank us.

I still have a lot of trauma – that is the word, trauma – towards Christianity, and church in particular. Although we're part of a new church now, I don't really want to go. I do feel like God prized me out of that church but I feel exiled constantly.

Jude (Australia) tells me about her path in and out of church employment:

> I went to uni at 40, did psychology and then had a discernment year, whether to do honours in psych or do pastoral counselling. I did that with spiritual direction. I've gone back to that decision frequently, going, 'I wonder what would have happened?'

After gaining experience elsewhere, she took on a role as pastoral care coordinator at her own church:

> It was exciting. I felt like I'm so lucky to be part of this: I've been a worship leader for years, and there was a sense of being with these people I loved and respected. When we say church is family, we don't mean that it's a dysfunctional family, but it is.

After a couple of years, Jude was offered a role as leader of a congregation, which she accepted:

> It was a very clear decision to be where I think Jesus is. It was a good year, then some new staff members came and dynamics on the team became very difficult, leading to me being asked to leave without due process, and the senior pastor as well. I experienced bullying that led to burnout, continually feeling threatened, and rather than being supported there was a lot of blame, gaslighting. It's taken a long time to recover.
> When we were taught the Christians were the good ones, what does it mean when the people who I grew up admiring, leaders I respected, people I trusted show appalling behaviour? When my yoga teacher and people in cafés who don't come from a Christocentric worldview, they show me a greater sense of compassion and dignity and respect? That has to go into the theological soup.

Austin (USA) tells me that he wasn't directly in the firing line of church abuse, but has had to reflect on what he was part of:

> I went to Mars Hill Church[1] for several years. We had heard stories of people having horrible experiences of Mars Hill for years, but the sense

---

1 Mars Hill Church, in Seattle, Washington, was founded by Mark Driscoll. Following well-documented controversies and abuses of power, Driscoll resigned in October 2014 and the church closed in January 2015. For more information, see 'The Rise and Fall of Mars Hill' podcast (Cosper, 2021).

was there's probably something wrong with them. I've had conversations with friends of mine who also were there and after everything imploded, we started asking ourselves how was it that we didn't see these troubling characteristics and things that Mark was saying? It's like you find some way to explain away the really horrible things. I've been processing that for a number of years, honestly.

I feel like in many ways, a lot of Christian communities socialize people to not think for themselves, to outsource authority to what typically ends up being a male pastor. The ways that we're socialized to have a very shameful sense of ourselves where we're always thinking about ourselves in the most awful, sinful ways. But then there can also be this release when you feel forgiveness or you're repenting and confessing. So, there's a lot of ways that feel very manipulative and very degrading, but also that keep people in these communities or that set people up for what I would say now is very spiritually abusive dynamics.

It's hard to even reconcile with the Jesus of the Bible, you know? Jesus, who feeds the poor and heals people, and then you have Mark who's so angry and his face gets red because he's yelling at everyone. There was a moment of reckoning for me and for a lot of friends of mine where we started asking, 'How did we get caught up in this?' and even feeling a lot of guilt, like, we invited our friends to Mars Hill. What were we doing? We shouldn't have done this.

Forgiveness for perpetrators of church abuse can, ironically, become just another area of violation for victims in a context where forgiveness is idealized and seen as a quick fix, instead of a hard road freely chosen if and when an individual is ready: 35% of survey respondents said they had felt pressure to forgive before they felt ready. Using Bible verses and the threat that God can't forgive you if you won't forgive others, churches can insist on immediate, unconditional forgiveness, often dismissing the real impact of harm and using it as a means to 'restore' (excuse) the perpetrator. Forgiveness is conflated with trust and the expectation that the relationship will be exactly as before, without new boundaries, inevitably leading to further violations. Those who cannot forgive are pressured to get past their 'bitterness':

> I am not able to forgive either of the guys that raped me. I'm not able to forgive my ex for locking me in a house for four years. I'm not able to forgive the people who tortured me in school. And a major flack that I've got from church is, 'Why can't you forgive them?' (Stacy, USA)

For Katie (USA), it is a long process of unlearning now that she has left church:

> I am learning that I don't owe anyone forgiveness for any reason, but that feeling that I should forgive someone no matter what, no matter how horrible, no matter how abusive, no matter how genuinely terrible a human being they are, that feeling is from my evangelical days because that's what they teach you.

I've come to feel that forgiveness is more about me making my own peace with a situation than it is me bestowing my forgiveness upon someone else.

Worship

I can remember times that seemed like wonderful times of worship, and you get carried away with it. Now there's a bit of me that's suspicious: is that so different from a psychological high you get at a concert or other events where everyone's excited? (Heather, UK)

I attended a church in London for a while where the Sunday service – maximum 10 or 15 of us – wasn't the main event of the week: there was a drop-in lunch for local workers, acting classes for vulnerable young people, art exhibitions. Services worked around this space, and we sat wherever the chairs were. The vicar encouraged me to bring my dog and was honest about his own life. It was the most participatory and least controlling church environment I have been in.

For most church members, Sunday services are the main source of spiritual input: the way that time and the church space are used has a huge impact on spiritual experience:

The way that church is set up, it's like a concert and a lecture. I think we're missing out on having a fuller picture of God because we only hear from one person every Sunday instead of it being a participatory, non-hierarchical thing that other people can engage with. (KP, USA)

Josh (USA) talks about church spaces themselves:

We've become so habituated to consuming all of our spirituality sitting looking forward, and we're not having an experience that's teaching us to turn to our neighbour and honour the God in them and trying to build skills together that help us make it through the week that we're actually going to live, and help us understand the perspective of some-body else and things that may help us have a more vibrant spirituality in the context of the community that we actually live in.

Over centuries, churches have been carefully curated environments, whether it is stained glass and soaring ceilings or smoke machines and bass guitars. For many, worship forms the core of their church experience and a time to connect with God, but the more technology is involved, the easier it is to manipulate not only human experience but even biology.

Shortly before the first UK lockdown in March 2020, I attended a lecture by two neurologists studying the effects of singing or dancing in groups. As churches around the world closed their doors and Christians complained about their right to worship being snatched away, I began to wonder: people can worship in their own homes, so what was it about corporate worship that they were missing? How much of it is a divine experience and how much is a neurological effect, or an overlap between the two? What does this say about human ability to create a seemingly divine experience, especially in the immersive worship sessions found in charismatic churches, and in church spaces where even natural light is blocked out, sensory and cognitive input controlled entirely?

As a noise-sensitive introvert, I often found the louder sections of this overwhelming. In some churches, there was the expectation to dance, painful to many Brits. Jess (UK) felt the same as me: '"We should dance like David danced and have wonderful, reckless abandon for God." I'm just not doing that.' There were worship times where we would sing the same four lines over and over, caught up in the emotion (or to conjure emotion). I doubt anyone intended it this way, but I now realize it's the same technique used by cults to brainwash followers.

A number of those I interviewed had been worship leaders. Tim (Canada) told me: 'I've led worship for youth conferences, and the joke would be that you measure your response in terms of how many teenage tears you elicited.' He goes on to tell me about times he has felt ill, and how that would lift as soon as he started to lead worship:

> My church background would ascribe that to the Holy Spirit and maybe that's true, just in a very different way to what we assume. I think there's something about me being part of creating something with this group of musicians around me. We're participating in a shared experience that is good and life-giving, with or without the woo-woo spirituality that can be connected to that, because I've had that experience regardless of the content of music I've played.
>
> It raises questions like what the concept of God means and how those different frameworks of story and experience end up framing the inter-pretation connected to it. If we think of God as not this male entity somewhere off somewhere, and if you push into the idea of God as love, and love in terms of emerging connectivity, then you can have the same experience even in the strictest church community.

That's very different than the idea of, 'Our posture was such that the Holy Spirit showed up.' I remember a lot of times people would come up to me after leading worship saying, 'Oh, you really brought the Holy Spirit.' Does that make me like this wizard shaman that can summon this deity? That's essentially the role that gets placed on the person with the acoustic guitar up front. That's a pretty disturbing environment, because then it depends on my powers, my capacity, but also my adherence to a code of moral purity such that if I can be without sin, if I have a sufficient amount of faith, I can summon the presence of God, as opposed to being able to approach a space with openness and a desire to connect to the people around.

Steve B. (UK) saw the effects both in worship and other events:

As well as worship leading, I'm a touring musician. I spent a lot of my career doing stadium tours and gigantic festivals, so I've observed what music does to crowds, and I read about the psychological effect that creates a tribe mentality. When you're singing, when you're part of the group, then there's almost a frequency that everyone sympathetically falls into.

The euphoria that you feel, it's a transcendent, transformative experience. And stood in front of the church many times I was like, 'I know what I'm doing here. I know what buttons to push to make people go a certain way. I know that if I put an intense amount of reverb or delay on my guitar, or I tell the sound engineer to put it on the main speakers, I know that's going to make everyone feel a certain ethereal feeling, to synthesize a spiritual feeling in the room.' In the end, I felt kind of disgusting, because I was like, 'I'm manipulating these people.'

Mara (USA) led worship at vast events all over the USA. For her, working the crowd was built into the core of leading:

When I was doing Urbana stuff, that's part of our training: when to say something, what to say. If there was a message and you were going to be on mic, you were taking notes so that you had points ready and you're like, 'What did people respond to?' so by the time you got up there, you tied it exactly into your song lyrics so that it would all be like, 'Look at how amazing God is, everything is connected.'

Obviously when I was doing that I didn't see it that way, I was like, 'This is how to give people the best experience, the best chance to connect to God', but that is really what it is, it's emotional priming, with music at the first end and then the powerful message.

As with a number of people, the content of the songs was a problem too. After several years, Mara decided she could no longer lead: 'I can't sing about how worthless I am anymore. It has affected me so deeply and profoundly to say this stuff over and over again, and I can't do it, even for a quick paycheque.'

Ed (UK) is an Anglican minister who struggles with a different aspect of the lyrics:

Historically, I've really enjoyed it, but now I just can't listen to it. I really struggle with that sense that 'I am God's person'. What makes you different to that next person who's homeless? Why you and not them?

It's another way of preaching. It's another way of enforcing a doctrinal point: you get somebody, usually a bloke, stands up with a big, thick Bible and tells you what to think about sin and then hands over to the band, and they reinforce that by singing a song about it.

And Evan (UK) said what I think we've all felt:

Part of my deconstruction was getting bored to tears of worship music. I'm into heavy metal and I'm a rock guitarist and I was playing in worship bands. Worship songs all end up sounding the same, the same chords, and the lyrics are terrible. It's all, 'Jesus is my boyfriend.'

Soaking

I remember being seven years old and trying to fake speaking in tongues as a sign that I've got it. And then I realized I was quoting some line from *Lord of the Rings* in Elvish. (Tim, Canada)

In our little Sunday school, we were expected to speak in tongues, to get us our language and be filled with the Holy Spirit. I can speak in tongues, but I really don't even know what that is anymore. At that time, I felt like I was mimicking what I had heard. So I felt like a fake, an eight-year-old fake. (Kirsten, USA)

Although a few of those I spoke to from charismatic backgrounds felt that they had had a genuine experience of the Holy Spirit, most either weren't sure or said they had not. The majority now weren't quite sure what to make of things they had seen or experienced. Like many of those I spoke to, I'm not sure I ever felt like a fake, but I wanted those experiences so badly that they may have been self-generated, and certainly dissociative at times. The focus on their importance can perhaps mean that people miss the small miracles of everyday life and love in favour of flashier 'signs'. This is the problem when you make something like speaking in tongues a signifier of salvation and relationship with God: over 79% of survey respondents reported having felt pressure to experience these things or felt guilt for not having been more involved in practices such as this and evangelism. Add to that the longing for experiences of God's existence and love which need to be repeated over and over, almost to prove that God is still with me. Ed (UK) tells me:

I haven't spoken in tongues for about four years. It's a really odd thing, it was such a massive part of my life, and it was an insistent part: 'You are only filled with the Holy Spirit if you can produce the evidence of speaking in tongues.' We literally had to do it in our church and somebody ticked a box on a sheet of paper.

Speaking in tongues was just the jumping-off point. Falling over – being 'slain in the Spirit' – became pretty standard (I never fell, and always felt inadequate). Then there was the Toronto Blessing, when things got truly weird: this was where the gold teeth and dust and feathers got going, as well as one-sided leg-lengthenings and people barking like dogs and crowing like roosters. Matt (UK) and I compare notes:

> There were people laughing joyfully, but also people sobbing hysterically, and it reminded me of a scene you sometimes see in Dickens novels of the madhouse, you know, those sort of noises that you get.
>
> At the end, everybody stood up and he would go round and he was praying, putting his hands out and one person would fall over and the next. He came to me and I desperately wanted to fall over and have that sort of experience, but I didn't want it to be fake. After a while, I hadn't fallen over and it was almost ruining the rhythm. I felt him give me a real big push. My eyes are closed and when you're doing that, it's easy to knock somebody off balance, so I pushed him back, and then I got told I had the spirit of rebellion!

I remember those 'soaking sessions', as we called them, often prepared in advance by chairs being cleared, expectation (or suggestibility) already high. I remember, too, watching as a group of vulnerable young people I worked with lined up as a visiting speaker prayed something generic for each one, and they all fell over. Yet I knew that they would go home that night to houses without food or sober adults, and even at the time I wondered what difference it was making. People would say it was God showing us blessing, which sounds like God blew the budget on effects and didn't have anything left for food. Bobbie (UK) gives an overview of the impact that the pressure had on her faith:

> In the late 1960s, as I was approaching my teens, there was this explosion of the charismatic. The vicar was such a lovely man, his face shone with a love for God, and he was not wanting to get involved in the charismatic stuff that the curate was, and sadly, there was a lot of arrogance about it.
>
> I'm a very logical, pragmatic person, as is my husband. I've been prayed for many times to receive the Holy Spirit: 'the second blessing', as they called it. I was told at that tender age I've got some unconfessed sin or I haven't got enough faith. It was always my fault because they couldn't cope with the fact that they were praying for me and nothing was happening. I'm standing there thinking, 'If God wants to push me over, he can, but you're not doing it: get off! I will stand my ground.'
>
> I think that probably started off the, 'What's going on, God? I'm doing what I think is right but you just don't want to bless me in that

way.' In the end, you think, 'Stuff this for a game of soldiers', you know? I think that for me, probably my husband as well, we would say that that has been underlying the problems that we had because we could never feel that we were truly accepted either by the church or by God, frankly.

Bobbie and her husband discovered the Northumbria Community instead: 'It just felt like coming home. You were allowed to ask the awkward questions there.'

Julie (UK) has been on both ends of the pressure:

I have a massive sense of regret at how I absorbed a lot of that and the effect it had on other people. I had a boyfriend who had a very different faith to me, but I was obsessed with being baptized in the Spirit and praying in tongues, and I'd really swallowed that whole thing because my conversion had been so dramatic. I was very judgemental about him and I've often looked him up, actually. I just want to say sorry because I think that must have been so hurtful for him.

When you're young, you don't have the confidence to speak out because you don't have a theological training that your leaders have. And you know deep down that something is wrong, but you don't have the tools to articulate that. I was very aware of the potential for spiritual abuse because I would go forward and I would never be the one to fall backwards. I remember faking it a few times because I thought that's the behaviour that's expected. I just want to get out of here, so I'm going to pretend to fall backwards and then escape.

Many people saw the 'Holy Spirit' used in ways that were directly harmful or manipulative. Emma (UK) describes the church she was in until her late 20s: 'They were so focused on wanting to see certain moves of God happen in the church that they tried to control the people in the church to facilitate this move of God.' She tells me how church leaders would select people to receive prophetic words, planned in the calendar well in advance. Emma and her husband told the leadership they were planning to leave the church:

They were very, very angry with us and they said, 'We were going to put you forward for one of these prophetic nights. Because you're in this sort of mindset and you're thinking about leaving, we've had to take that away from you.'

I think there's probably something in prophecy that is real, but it is absolutely abused and idolized in many churches. The idea that you as a human, as a pastor, can choose who God speaks to is just insane.

Eventually, the leadership allowed them to attend the next meeting, where American guests would be prophesying:

> I think that they were fully expecting we will turn up to this meeting and one of these prophet dudes will be like, 'God says stay.' We waited three weeks till that meeting. I remember physically shaking with fear, just being so terrified. Before we went to that meeting, we literally prayed: 'God, if it is right for us to leave, shut the mouths of men. No lies, no fake prophecies, right?'

At the meeting, no one prophesied over them. Emma's husband decided to put them to the test by directly asking each prophet for a word:

> These two leaders looked absolutely mortified, but he did it on purpose because he wanted them to see that he'd 'tried' to get a prophetic word. And it was just crazy because they were these guys from America, and they were just like, 'Bam, bam, bam, prophecy, prophecy, prophecy', and when my husband asked them, they were just like – nothing. It was proof to the leaders that they couldn't manipulate us anymore.

Some of what goes on in the name of the Holy Spirit tips over into action that leads to lasting damage. Being finger-snapped at or blown on is bad enough. Being discouraged from questioning if reported miracles and healings are real is oppressive. Being pushed or having hands placed all over you without consent is potentially in breach of a church's own safeguarding policies, and possibly the law, especially when young and vulnerable people are involved. David B. (UK) mentions an incident that was as laughable as it was concerning:

> Somebody said, 'You can feel God's presence on the stage', and then, 'No, it's right in the corner of the stage', and everyone crowded into this corner in a great big huddle, and I was just thinking, 'This is madness. Why would God be in one carpet tile square on the corner of that stage?' And in terms of safeguarding stuff, why have you got all these people physically hugging together on one tiny spot?

Nina (UK) recalls her childhood memories of the Toronto Blessing:

> I had these confusing, intense experiences growing up where I wasn't sure what was happening and didn't necessarily feel in control of my decisions. I feel like it's a coping mechanism to people and potentially pretty harmful, manipulative. Almost like a drug, I guess. So I don't want to be near any of that. It's too triggering.

I remember several instances towards the end of the night when you're so desperate to have this encounter and you confess all the sins you can think of and end up crying. I felt good that I was crying, like, 'Oh good, I'm feeling bad enough to cry. Something's happened.' Now I just feel really sad for that child.

Exorcisms and unqualified interpretations of health issues or disabilities as 'demons' or 'sin' rate among the most harmful. Jemma (UK) had recently spoken to a childhood friend about their shared memories of big Christian festivals:

My friend had particularly traumatic experiences with people trying to exorcize demons from her and her mental health condition being interpreted as satanic practice going on in her body. Her story is not at all uncommon among the thousands of young people that attended those camps, whether it was kids suffering from mental health issues or people with physical disabilities being prayed for, for healing, and the terrible theological message that gives.

We were both surprised that it does not seem like in any way those organizations who run them have been held to account over the trauma that they have clearly caused. We feel quite angry that there have been no repercussions, and I'm sure they followed the official safeguarding rules or whatever, but having a bunch of teenagers in a big tent where you're telling them they've got demons in them just doesn't really seem like it.

I don't know what to make of it all now. Perhaps it is helpful for some people, but it seems that for the vast majority it is neutral at best: not positive or transformational, just bizarre. For Laura (UK), it prompted questions:

I was brought up in an environment where speaking tongues was just weird, and nobody did it anymore because it stopped when the Bible finished being written. Then I visited churches where it was normal. That opened a little crack in the door to say, 'OK, people have different views on this. What do you do with that contradiction?'

It is not confined to 'the saved'. Mia (Costa Rica/USA) was one of several people who discovered that her 'spiritual gifts' remained after she deconstructed:

Because I tended to pick up on nuances of how people were feeling, I was believed to be extremely prophetic and extremely insightful, and have all these gifts of wisdom and knowledge. I don't really know how I feel about it at this point. Maybe there's some element of it that is a spiritual thing, but I think, frankly, a lot of it was I paid attention and I cared.

As an atheist, Gary (Canada) was asked to teach some university students to speak in tongues as an experiment. He explained it to them and encouraged them to go ahead:

I'd never given what speaking tongues sounded like, but they started doing it, and then they started singing in the Spirit and they were really moved. One of the girls was crying, one girl said, 'I was about to dance.' I go, 'That's a thing, where somebody gets up and dances in the Sprit.'

David (Puerto Rico/Netherlands) asks:

What is this feeling touched by the Lord? I actually sometimes felt those things even when I was an atheist. Learning a little bit more psychology or meditating, you have this really similar experience of those things. You can get suggestions or altered states of consciousness.

As a child, Elisabeth (UK) was often asked to pray for adults, who felt she could give them words of knowledge and prophetic spiritual insights. Now, she's not sure where that came from, but has had similar spiritual experiences more recently:

I did chakra dancing the other week, and it reminded me of the Toronto Blessing because it was almost ecstatic in the music and everyone was waving their hands. It dawned on me how my whole life I've been experiencing so-called spiritual ecstasy within a church environment, but to experience that same thing in a different environment was liberating and confusing at the same time.

Warfare

When I was in my 20s, an ongoing back complaint flared up. I was over-seas, so someone took me to a doctor they knew through church. She was a qualified medical doctor, so her diagnosis was unexpected: I had one leg longer than the other, which is a sign of spiritual oppression. The remedy would be deliverance ministry. I didn't take my medicine. Looking back, I agree with Phil (UK):

> I don't think there was anyone behaving maliciously on purpose, but we were probably doing all sorts of things that were unwise under the banner of pursuing God, and that prayer and ministry is the answer to all sorts of major complex issues in people's lives. And it turns out not to be.

This kind of spiritualizing is common in evangelical circles, with everything from health conditions to accidents to the finding of parking spaces attributed to either curse or blessing. When all your words and actions are part of a bigger narrative in the battle between good and evil, it is inevitable that spiritual forces are going to get involved and help or hinder you. Statements like, 'Don't speak that (negative thing) over me', 'Speaking blessings into your life' and, 'I'm claiming this for Jesus' sound an awful lot like the 'manifesting' craze on social media, and Jesus' name ends up invoked like a magic spell, Bible verses used like magical hand grenades a person can lob into the battle.

As well as the battle, other militaristic language includes spiritual warfare or attack, victory and glory (add your own favourites/triggers). The first Christian novels I read were Frank Peretti's *This Present Dark-ness* and *Piercing the Darkness*, which, with their vivid portrayals of the spiritual dimension, freaked me out completely and, given that this kind of perspective was not uncommon in the circles I was in, informed how I saw the spiritual realm. (The books also reinforce the view that abuse allegations against white Christian men are spiritual attacks; accusers are demon-possessed; demons can enter a person through sexual abuse; 'secular' authorities such as social workers are in league with Satan;

Christian women are submissive and pure and non-Christian women are temptresses.)

Peretti is far from the only person to write about spiritual battles. Thanks to evangelical fascination, non-fiction books on the demonic and the occult are almost an industry by themselves. Amanda (USA) is a pastor who has seen this in her congregations:

> The Antichrist is everywhere. Really? Come on! You find what you're looking for. So then why are we looking for evil all the time? Why are we not trying to be aware of where the beauty is in the world? Christians, particularly evangelical Christians in America, are fascinated with overcoming evil and rooting out evil and finding evil in people's lives that we can be pure. Just exhausting.

I got off relatively lightly, despite my wonky legs and the generational curses I was told I had due to my 'unsaved' family. While I certainly bought into some of it, some things just seemed too far for me (or maybe I just wasn't spiritual enough), like refusing to abide by common sense or local laws and then viewing the negative results as spiritual attack or persecution. But particularly for those who grew up with this, the impact has been serious and long-lasting. Eva (USA) tells me how she felt on high alert at all times:

> Anything went wrong, that was the devil attacking you. I think a lot of people my age grew up with a really heavy emphasis on spiritual warfare. Satan is coming after you. If you were weak for even a second, he will attack you, demons can get you at any time. I still have dreams where demons are choking me.

Abi (USA) similarly grew up with this narrative, and as she told me about her anxiety it struck me that something like apparent demonic activity is such an easy thing for anxiety to latch onto: it's unseen. You can never quantify it. It's the kind of thing anxiety loves:

> Demonic activity was the thing that my anxiety grabbed onto as an explanation for why I felt the way that I did, because we didn't really talk about any chaos in the home. And my parents, because we were at this charismatic church, they believed in demons, too. They couldn't be like, 'No, the monster's not real. It's normal to be scared sometimes.' There was no comforting, it was like, 'Yeah, there could be demons here right now.' To be honest, I was scared at night into my early 20s.

Kirsten's (USA) story is perhaps the most sinister, although I'm aware of others who have suffered similar treatment, whether for undiagnosed autism, trauma symptoms or a range of other reasons:

> I had nightmares as a child, and it was because I was sexually abused by the music minister and nobody knew that. They assumed my nightmares were demons, so they put me in the middle of the room – I'm five years old – they stood around me and prayed out demons.

Anyone who has been present when people are 'praying out demons' knows it can be overwhelming, even for an adult observer. For a child who had already been abused, surrounded by shouting adults, it had a devastating impact.

Dodgy

My mom burned my Sesame Street curtains and my bedspread and all because they said, 'If you're Christian, you can't have monsters around.' But see, I was little and Sesame Street was my world. (Stacy, USA)

When the big things are split into binaries – God/Satan, angels/demons, good/evil, heaven/hell – this has a trickle-down effect into smaller and smaller things. Everything becomes classifiable in this way, with little room for nuance or grey areas. Joy (USA) tells me that, despite believing in grace and forgiveness, the constant teachings on how sinful we are drove her to believe she was a terrible person. She wondered how people lived with themselves, knowing how terrible they were. Eventually she checked herself into hospital, afraid she was going to take her own life:

> When I got there, I decided that I was going to survive, and that meant ignoring a lot of the right and wrong that religion had instilled in me my entire life and that had been so heavy on me.
>
> The idea of neutrality is something I never got to experience and think about until after I got out of religion, because everything had a moral value. To just look at everything and say, 'Those are neutral things, those are entirely amoral, and if you choose it, you can do it in a moral way or not, but it, in itself, is neutral', that has been very freeing.

I look back at the things that were considered evil, or just 'dodgy' for Christians, and realize how many of those things are, as Joy says, neutral, depending on what you do with them. I put a checklist into the survey, asking which things people had been taught were wrong, and asking people to add their own. Here's a sample of the most popular options we came up with: yoga; New Age practices; alternative medicine such as acupuncture; crystals; meditation and mindfulness; Harry Potter, Pokémon, He-Man and Barbie; secular music, tv and movies; horoscopes; the Enneagram; tattoos and piercings; feminism and liberalism; science and Evolution; dancing; drums; Halloween; women working outside the home; (American) public schools; therapists and psychologists; lotteries;

martial arts and 'anything worldly'. (Any object of non-western cultural origin was automatically viewed as demonic: we will look more at this in White Jesus.)

Andrew (Australia), who grew up Seventh Day Adventist, tells me that he didn't go to the movies until he was 15, and then only because the movie had an Adventist theme. I have to tell Andrew that I was taught that Adventists themselves are dodgy.

A few people confessed that their teenage rebellion had consisted of secretly reading Harry Potter books (mine was watching *X-Files*), while others remembered their churches holding burnings of secular CDs and books, putting churches right up there with a long list of unpleasantly authoritarian groups throughout history who have done the same:

> I'm a big heavy metal fan and I felt convicted to get rid of a load of my CDs, which I've since got back. The 'sin' aspects were sucking bits out of my personality or my being. You're made to feel like some of the things that you do or you're into are really bad. (Evan, UK)

The control of influences and input in this way is easy to dismiss as unimportant, but it creates an isolation from 'the world', making it hard to engage with peers and allowing only the 'correct' influences and view-points to be heard. It also just makes the world a less vibrant place:

> One of my great sadnesses is how restricted my teenage years were in terms of culture. All the music I heard and sang were hymns and some truly dreadful choruses. The books I was given were all published by Inter Varsity Press, so a very restricted range of stuff to read. Now, in my adult life, I feel like I've got a whole lot of catching up to do. There's so much wonderful stuff out there. There was a huge narrow-ness culturally: the demarcation of boundaries was so firm about what was allowed. I feel that that was a diminishing of my life in crucial years. (Sally, UK)

In my early 30s, a friend and I created a heavily edited photo of me flying on a broomstick which I used on my social media profile. Others at the mission training base I was on at the time had no problem with it. How-ever, someone from another base spotted the photo, and colleagues told me that they had received emails from him asking, 'Is Olivia practising witchcraft?' and warning of dire consequences if so!

While I was well able to laugh this off, there have been times that this mindset has led to far worse. Bridget (New Zealand) told me what happened in a group she was leading: 'One lovely person in the group told another person, who had recently lost her son in an unexplained death, that the reason it had happened was because she had crystals sitting in her lounge.'

The warnings are always that these things will somehow open us up to the demonic, but it seems that it has a strong element of quashing the competition: so much of what takes place in evangelical circles has strong similarities with the things that are supposedly 'dodgy'. The generic nature of many of the prophecies I have heard sounds a lot like newspaper horoscopes, and I have never received a 'prophecy' that was either specific and true, or non-generic enough to mean whatever I made it mean (although I'm aware others have had astoundingly accurate experiences). There's the view that meditation leads to emptying the mind so that demons can enter, but practices like speaking in tongues and some forms of prayer are comparable. *Lord of the Rings* and the Narnia series are usually allowed because their authors were Christians (although not evangelicals), but Harry Potter is a fast-track into witchcraft.

On the other hand, I lost count of the number of people who told me they have found yoga helpful for a variety of reasons, not least countering the disembodiment and body-shaming in much of evangelicalism. When I eventually discovered it, it certainly contributed to sorting out my 'spiritually oppressed' back problem. Sharon (UK) discovered it had the opposite effect to that she was warned about:

> It has really helped me engage with God and it's interesting, actually, the people that have suddenly contacted me out of the blue to tell me I shouldn't be doing it. They can't tell you why not, they just have been taught in church that it's not right. Some of them have come up with things like, 'Well, when you do these positions you're worshipping these different gods.'

Non-Christian therapists and therapy models are also viewed with suspicion despite the fact that, in my experience, plenty of 'biblical counsellors' are not qualified or registered and are liable to push a particular theology. I share Eva's (USA) feelings about it:

> The thing that frustrates me the most is that the Church demonized all the tools that could help us, like therapy. They basically created these mental illnesses that we didn't have to have and then they said, 'Therapy is not good. Meditation is basically meditating on a demon.' Everything that could possibly have helped us was a tool of Satan. We suffered a lot longer than we had to.

Them and Us

The fence around the tribe is a set of beliefs that determines whether you're in or out, and more time is spent on discussing those beliefs than is spent on the practice. (Sam, UK)

The binaries continue with people: saved and unsaved. Christians are safe: 'the world' is a threat (and 'Christians' means 'Christians like us'). One of the first things I learned when I 'got saved' was that not all Christians are 'real' Christians: 73% of survey respondents were given a negative view of other Christian denominations. (It begs the question as to how evangelicals can claim that the Bible is the inerrant word of God, when those who chose which texts made it in were not evangelical.) I look back at the sheer irresponsibility of those adults (not all, but enough) who told me, as a child, that I couldn't really trust my own mother because she 'isn't saved'.

Ruth (USA) tells me how she felt growing up:

Most of our friends that we would socialize with were Christians. I do remember that there were some that were not, but I also remember being absolutely terrified of being around them, like they're either going to influence me or they're going to put a hex on me, and they're going to hell and it's on me to change them.

Not only was Christianity the only way, but it was Assemblies Of God as the only way. I had Baptist friends who I needed to convert because they didn't believe in the power of the Holy Spirit, and no Catholics are Christian because they worship idols, they pray to other people.

For Austin (USA), this kind of attitude was part of his education:

We took a class on different religions in my high school, but it wasn't called Religious Studies: it was called Cults. So, we talked about Mormonism and we talked about Islam and we talked about Jehovah's Witnesses. Then at the end of the class, we talked about Catholicism, and I remember my Bible teacher was like, 'It's not technically a cult, but it's close.'

Phoebe (USA) found it was present at work:

> In the church where I was on staff over 13 years, I was taught that there was no other denomination like the Methodists. Calvinist teaching was just garbage. Catholics were horrible people who were led astray. The way that the leadership would talk about other denominations and other teachings, it's like everyone else was crazy. Everyone else was less than. It was very tribal, it was very us and them. If you weren't part of us, you were just blown off and dismissed: you've got nothing really of value to offer the Christian community. It felt like death to my soul, and I needed that job so badly, we needed insurance and I felt like we didn't have a choice.

Even former evangelicals who have changed their minds on particular issues (usually sexuality) find themselves suddenly cast out, regardless of previous popularity and 'anointing': Jen Hatmaker, David P. Gushee, Steve Chalke and Rob Bell all come to mind, alongside the shockingly nasty comments made by some evangelicals after Rachel Held Evans's death. Just a little engagement with the 'other' can quickly make you into the other, and cancel culture has been going on in these circles well before social media existed:

> Community, when it works, is brilliant. It's a shame, but certainly in my experience, it seems to be that there's us and them, in and out, and there is a line, and once you're one of us, then it's a pretty good place to be. But if you stray too close to the line or step over the line? Suddenly not such a good place to be. (Matt, UK)

Steve B. (UK) remembered the double standards applied to those who didn't measure up:

> As soon as I would bring anything to the community group, I would just be immediately met with, 'Richard Rohr has heretical views', or, 'Rob Bell is a heretic', or it would be attacks on their personality or 'this person had an affair' or 'this person stole money', whatever. I remember around the time of the Ravi Zacharias scandal and I said, 'But what about Ravi Zacharias?' It's like, 'Yeah, but we're all broken.'

Hope (USA) comments that, 'We end up rejecting people who actually are truth bearers', while Gary (Canada) speaks directly to those double standards:

> Evangelicalism specifically empowers our worst belief systems that the other is wrong, that our smallest group is right and that we're under attack. And so you become this, 'We are the victim, we need to close together, and they are judging us so bad, so we shouldn't judge ourselves too much.'

(The other side of this coin is support for anything a Christian does, triumphant claiming of any celebrity who so much as hints at faith, the lauding of any book or movie with a Christian theme, however cheesy or problematic.)

The terms 'dodgy theology' and 'wishy-washy' were ones I grew up with. I remember a highly qualified and enormously intelligent curate joining a church I attended in the 1990s. After a couple of sermons in which he suggested that climate change was real and gave a range of theological stances on hell, I heard 'dodgy' muttered by a few people far less qualified than he was.

Michael (UK) is a pastor who has faced this from his own church:

> When I came to this church that I'm in currently, it was conservative in theology. One of the deacons asked for a list of books I'd read in the last year. I said, 'That's an unreasonable request', but I provided him with a list, and he highlighted authors that were heretics, and then voted against me.

This disallowing of the wrong ideas is common. Paul (USA) sums up the reasoning: 'You shouldn't read certain books, you shouldn't listen to certain people because if you do, you'll become evil.'

Those who are explicitly not Christians of any sort are even more suspect: over 86% of survey respondents had heard negative teaching about those of other faiths or none. Some of the things I've heard more than once about non-Christians are that they are in rebellion against God; they can never be truly joyful or at peace; they are hurting, lost and feel empty but are in denial about this. Most will actively try to lead you astray, friendships with non-Christians are for evangelistic purposes and romantic relationships with them will lead you straight into sin and heartbreak.

External sources of authority and lived experience that disagree with what 'we' think are untrustworthy and must be rejected. During a mental health crisis, Sharon (UK) sought treatment. But her experience of God was dismissed by those at church:

I spent time in the crisis house twice. The first time I went, I felt God strongly speaking to me through a Pagan witch and a member of staff who was Sikh, who sat with me and said her prayers. When I told people at church they were horrified, like, 'God wouldn't speak through a Pagan witch and a Sikh.'

Perhaps the one that makes me most angry, and which I never managed to understand, was the line that non-Christians are incapable of real love or of moral action. The line goes that God is love, so those who don't know God cannot love (and God is where we get our moral standards, which applies the same reasoning). Apart from anything, it is a direct inversion of the verse it is taken from, 1 John 4.7: 'love is of God; and everyone who loves is born of God and knows God'. This flings the boundaries of who knows God wide open.

I heard the inverted version in a few places, one of which was in the missions organization I worked for. Sophie (UK) trained with them over 20 years later and on a different continent, but confirms that this is still being taught:

One of the teachings was about relationships, and it was basically that thing of real love is God's love and so unless you know God's love, you can't have that in your relationships with people. My best friend wasn't a Christian, and I remember being like, 'My closest person to me in the world who I trust more than anything is not Christian. What are you saying about the level of that friendship?' and the response was, 'Non-Christians can still have really intimate friendships and relationships and love, but how much more would it be if they knew Jesus?'

Sophie's friendship was damaged as a result, and it took time to repair the rift. Lucas (UK) sums up the moral superiority and exclusivity that go with these attitudes:

I always intentionally kept relationships at school pretty superficial, and I really felt I had nothing to gain from these people because they weren't in the church and they had nothing good to offer. If I was being honest, that's totally how I would have seen it. They were of the world of darkness, you know?

It can also lead churches and mission agencies not to work well with other groups, which is a sad waste of opportunity. Josh (Netherlands/ New Zealand) has seen this, too:

All sorts of church community action, they would never link up with non-Christian groups because they said they couldn't be trusted and how that undermines the effectiveness. I've seen that so many times. I think it's relinquishing ownership or relinquishing authority, and if they're going to do something good, if they're going to be an agent of change, surely a secular organization or group of people would be vastly inferior to that. That is such a poor excuse for apathy or duplication.

It's no wonder, with such a dangerous world out there, that a strong persecution narrative forms part of evangelical thinking. The dire warning that 'persecution is coming' is often given, complete with instructions never to deny one's faith on pain of damnation, and to learn as much of the Bible by heart as possible, in case 'they' take it away. It feeds straight into that fear of outsiders and 'secular' authorities. I realize now I had a constant, background anxiety about this, until I worked with people who were facing real restrictions of religious freedom. But it seems that white, western evangelicals increasingly take any critique or holding to account as persecution, an undermining of their freedom of belief, paralleling themselves to the Bible's oppressed Hebrews rather than the powerful Egyptians.

For some people, the othering formed a breaking point with their church. After seeing 'them and us' attitudes on the mission field and experiencing othering first-hand when she married into a different culture, Isabel (UK) told me how it impacted her deconstruction:

> One of the fundamental things that I was finding difficult in church is the divisions between the people who are in and the people who are out, or that people can be excluded. 'Well, you can't preach because you're a woman' or 'We don't want you here because you're gay' or whatever, and that's just a problem for me.

Deconstructors who leave are often ill prepared for the world they have been trained to view as dangerous and/or an evangelism opportunity. Many people reported on the survey that they had difficulty adjusting to life outside church when they left. Perhaps, subliminally or not, that's the point.

Politics

I talked about politics and it bit me in the ass. (Russell, USA)

In the fundamentalism I grew up in, politics was never mentioned. Russia was a big fear that played into the apocalyptic scenarios of the 70s and 80s, but even as beloved as Ronald Reagan was, I never heard his name in a church service, never. But gosh, a lot of people here are wearing Trump shirts to church. (Ronnie, USA)

For so many Americans who contributed to this book, politics in church was a major issue. I interviewed people from all over the white-majority world, and while most countries do not have this blend to anything like the same extent, it does affect evangelical churches everywhere due to the homogeneity of the culture and the sharing of resources, from American Christian websites to American-linked ministries (and often where America leads, the rest of the world follows, with or without context).

Some of the current context has been decades in the making, though, and is not confined to the USA. Tim (Canada) tells me he grew up in the Canadian Bible Belt, in a church and family steeped in dominion theology:

The terms used were things like 'penetrate culture' or 'influence culture'. Terms like 'dominion', the Church as a governmental authority. I'm thinking R. J. Rushdoony; voices where it's like, 'We need to establish the kingdom of God in terms of cultural domination.' But it was also connected to spiritual warfare as well, and so if you had a church community that is having influence within government or within the business world, that also was connected to fighting against the spiritual forces and powers.

I hadn't heard Rushdoony's name until about a year ago, but I am well acquainted with versions of his teachings and I realize how much they have, in one form or other, seeped into mainstream evangelical teaching across the world. (Rushdoony, who died in 2001, was also a eugenicist and Holocaust denier, wrote that Southern slavery was 'benevolent' and put interracial marriage under the category of 'unequally yoked'.) His teaching and influence have to go into the mix of modern evangelical rhetoric around politics. Add to that the last few decades of Christian groups manoeuvring into positions of political influence, persecution narrative combined with a steep decline in both numbers and cultural domination, then layer on top of it the militaristic rhetoric in worship songs, and it all spills over into the blend of American politics and evangelicalism that we see today:

A lot of Christians are given the idea that you have to defend the honour of the Bible and you have to defend the faith. It's very much this narrative of war, so when it feels as though Christianity is giving up territory to these progressive ideas that seem to go against literal interpretations of a few scriptures, they've been mobilized to defend this at all costs. You have people who literally voted for a man who talks so crassly about how he treats women. You have women voting for this man simply because the other person would allow abortion to take place or is supportive of gay marriage or whatever. And so for them, it's like, 'I don't like this man, but he's going to help regain some territory for Christianity within this country', because the narrative that they have been fed is that America is a Christian nation under attack. I think that's even been exacerbated by the pandemic. (Anselm, USA)

Ronnie (USA), a pastor, talks about the overwhelmingly politically conservative area he lives in:

It's a radical, dangerous fusion of Christian nationalism, political power, conservative evangelicalism, it's all in the pot together. It's volatile. I think that evangelicals were primed for a Trump type of character to come along. He is so much like Mark Driscoll and what you would see in a pulpit. It's been frightening to live in the midst of.

He goes back to the broader teaching he received growing up:

Looking back at it now, the constant apocalyptic state that was projected was just abusive. I think it was emotional abuse. I think it was spiritual abuse. I think it was a form of religious terror. These churches were just an extension of the Whitfield revivalism where you had to have this emotional response, this repentance every week, and the big muscle was the apocalypse, hell, end of the world.

There was something to be terrified of all the time and it did a great deal of damage. I can remember the inability to sleep at night, I had to check in on my siblings or my parents late at night to make sure no one had been raptured and I've been left behind. I'm not surprised at all that evangelicals are the ones that just love conspiracy theory as a result. We've been primed for it.

But frightened people are much easier to control, either by churches or by governments. Give people an enemy, keep them afraid, offer them safety and salvation of one sort or another, and you have their loyalty. It seems that, like Peter in Gethsemane, fear means that too many people are willing to kill for Jesus, but not to die for him. This climate has cost Paul (USA) dearly:

> I still had friends from church on Facebook and stuff, and when I would start talking about being affirming, and I'm also anti-violence, I'm against wars, I'm against the death penalty, so when I talk about that my former friends would say, 'Well, you're not a Christian anymore.' And even if I point out things from the Bible, they say, 'No, you're deceived, you're leading people away.' I lost a lot of friends. I actually lost my mother to Trump, so that has been painful and isolating.

Russell (USA), who found that talking about politics 'bit me in the ass' (above):

> This is just lunacy. I don't understand how Christian people can embrace that. That's not the hippie Jesus that I grew up with. It's not the loving Jesus I grew up with. And we're trained from when we're little to follow authority within the Church, so the road is already greased for them just to pull along.

Neither the USA nor the Church are the only places to see increased polarization on a number of fronts, but perhaps it is even uglier in an institution that claims unconditional love as a core part of its identity.

Saved

Whenever I met people who didn't believe in Jesus, I knew my Bible, I knew the arguments for why it was true and I was very eager to tell them why they were wrong. We also got the teaching that it's a shame to be outside, poor them, they need Christ, they don't know what they're missing. (Emilia, Sweden)

I didn't ever have a conversion experience, and that's not a surprise, growing up in a Christian family, is it? But that was a thing at church and in the youth group, and you had to have one. So I made one up, because otherwise you weren't a Christian. (Margaret, UK)

If you died today, where would you end up? It's quite possibly the worst way to persuade someone to follow a cause, and doesn't exactly scream 'unconditional love', but I remember hearing it numerous times and even using it myself on occasion. Liz (UK) tells me about an experience she had in her early 20s:

Somebody wanted some prayer because their grandad was dying. They were saying, 'I find it difficult because they're not a Christian and I'm worried about them.' The person I was with basically told this person that their grandad is going to hell, and it was their responsibility to make sure they got a conversation in.

Mia (Costa Rica/USA) was on the receiving end of similarly emotive instruction:

When I was 12 or 13, my mum sent me to summer camp. It was one of those camps where there's a ton of high feelings, a lot of emotional manipulation, trying to get you to cry and feel terrible about yourself.

My stepdad was pretty abusive. That was just part of that church, that you're encouraged to physically discipline your children and be very strict, so he would hit all of us frequently. I was also sexually abused by another family member. So, I was at this camp with all these really high feelings and all of this trauma, and very much it was being used as, 'Oh, you really need Jesus to save you from all of these things.' I just felt so guilty and ashamed because I genuinely believed all this was my fault, so I ended up doing the whole 'come to the Lord' thing at this camp.

Over 75% of survey respondents said that they had participated in evangelism. For me it was such a mixture of feeling guilty if I didn't (because unsaved people would suffer eternal conscious torment and my leaders said that if we really loved our friends and family we would tell them about Jesus) and also horribly awkward. The targeting of children, in particular, felt uncomfortable: 'the 4-14 Window', as it is known. In my first few months in mission, we were sent door-to-door. My group spent some quality time in a fast-food place instead, which pretty much set the tone for my evangelism efforts thereafter. At the time, I did honestly think that 'getting people saved' was for their best, with a barely acknowledged side-order of 'if they join us then we will face less opposition'. Now I cringe at the implicit 'I have what you need whether you want it or not.' Elisabeth (UK) is emphatic when we compare our experiences from the same organization:

Oh, I flippen hated it so bad! I actually ripped up my journals a few months ago because everything I wrote pretty much was like, 'I feel so bad, I haven't evangelized. Surely if I believed it this much, I would talk to everyone', you know, like going to a shopping centre and singing and then trying to walk around and ask people.

Now I'm experiencing what it's like to be on the other side, how I used to be with other people starting to lose their faith: 'Oh, let's pray with you. It's not just about church', and trying to reel them back in. I now feel like people are doing that to me, and it's really horrible.

Evangelizing friends was a recurrent theme in interviews, and Joshua (UK) remembers, 'It became quite hard to form authentic relationships with people, because every single relationship you have is an opportunity to evangelize.'

Julie (UK) also found it distasteful: 'I remember at the time saying, "I hate the term 'friendship evangelism'. You're either friends or you're not: don't dress it up." I remember thinking that it's really deceptive to call it "friendship evangelism".' (Then there's 'missionary dating': next level friendship evangelism.) Jess (UK) touches upon a problem many of us ran into:

It was a bit like, 'I don't really know what I'm offering people. I feel like I should be offering them eternal life and you say these magic words and you become born again and it's all OK.' At the same time, I did have all those nagging fears that if I didn't, then terrible things might happen to my friends. I just lived with that weird cognitive dissonance for quite a long time, didn't really resolve it.

My mum tried to evangelize my friends to the point where they were a bit scared of being left alone with her if they were at my house and I went to the toilet or something.

At a church level, things are more strategic. Having started going to a branch of an international megachurch in her early 20s, Vivian (Netherlands) quickly ran into this: 'Growth was the goal and everything had to be about attracting new people. There was a lot less attention on the people already inside who did have questions and doubts.'

Austin (USA) spent seven years working as a minister. He told me how much he enjoyed meeting people and working alongside them, but after some time he became disillusioned:

I started feeling the pressure to meet a quota for how many people I'm bringing into the church. I saw the man behind the curtain. We talked so much about, 'Here's how Jesus would minister to people', and yet I found so many contradictions in the fact that, from what I read of Jesus, he didn't care about how many people were following him, he didn't care about pushing people to donate money.

While some churches are more explicit about a growth model, others combine it with community work, which tends to dilute the (probably) genuinely held altruism:

My church really valued mission and outward-looking things you could do for the community, which sounds great, but it's all with a view to saving people, not actually being there, present and listening and serving people unconditionally or selflessly. It was more about, 'How do we get the gospel in there?' (Romilly, UK)

Sharon (UK) saw the fallout of this when she worked at a church:

Through the parenting courses I did, a couple of women became Christians and one of the mums had three children with special needs, she was on her own, and she started coming to church. It's awful in a way, but I almost had to teach people how to be with her. As in: 'Her kids are not going to sit still, they're not going to be quiet, she'll be late.' People were brilliant until the day she got baptized. A few months after this, she said that she felt she had been conned by a really good salesperson. She said she wasn't talking about me, she was talking about church. Everyone was so caring and supportive, ringing her up and texting her, taking her meals. Once she signed on the dotted line and she'd been baptized, all of a sudden it was like she was a project and they'd moved on. I literally felt like I'd been kicked in the stomach. I took it to the leadership team and they just sort of said, 'Well, it's not just about us caring for her, she needs to care for us.'

When I remember it, I feel the same emotions again of how we let her down because it was all about getting her into church on a Sunday and all of a sudden she didn't matter, people weren't making space for her kids and people started tutting when they were running riot.

Having deconstructed the evangelism models and motives we were given, Julie (UK) sums up how an awful lot of us feel: 'It's liberating to feel like it's not on you to save the world and to evangelize everybody.'

Lemon Meringue Pie Gospel

The more I read about who Jesus really was, he was a social activist, and I didn't understand how people were using Christianity to live their comfortable life. The triviality of American Christianity just annoyed me. I wanted to talk about real issues, and people were annoyed because they just wanted to plan their next fundraiser. They cared more about whether you could bake a pie. Your score goes way up if you can make a lemon meringue pie. (Kathy, USA)

In my late 20s, I had been working on a community-run project for a number of years, seeing a cycle of disenfranchisement and poverty that had gone on for centuries. I was starting to move towards advocacy work and spoke to someone back home about the need for justice and systemic change. 'Isn't justice just people getting angry and going on marches?' she asked. Getting people saved was far more important.

The split between a 'salvation gospel' and a 'social gospel' is, for many churches, mending. There is no doubt that faith-based social action does a huge amount of good in the world. There is also no doubt that quite a bit of it is misguided and ineffective, if not downright harmful, from ulterior motives to unqualified assumptions about people's needs.

Churches are not alone in doing harm: recent scandals concerning NGOs are only the tip of the secular iceberg in terms of damage done. But the Church too often claims to be better than others, while setting itself a frighteningly low bar. An over-emphasis on the divine nature of Jesus and a spiritualized, personal relationship with him, at the expense of an incarnational faith and acting as the Gospels tell us Jesus did, means we can spend hours singing worship songs and then step over the person who is homeless as we leave church.

It's this spiritualizing instinct that says if we understand things in a spiritual way, that removes our responsibility to do anything practical about it. We watch the news on the television, and then we look at our Bibles and we go, 'Oh my goodness, amazing parallels', and that gives us an incredible feeling of vindication without actually having done anything practical whatsoever. (Andrew, Australia)

The pastor, when all the climate change stuff kicked off with Extinction Rebellion, said, 'God's got this.' What the hell does that mean? What it means is you're switching people off to one of the most critical issues in the history of the Earth, you dozy twonk. (Aidan, UK)

While spiritualizing away the problem is one thing, other people's frustrations lay in their church's total disinterest, or the attitude that only God can fix complex social issues so we shouldn't try. I remember being invited to a church to speak about violence against women. After the service, a woman walked up to me and said, 'I didn't want to know that', and then left. It may just have been a rubbish talk, but I remember thinking that surely engaging with issues like this should be an integral part of church? Julie (UK) tells me her experience:

My first big moment feeling I couldn't carry on with church was when Islamic State kicked off in 2014 and there was the massacre of the Yazidis. All this stuff was massively affecting me, and nobody in church was even talking about it. The refugee crisis in Syria was kicking off, and I remember crying on the sofa to my husband, and I hardly ever swear, and I remember saying, 'Why the fuck does nobody care?' People in church were still like, 'Can you pray for my auntie who's got a headache?'

I remember saying to the leader, 'Nobody's talking about these massive crises', and he said, 'Oh, you want to speak to Donna', because she was this social action woman. It wasn't, 'You're right. We should be engaging with these subjects.' It was, 'You should talk to Donna because it's clearly her thing as well.' Special interest. Niche.

What MJ (USA) experienced is a more explicit version of this passivity about what is going on in the world. It shaped her future:

We had a hurricane scare and it ended up not hitting us, but people evacuated, and it hit Florida. On my way to Bible college, I had seen a sign from this really small church in my neighbourhood, and it said, 'We're collecting donations to help the hurricane victims.' I thought, 'Wow, that's really nice. I wonder what my church is doing, my big church.' That day, the pastor's wife told us that her husband, the head pastor, was angry about the hurricane scare because people were evacuating and church attendance wouldn't be high and they wouldn't get enough offerings. That was my last day at Bible college, I dropped out.

They didn't even have to pay for their house. Somebody gave them a house. So it's not like they were worried about money. It's not quite a megachurch, but damn near a megachurch, you know? And your concern is not about your congregation who had to miss work to evacuate, who maybe lost wages, not about the people who were actually hit by the hurricane, but that your offerings would be lower for a week. That's not Jesus. That's not God.

Tessi (USA) also faced this lack of compassion when she worked with vulnerable young people:

> I have kids that are showing up on my doorstep in the rain, at three o'clock in the morning, blood flowing down both arms because they have been cutting for hours. They have walked two miles to my house because they know I'll bandage them and be with them. And Church Lady calls the pastor to complain about how I'm bringing kids to church that aren't brushing their hair, or I'm supporting self-injury by letting it happen in my house, or I'm allowing goth kids to hang out with non-goth kids.

At the next level is the well-intended but ineffectual:

> When we left our church, what became very clear to us was that if you weren't in the church, it actually wasn't being and doing anything. We thought it was quite vibrant and doing things all the time, but we stepped out of it and it was remarkable how little impact it seemed to have, and you think, 'What have I been doing all this time?' (Scott, UK)

Nina (UK) experienced this lack of impact amid the activity:

> At uni, my faith reoriented from that very charismatic, intense emotional experience to more of a social gospel: live among the poor, live in community and if you live in the way that Jesus lived and follow his teachings, then that would bring about the kingdom of heaven. I still understood that as 'people become Christians'. So we moved to London wanting to live in community on a council estate. When we actually got to that situation, it was hard to see what was really being done, what was really the point of us living in community. They had a real cookie-cutter idea of what a church plant was: toddler groups, the marriage course, the Alpha course, the parenting course. It was very formulaic.

Nina found herself running more and more church programmes, as well as being, worryingly, bookkeeper, treasurer and trustee simultaneously:

I was like, 'All this money that people are giving, good tithers that we are, that is just to pay this guy's salary and pay for the buildings. That is the sum total of church.' I started to see church as a professional service for people to manage their guilt and as a club to have belonging. It wasn't affecting the community or making the world a better place. I felt really jaded by that.

My issues with church at that point were around structure and depth of spirituality, I really hadn't started deconstructing the big things. I felt that spirituality and relationship with God was supposed to be transformative. It was supposed to be life-giving and it was supposed to lead to deeper relationships and community. And I felt like all those things were lacking.

It's not a bad business model: tell people they have guilt, then offer the service to manage it.

Steve B. (UK) points to the classism inherent in some church activity:

This particular church is extremely middle class. If someone that would be considered working class walked in, they would just feel massively alienated. I feel uncomfortable with essentially seeing the solution as to pull the lower class or low income into the middle class rather than challenging the system as a whole. They just go, 'Let's train everyone to make beautiful gardens.' That's not really what people want.

People are just very misguided sometimes. How do you square away spending £300,000 on a building when you've got children in this city on free school meals, when you've got single mums down the road struggling to feed their kids? Why are you building a lavish horsebox as a prayer cabin, with a wood burner and a coffee machine, to pray for the poor? The thing that really bothers me is I see how complicit I am in that because I am middle class and I can't do anything about it, and if you question it, you just get told that you're negative.

Tim (Canada) has seen both the spiritualizing of the issues and the way that Christianity has directly contributed to people's vulnerability – creating a problem and then claiming to be the only answer to it:

The churches had this great testimony of, 'There was spiritual deliverance for him. He was delivered from the demon of addiction, and then he was welcomed into the fold of God', but they didn't know what happened the day following. There would be missions teams that would come up from different parts of the world and did street evangelism, and some of our youth, I saw their experiences of people who wanted to pray and took advantage of their circumstance. They were like, 'I'm homeless, I have a target on my back.'

Later in our conversation, he gives the bigger picture:

When you engage with the homeless community, you see the fallout of conservative cultural posturing. Within Canada, 48% of our homeless youth are a part of the LGBTQ+ community. There's a direct line between the two: they're on the street because they've been kicked out specifically because of their sexuality. There's that disparity between this idea that 'cultural Marxism', or liberalism in general, is eroding our values by pushing the LGBTQ+ agenda. But then if you look at the main communities that we were working with, we were working with the LGBTQ+ community and the First Nations community as the two most represented peoples. And for all of them, there was already a contact with Christianity, but they had experienced the rejection, the damage and the violence.

It was thrown around a lot that we need to go back to our founding as a Christian nation, and then I would see what the dark side of that was, what this Christian nation had done in order to protect a certain cultural hegemony.

Why didn't you just leave?

Looking back, I can see red flags, but it was just my normal. (Ruth, USA)

The people who are done with church are not done because they lost their faith. They're done because the Church is done with faith. (George, Australia/UK, church minister)

I listened to story after story that contained the same broad pattern. It is not simply a few rotten churches, a few 'broken' individuals in leadership: it is the system itself. But the system and its leaders can never be criticized, so the complainant is blamed.

People do not deconstruct or leave church lightly: after decades of loyalty and defending church or mission organizations, there is huge sadness and, at times, sheer terror about leaving, even if just to a different church. People told me about diagnosed PTSD and years spent in therapy. The majority deconstructed church before they started to deconstruct theology, often finding a seamless progression from toxic institutions to toxic theologies. This is circular and self-reinforcing: we become the God we worship and we fashion God in our own image.

The constant theme that ran through almost every negative experience people spoke about, including my own, was control and the avoidance of vulnerability: the black and white rules; binary thinking; othering; authoritarian leadership; sin management; paranoid persecution theories; lack of real engagement with complex social issues; violent theology; militaristic language and the urge to dominate wider culture. These are not places structured around vulnerability, authenticity and unconditional love. While there are plenty of loving, compassionate and self-sacrificial people within churches, the structure and leadership of too many is not ultimately built for this.

This is a pattern, and too many churches and Christian organizations have strong similarities to cults, their methods fitting neatly into Robert J. Lifton's criteria for thought reform/brainwashing (Lifton, 1961). The recruitment, monitoring and control may start off being driven by a genuine concern for people's spiritual wellbeing, of saving people from eternal conscious torment, but it is a concern that puts compliance before autonomy, rules before ethics and coercion before liberation. Moreover, listening to their own PR about the good they do prevents many from really looking at harm or even believing it exists. When you have been told enough that what you are experiencing is freedom and abundant life, that what those outside experience is misery and emptiness, it becomes easier to start justifying problems and harm (more so if church was, initially, a place of safety and refuge).

Whether intentional or not, far too often leaders maintain power and control through shame and fear: of hell, of being outside the will of God or God's protection, of losing community, of the outside world. This may not be overt: all it takes is for previous leavers to be publicly denigrated or pitied and their story told for them (they rarely get a chance to tell it for themselves) for those still 'in' to cleave more tightly. We all have a deep survival need to belong, and when the evangelical bubble is your entire world, the threat or risk of losing that keeps people compliant and leads them to ignore a great deal of harm, especially when everyone else (apparently) sees no problem.

No one intentionally joins a group like this: initial experiences are of warmth and encouragement, of promises made and sometimes of real change happening. As commitment and loyalty increase, so do demands, and the shift is incremental, insidious: promises of love, purpose and transformation get twisted into their opposites. If this is the only place that God is really at work, leaving is not an option, more so when you have years or decades of commitment invested already, or if that is your career. Michael (UK) and I discuss ideas around power and church:

> Jesus constantly subverts the idea of human power, from the moment of being born in Bethlehem and not Jerusalem, being raised in Nazareth and not Judea, being crucified – a method that dishonoured the Jewish man. Then being buried not in his family tomb, but in the tomb of some stranger. He's constantly undermining the power structures of our world.

How is it that so very many churches, denominations and Christian organizations that claim to follow Jesus have inverted this so completely?

PART 2

Stumbling Blocks

He/Him/God

I am 17, and a leader tells me that my friendships with boys are a good place to practise submitting to my future husband.

I am 29. Two male colleagues sit four of us single women down and explain to us that we will never find husbands if we continue to be so independent and opinionated. Gutting.

I got approached by the Sunday school teacher, absolutely horrified, saying, 'I think you need to talk to your daughter because she told people in the Sunday school class that you could call God "she".' (Alison, UK)

The inequality and the pain that it brings, what patriarchal thinking damages for humanity. Those questions of power – who holds the power and who doesn't, whose voice is welcome and whose is excluded – is part of my experience of gender. (Jude, Australia)

I was always supposed to be less than. Now I'm supposed to be a whole person, and I'm learning how to be. (Joy, USA)

Above my desk is a 1992 quote by former Republican presidential candidate and Southern Baptist minister Pat Robertson: 'Feminism encourages women to leave their husbands, kill their children, practice witchcraft, destroy capitalism and become lesbians.' I don't think Pat would appreciate the fact that I have it there because it makes me laugh: it reads like a parody of misogyny. And yet over 43% of survey participants were taught that feminism belongs on the list of things that are 'dodgy' for Christians. Tim (Canada) explains, 'The greatest threat to Christianity was feminism, because feminism takes away the proper roles of men, and if we don't have strong men, then our country is threatened.' Given that reading feminist and womanist theology and legal theory was the start of my deconstruction, maybe those churches are onto something.

Much of this chapter reflects the experience of those born and socialized as women. I am aware that evangelical teaching on gender has a negative impact on all genders. However, the majority of those who filled in the survey and who raised the issue of gender were cisgender women. While the survey asked for participants' gender/pronouns, I did not dig further to find out if participants were trans or cisgender.

When I asked on the survey if respondents had sometimes or regularly heard teaching or advice on appropriate gender presentations and roles or God's purpose for the different genders, 85% responded 'yes'. 48% reported that women were held to a higher standard than men in a church context, 6% said that men were, 34% responded that there was equality, with added comments such as 'equality of standards but different expectations'. Highlighting that this is less biblical and more cultural, Americans had a more gendered message, while Scandinavians reported more egalitarian teaching.

I've got away relatively lightly, although certainly not unscathed, in this area. I was raised by my mother alone since I was six and had some strong female leadership along the way. Most of the male headship teaching just seemed ridiculous.

The subtle expectations about roles and demeanour are just as corrosive, however: dress codes, blaming women for the thoughts and actions of men and, ultimately, the gendering of God. Elizabeth A. Johnson writes:

> The symbol of God functions as the primary symbol of the whole religious system, the ultimate point of reference for understanding experience, life and the world. Hence the way in which a faith community shapes language about God implicitly represents what it takes to be the highest good, the profoundest truth, the most appealing beauty. (Johnson, 1992, p. 4)

She goes on to quote Mary Daly: 'If God is male, then male is God' (ibid., p. 37). It isn't difficult to get into trouble in an evangelical space by referring to God as 'she' or 'they': the most concession likely to be granted is that God has some female or feminine attributes. Yet English Bibles too often lose even these feminine attributes of God in translation, interpretation or church teaching: the word in the Hebrew scriptures translated as 'compassion' or 'show mercy' literally means 'womb'. It took me years of being told that Bathsheba seduced David before I realized that Bathsheba was raped by the King (in a reflection of the victim-blaming of many assault survivors in the Church), or that the unnamed, seven-times-married woman at the well had no legal right to file for divorce: she had been divorced and likely made destitute each time, yet I was taught that her sin is the problem. Any suggestion that this view of God and scripture may lead to a devaluing of anyone who does not fit the cultural norms of manhood is strongly denied.

The 'Proverbs 31 woman' ('the wife of noble character') is held up as a model, although her virtues are often moulded to fit whatever the speaker thinks a woman should be: 'she considers a field and buys it; out of her earnings she plants a vineyard ... she sees that her trading is profitable' (verses 16 and 18) are not generally listed as desirable in godly women. We are taught to be good girls. We are taught to comply, smile, please, ignore our own needs, not know our wants, take what is not enough and declare it abundance.

Women are 'equal in value but different in authority/role' (known as complementarianism), regardless of the individual's actual personality and strengths. Lynn (Canada/Ireland) and I discuss this treatment of the Bible and the view of women:

> These are things that you don't notice, you assimilate them without understanding the philosophy and the theology behind it. So, it continu-ally reinforces the subordination of women without you even vocalizing that in your head. It bypasses speech and just goes right to the psyche.

Katya (UK) explains the impact of a lifetime of this on her:

> I feel like we've been robbed. I've been robbed of my ability to cele-brate womanhood in all its guises. I've had body dysmorphia. I've had enormous shame and stigma about losing my virginity when I was 17. But having daughters is just mind-blowing in terms of the speed and the urgency with which I've had to really go back and address this absolute pile of lies and try to seek new information and practices to help them in their journey of understanding of what it's like to be a woman. It's been such an effortful process, and I'm tired. I'm emotionally tired from having to keep pulling out layer after layer of dysfunctional belief.

Let's go back to Eve and women's 'primary' role: 'I was told repeatedly that birth was so horrible because of Eve, but it's our duty to have children', MJ (USA) says. The number of people who told me that they had a high number of siblings was striking. Abi (USA), one of seven siblings, tells me that hers was considered a smallish family. Now she has children of her own: 'The pressure to procreate is intense in Christian circles. I don't know that I can say that I chose to have kids: it was a matter of course. But anyway, I joke that my quiver is full.'

Tim grew up in Canada's Bible Belt:

The dominant way that spiritual warfare was talked about was in terms of how you can establish this culture-war Christianity. That language permeated the family culture to the extent that we had things such as the term 'open womb': having as many kids as possible was an act of cultural warfare. Using birth control is a disqualifier for participation within the church. Growing up, to practise faith was inextricably connected to the expectations of distinct gender roles that are setting you towards a trajectory of being a father or mother. This is the way that we save the culture; this is the way that we save the world.

With my mum, there's not yet a capacity to engage in processing all of that. This theology has cost her a lot more, so for her to question that is to question the entire value of her existence or her personhood. Even if there's a semblance of her choice, there's a limited range of expression for what a woman can be. The entirety of her existence then becomes defined as this home-educating mum. So, if the kids are seen to stray in any way, that's a direct reflection on her and her capacity or incapacity to be a godly woman. Her identity and reputation and validity as a woman are on the line because there's not an option to fail. You have all your kids turn out as full participants within this cultural battle that we're a part of and walking in the way of God. The only reason you're on Earth is to do that, and it's your access to honour and respect within this patriarchal family structure.

Even in systems less extreme than this, male headship teaching is normal: the idea that a loving partnership needs fixed roles and one person pre-assigned to make all final decisions. It put Christine (UK) off marriage:

> I remember at a wedding hearing this sermon about the woman's role in the marriage and thinking, 'But this is a really intelligent young woman. Why is her opinion worth less than her husband's?' So, I was reluctant to even pursue relationships. I could see what being married would be in the context of Christianity and that's not what I want.

Ruth (USA) did marry, but risked being deemed a 'failure':

> I was constantly being told to change. My husband was constantly being told to change me. Once we were able to be like, 'What is my strength? What is your strength, what are our weaknesses?' it has made a world of difference.
>
> I'm better with numbers, and so I do finances: he was tired of me not getting the laundry done, so he washes clothes. That could have been a 'failure as a wife' thing. Our marriage is so much better after being out of that.

Training up godly women and men starts young. Caro (Australia) tells me about her own childhood:

> A lot of the healing work I've had to do in my own life has been around how the culture I grew up in patterned me to be a certain type of person. I was patterned, as a young Christian girl, to assume that I was going to be married by 20, and I had to find a passionate Christian guy, more passionate than me because I had to have a spiritual head. The highest call any young Christian woman could have was to be a pastor's wife. I never wanted to be the pastor's wife, but I certainly thought I'd be the pastor until I realized women didn't do that. But it was all really subtle.

Joy (USA) is still living with the effects of being socialized as the 'good Christian girl':

> With purity culture and being raised defined as female and a very limited context of the role assigned to us, I diminished myself and my sense of self-worth to a point where I didn't even have a personality because I was so sure that the only way to be a good person was to be this passive, very forgiving, un-opinionated person. If I had a strong preference, it might come up in opposition to a man's preference and then it would be wrong.
>
> I don't know what I want: I've never been asked. Just to allow myself to exercise opinion and decision-making, it's very new.

People across the gender spectrum told me about the shame they felt for not fitting into prescribed standards. The existence of trans and non-binary folk is often denied altogether or dismissed as 'they need healing'. Steve B. (UK) says:

> Someone in our church defined as trans. I heard through other people, because churches are rife with gossip, that this person was in some kind of conversion therapy. I mean, why? Why can she not be who she is and why do we feel that we have to get involved? It was almost like you were talking about someone who was having an affair – it was in hushed whispers at the back of church. I just thought that must be really uncomfortable being her right now.

Fran (UK) tells me about when they started to question their gender identity within an evangelical context:

I had no framework for anything other than being cisgendered, so I didn't know what to do with those feelings. They ended up getting compressed into, 'Don't think about it, don't think about it, don't think about it: explosion of "what on Earth is going on?"' and then it goes back in the box. I had no lens for that other than shame.

Now I consider myself non-binary. I don't think I could have understood my gender identity without unpicking my faith. I couldn't have started to really get to know who I was until I began to make my thinking less rigid, and I think a lot of my rigidity came from faith, from this very particular understanding of how the world is.

For a while I attended a women's Bible study. I would turn up in ancient, muddy jeans, dog hair attached. Everyone else had neat dresses and brought homemade baking. Tamsin (UK) and I have similar feelings about such events:

Women's events in church were a weekly coffee morning where they did some singing and then a talk on quite a soft, feminine issue. The advertisement was, 'Children are well looked after and there's wonderful cake that people make. It's the highlight of the ladies' week.'

At the 'Man Up' events there was no provision for childcare whatsoever. You were all singing together in good, hearty male voice and eating bacon sandwiches. When I think of that, I'm so pleased I left!

Tamsin also mentioned John Eldredge's book *Wild At Heart* (cover image: a man leaps off a rocky crag). In the early 2000s, it felt like every Christian man was reading it. While it was not as aggressive as some material, it pushed a particular type of alpha masculinity and formed part of a movement against what some evangelicals perceived to be the feminization of the Church (if only). In 2005, it was followed by *Captivating* (cover image: in soft focus, a willowy woman heads towards a fairy-tale castle), co-authored with Staci Eldredge. Looking back, even the titles are telling: a person can be 'wild at heart' autonomously but is 'captivating' in relation to a third party. Tamsin told me about the impact on her university Christian Union:

It's powerful because it's tied to faith and Jesus. For some friends of mine, they wanted to be taken seriously as Christians and within their friendship communities as people who belonged there, so they chose to enact those kinds of behavioural ideas that weren't legitimate in the first place, because there's nowhere in the Bible that talks about 'take up your tent and go wild camping', and that type of masculinity isn't evidenced by Jesus. But people wanted to be in that culture and to connect to the God who was presented to them in that culture. I think probably some of the girls did the same.

These male stereotypes don't always appeal to women, either:

> I always had a hard time dating Christian men because of the rhetoric that is preached to them around what their role is in relationships with women. I've always wanted pure equality and companionship and intimacy and I never wanted any kind of 'role'. Those relationships always felt like only part of me could come, or that I was becoming a shell of myself, because I had to become this very polite, very whatever version of myself instead of showing up fully as an equal partner in the relationship.
>
> I've had to reframe the way that I show up in romantic relationships because there was a pattern that was established, a role that I would slip into with men that never suited me. My first queer relationship was with somebody who is trans and non-binary, and that was the best relationship I've ever been in. (KP, USA)

Greg (USA) also read *Wild At Heart*. It made sense to him, until he fell in love with his wife, and found that many of the stereotypical roles were reversed for them:

> She's a leader, she's right up front, and that's what I loved about her, because I was the shy, smart kid. I get so tired of hearing about that's what women do, that's what men do. It's not God's created order. This is just mostly how men have set it up to benefit them.

Nowadays, Greg tries to counteract the gendered messaging his daughters hear in their Christian school.

It is not just about roles, either: several people told me – and I have seen it myself in Christian charities – that where men were paid, highly qualified women did the same work as volunteers. Abi (USA) faced another problem common in churches: 'It was just a really unhealthy working situation: as with a lot of churches, there just weren't good boundaries.' She increasingly found herself isolated with her boss, despite her resistance: 'It came out that he had a thing for me. We were thrown into mediation together as if we were equals, but they couldn't understand that we were not equals: he was my elder and my boss and a man.' The church blamed her for his feelings:

You can't have it both ways. Do you want all the power? Do you want to be the only leaders? Then you'd better be willing to take some responsibility.

I started to realize I'm being treated this way because I'm a woman and they think that I had to have done something for him to like me like that. They thought that I was ambitious and not listening to my husband: those are things that were said to me. I got pressure to confess to things, and when they couldn't come up with anything else, they were like, 'You're just immature.'

I keep saying I'm lucky because I've only been hurt by people with good intentions, but I'm still hurt and I still have Complex PTSD.

The way she was treated started her questioning the structure that had created this unfairness:

All the churches I had gone to were very complementarian. I was terrified because I was like, 'This feels like a slippery slope, because if I think that women are equal and allowed to be pastors, I'm probably going to think that being gay is fine too.' Spoiler alert: it was a slippery slope and I did come to believe that being gay was totally fine. Egalitarianism was first, then hell, then everything else.

Veneda (USA) tells me, 'Being a Christian woman is a whole different deal than being a Christian man.' She eventually gave up trying to squeeze herself into church gender expectations:

I finally just said, 'Church isn't for me. I'm really different than everybody else in church, and I've been trying hard to put my jagged and weird self into the polished Christian woman mould.' I just couldn't do it.

I started growing up as a woman, and the more I grew, the more I knew that I could not continue to be that small. During this time of leaving church, I realized that I was very unhappy. I hated my life. I didn't know how to fix it. My marriage wasn't all that hot. I'd done all the good Christian woman things to make everything perfect, and it wasn't working. I started walking around my neighbourhood every night for a year. I walked and I prayed, I yelled, I screamed. But within that, I went back to school, and gradually started trying to put together a belief system for myself that actually worked.

Despite the fact that the Early Church had women priests, women in leadership remains a contentious topic in evangelical churches. Erica (UK) told me of her excitement as a teenager: 'I remember going to Greenbelt Festival and there was a woman presiding over communion. It seemed terribly natural, but later I thought, "That was a woman! That was a woman!"'

I was rarely directly taught that women couldn't lead (although I certainly heard grumbling when the Church of England began ordaining women), but when I think back to different 'biblical leadership models' I was given, I don't remember ever hearing a woman mentioned: it was never Deborah, Huldah or Jael and her weaponized tent peg. Many people told me how they had been taught that women can have certain roles within church, maybe even be pastors, but not the lead pastor, or that in university Christian Unions, women can teach but only alongside men, usually their husbands.

The contradictions are rife:

When I was a pre-teen, we started going to a Pentecostal church, which my mum and dad got super into. They ended up being elders of the church, well actually only my dad did because they wouldn't have any female elders, even though my mum was a lot more spiritual and involved in the church. (Jess, UK)

If you were a missionary, then it was OK for you to preach and lead if there was no man around to do it. But if you went home to a church, the women had to keep silent unless they were telling you about the missionary activity they'd be doing when there was no man and they had to preach and lead. (Laura, UK)

Ruth (USA) tells me of her response to women who pushed back: 'Women were like, "God called me to be a pastor" and I'm like, "You're not listening to God. Your selfishness is getting in the way." My husband actually changed my mind.'

Amanda (USA) is one of several pastors who almost wasn't one:

I was called rebellious. I was called stubborn. I was called anti-authoritarian. All those things women should not be, un-submissive. But at the same time, I really loved God and wanted to serve the Lord.

I went to Bible college at an Assemblies of God school and went into the ministry field, but my goal was to marry a pastor because I wanted to be in ministry. Even though my denomination ordained women, I never saw women in the kind of ministry I wanted to do unless they were pastors' wives or missionaries. I didn't want to be a missionary, so I had to be a pastor's wife. So, I went to college to find a pastor.

Another such pastor is Caro (Australia), who felt drawn to pastoring from a young age:

> But then at some point realizing that women didn't do that. No one told me that explicitly, there was just not an equality of men and women, and there were certainly no women ministers. So, I ended up just giving up on that.

Caro became involved in a church while she was at university, later becoming youth leader there as her draw to ministry slowly resurfaced. Eventually, she began leading the church:

> I have really bucked the cultural trend: I'm the pastor, my husband is the pastor's wife. That's not normal in Australia. I rarely come across another female minister. So even though we've forged a very different way of being married from the script I was given growing up, there's deeper stuff in me. There's another layer of talking, rethinking, reimagining to do. Yeah, it's messed up.

Caro remains a pastor and has led her church through a painful process of collective deconstruction. Jude (Australia), however, was eventually bullied out of her position as pastor:

> I remember talking to an elderly senior pastor, and he was telling me how open-minded Baptist churches were because we let women be pastors, and instead of me being happy and grateful, which would have served me very well, I just had this hot rage. Anything that can be 'allowed' can be taken away. Something about that was a watershed moment.
>
> We had a staff of eight. Only three female, we were all part time and if you look at what female pastors were allowed to do, it was fine when I was doing pastoral care or children's ministry, helping, supporting, welcoming, nurturing. But I learnt as a pastor of a congregation that a lot of people coming to a Baptist church would not want to put themselves 'under the authority' of a female.
>
> What is harder to put my finger on is the boys' club. That became part of the unhealthy dynamic of power struggles. And the ways that the females on the team thought it must be us. We must not be forgiving enough, we must not be gracious enough. You don't believe it's actually happening or you can't give proof, but your gut knows disrespect. It knows the subtleties of being shut out of the boys' club, slapping one another on the back, 'brother this' and 'brother that'. I could never understand what it was about that word that made my guts churn until

I thought, 'Oh, because it's not inclusive.' It's a continual label that says, 'Not one of us.'

I also had women in my congregation who surprised me with their sexism. They could be more conservative than the men and would struggle with whether it was OK for them to have a female leader. I had nice church ladies instructing the other women that women weren't meant to be speaking in church. What does that mean when I preach? What does that mean when I tend to them, when I pray for them?

The subtleties of that and the impact of the continual undermining. If it was overt, you could call it out. But it was slippery and shady. It does a number on your mind because you can't quite catch hold of it, and that fear of being petty and when you try to raise things, when you're speaking of an experience that others haven't had, they don't get it.

It's easy to feel that attitude of 'allowing' women to be pastors and ministers is more about window dressing than fundamental change, and that women are expected to simply fit into a structure created by and for men (especially given that religious organizations in the UK and some other countries/states are exempt from gender equality law). There is perhaps no greater symbol of this than the clothing many ordained women are expected to wear. Despite the majority of Church of England ordinands now being women, they are still required to wear clothing designed for male bodies, making their external appearance male. Liselotte (Denmark) is a thealogian[1] and Lutheran minister who has experienced this too:

It could not be a greater victory for patriarchy than when women vicars don not only the male garb dating back 500 years, but also this through-and-through male theology, then feel great about it because we've had female vicars in Denmark since 1948, aren't we just a very liberated feminist church? No, we're not.

Women who want to lead are not the only people who miss out in this system: church members do too. KP (USA) reflected on what she gained from women pastors:

I felt like the male pastors feel their perspective is everyone's perspective and they preach as if that's the case. Part of having more female leadership felt like there are angles to my faith that are now being considered that were never considered before. There are things around being

---

1 Someone who studies theology from female/feminine perspectives including, but not limited to, feminism.

embodied that keep coming up for me: the first time I ever heard anyone talk about being a being that lives in a body was at the church with the female senior pastor.

Isabel (UK) told me of her shock when she realized that her church would not allow women to speak:

I feel like that was a loose thread, then you start to pull. It brought up more and more questions. I felt I was aligning myself with things by being there that I wasn't aligned to. My integrity was compromised, and it was making me anxious.

Her anxiety became so debilitating that she had to stop attending church:

A really strong thing that I found since leaving the church is a much stronger sense of myself, the feeling of being a powerful woman. That's one of the reasons I never go back: I felt like something had been suppressed and I wasn't even really aware of it.

Towards liberty

Isabel and I are among the many – not just women – who become more fully ourselves once we deconstruct evangelical theologies and practices around gender. Strict binaries serve no one, and only reinforce the hierarchies and othering that pervade so many church spaces. Tim (Canada) tells me about the changes he has seen in moving away from this thinking:

My wife and I have been active to try to remove male language in relation to God. I've been noticing how much those changes of language really alter our way of seeing the world, like seeing God as a community or as a presence that is thoroughly outside of biological binaries: that changes things like prayer. I'm pushing myself to reimagine the world in a different way.

Ruth (Canada) tells me about when two of her children transitioned, and I ask how she dealt with that with her church background:

The big thing is getting rid of a binary, right? So if there isn't a heaven and hell and there's not a good and bad, there's not a Christian and non-Christian in the same way. Gender was just another thing I thought of on the spectrum.

It takes time and work to undo the impact that such a culture has on individuals, and the backlash can be savage. Fran (UK) tells me, 'In a freer world I would feel free to express myself in a more gender fluid way.' They are in a position of leadership, but, when we spoke, had been unable to be open with their church about being non-binary. Jude (Australia) met strong resistance when challenging power dynamics:

When congregants are taught that hierarchy is the way to go, you're this flimsy little person trying to subvert a giant empire that is based on hierarchy, and so coming in with a different power dynamic, a shared power that makes place for the other, for every voice, for the children to participate, it's seen as soft. It's seen as ineffective. It's seen as struggling. In my case, when I spoke up about struggle, I was told, 'You're not thriving.' Who is thriving in this kind of environment, I would like to know?

Chewed Gum

I am 16, watching my friends act a drama in front of a church congregation. Vicky holds up a big, red, paper heart. Every time she interacts with a boy, he rips off a piece of the heart, until the paper is reduced to a small shred and Vicky to melodramatic sobs.

I am 23, sweating in my baggy, crew-neck t-shirt on a hot day. One of the male leaders walks up to me. 'Can you deal with your clothes? You're causing the boys to stumble.' My face grows even hotter as I look down at my clothes. Too tight? Too low-cut? I notice that one greying bra strap has slipped off my shoulder and is just visible beneath the end of my sleeve. I push it back up and avoid the leader for the rest of the day, hiding out of sight as he tells us that 'the girls' (all adults) must wear long skirts and covered shoulders to church. There's no dress code for 'the boys'.

> All those teachings around purity and abstinence were horrible, just horrible. I almost feel like I have no words for how deep the shame goes. (Austin, USA)

> There's this persistent reductionist approach to the way that we teach relationships and marriage. It's all about whether you've had sex before marriage or not. It's not about the complexity of doing life with someone in relationships. I know you can't impart all of that, but you can give a more holistic picture. (Marie, Australia)

Purity culture was the single biggest issue mentioned in people's deconstruction stories. It starts with the idea that the only appropriate place for sexual activity is within lifelong, monogamous, heterosexual marriage: 97% of those who responded to my survey, of all ages and nationalities, checked the box stating that they had been taught this. Sexual activity considered sinful includes pornography use, masturbation and sexual thoughts – 84% had been taught this. Evan (UK) recounts how this worked its way out in his church:

It was all about sin and sin is the reason that the world is terrible, especially sexual sin: that was the worst thing you could do. One of my mates was the worship leader, and one morning he didn't turn up. He later said, 'Oh, it's because I masturbated the night before. I wasn't in the right place to lead worship.' I don't think God really cares.

In the name of protecting young people – especially girls and women – and strengthening Christian marriages, it spreads out from this core idea to become an entire system and way of life encompassing thoughts, clothing, movie and literary choices (I was told that we shouldn't read Song of Songs until we were married – and that was before I knew that theologians had suggested that it was written by a female author, about unmarried female sexual pleasure, in a context where God is not mentioned once (Brenner, n.d.; Weems, 2004)). It is hard to know where the external pressure ends and the internal pressure begins: actions and interactions are policed both by individuals themselves and by their leaders and peers: 'Purity culture was definitely a thing. I was a huge proponent. I judged other girls on my soccer team no end. I was a bitch' (Freya, USA).

Female clothing is subject to endless scrutiny to make sure it is 'modest' and not likely to 'cause the men to stumble', and girls find their bodies judged from pre-pubescence, especially those who develop earlier or are curvy. This can only have a negative impact at an impressionable age. Liz (UK) tells me, 'We have dissociated from our bodies. Being female, I remember feeling like your body is disgusting or negativity about your body. Enjoying your body or being proud of your body or celebrating your body is a bad thing.' Responsibility for male desire is put on women/girls, whether women/girls want the attention or not. Girls are told that they must stop boys from 'going too far' (while simultaneously submitting to male headship – it seems men can control women but not themselves), normalizing the violation of boundaries: less is said to boys about respect for girls. The concept of 'lust', in the way it is used in these circles, conflates the normal physiological process of arousal and healthy human sexual development with out-of-control, predatory sexual activity: a number of the men interviewed said they simply didn't recognize themselves in the rampaging images they were given as teens.

Pre-marital sex is often treated as the worst possible sin, especially when committed by women or by people of the same sex. The message is that the only alternative to sexual 'purity' is unsafe promiscuity. But purity teaching doesn't address a healthy sexual or relationship ethic beyond 'no sex before marriage and marry a Christian': God appears to care far more about virginity than healthy relationships.

The sheer amount of focus put on sexual purity would suggest that evangelicals are even more obsessed with sex than the secular world they condemn for being so. Jack (UK) faces this all the time:

As someone who is asexual, I am deeply frustrated by the general Christian obsession with sex and family, regardless of orientation. I feel ostracized for not wanting this, let alone not thinking that it is what Christians should spend so much time worrying about. If anything, this has been a large part of my faith deconstruction.

While most modern purity messaging seems to have been in reaction to the HIV/AIDS crisis (those subject to the teaching are told that if you have sex outside of marriage you will – guaranteed – catch an STD and/ or get pregnant and ruin your future marriage), it also has roots further back, both in reaction to the sexual revolution of the 1960s and the ending of American anti-miscegenation laws: if you can control who people are having sex with, then 'sexual purity' also ensures 'racial purity'.

This is hardly surprising when you consider the source of much of contemporary Christian teaching on marriage and family more broadly: the early/mid-twentieth-century eugenics movement. Paul Popenoe, a noted atheist 'positive eugenicist' (breeding in favour of desirable racial, economic and physical characteristics), promoted white, heterosexual, reproductive marriage. Alongside gender essentialism and male supremacy, Popenoe dismissed domestic abuse and encouraged wives to endure abuse and unhappiness patiently, to look desirable for their husbands and to provide them with sexual fulfilment. Feminism and homosexuality were condemned, as was racial 'incompatibility' and 'undesirable' qualities such as illiteracy, poverty and being an immigrant. He is quoted in standard Christian marriage books such as Tim and Beverley LaHaye's *The Act of Marriage* (LaHaye, 1998, p. 220) in a chapter on women's lack of sexual fulfilment, in which women are blamed for being both too passive and too dominant, and his theories are mirrored throughout the work of his former assistant, Dr James Dobson, founder of Focus On The Family (Popenoe even wrote the Foreword to Dobson's 1970 book, *Dare To Discipline*).

While much of the 'industry' that goes along with purity culture comes from the USA (such as the Southern Baptist 'True Love Waits' campaign, with its purity rings, pledges and 'daddy-daughter purity balls' complete with pre-pubescent girls in white, wedding-style dresses – monetizing girls' virginity just as surely as selling it off), its message has spread worldwide. The object lessons don't seem to vary much across the world: 55% of survey respondents had heard those who have pre-marital sex compared to a cupcake or an apple with bites taken out of it, a rose with the petals torn off, water with dirt added, a pre-chewed piece of gum and a glass of water passed around a youth group with each person spitting into it in turn. At the end of all these, the question is asked, 'Would you want this cupcake/rose/gum/water now? If you have sex before you're married, no one will want you either.' Most of these play on a visceral sense of disgust. The object is permanently tainted: it can never be unchewed, un-spat in, made clean again. No other 'sin category' is taught like this – we are given messages of forgiveness and restoration. It is not hard to internalize the illustration: I am dirty, contaminated, shameful, unlovable.

One of the stranger theories is about the 'soul ties' that are supposed to develop via sexual contact: your soul will be bound to anyone with whom you have sexual contact, consenting or not, and will remain bound to them even when you marry someone else. The only Bible mention of two human souls being joined together is between David and Jonathan, and the tone is positive (1 Sam. 18.1), but this seems to have been missed by the theory's proponents, and it is widespread enough for over 58% of survey respondents to have reported hearing it.

Even those who 'saved sex till marriage' reported feeling sinful: shamed for impure thoughts or for being attracted to someone. At the very least it leads to constant self-policing. It goes further than rational, waking thoughts: I used to have a recurring dream where I realized that I had had sex with someone, and the overwhelming shame and fear of pregnancy or disease was enough to wake me in a panic. I never actually dreamed about having sex, but that seems to sum up purity culture: no sex, just shame and fear.

Girls and boys

Despite expressing his own deep-seated shame, Austin (USA) tells me:

> I think the burden is much heavier and much more crushing for women, because often the unconscious or subtle messages are that men can't really control their sexuality so it's up to women to dress in a way that doesn't provoke that in men. It often feels like women have to bear the shame that men are feeling, but aren't able to name, because men are socialized to consider themselves powerless about even controlling their own urges. It's bad. It's really bad.

It's a low view of both sexes: men as uncontrollable animals, women as temptresses who lead men astray. What is noticeable though is the gender imbalance which Austin pointed to. 64% of survey respondents said they had been taught that girls/women are in some way responsible for boys'/men's lustful thoughts and must not cause them to stumble by how they dress or act. Only 7.1% said the same the other way around.

Little is said about women's sexuality beyond the fact that women simply do not 'lust' or want sex to the same extent as men: many women I spoke to suffered serious shame and a feeling of being aberrant, even wondering if they had a sex addiction, for having felt aroused, watched pornography or masturbated (sometimes termed as 'touching your sin cave', which is supposed to be reserved for your husband, further removing bodily autonomy: only someone else is allowed to touch your body). Holly (UK) tells me that, 'Men lust and have desires and girls don't. So if you do, you then feel extra doomed.'

While boys and men do receive shaming messages, a sexual 'slip-up' is just that: a slip, a mistake, boys will be boys. Girls and women, on the other hand, are permanently damaged goods if there is any sexual misdemeanour (although 23% of survey respondents reported being taught that Jesus can restore the virginity of those who lose it prior to marriage. Perhaps this is because Jesus recognizes that virginity is a social construct in the first place). Girls, more than boys, are taught from a young age that their virginity is a gift to their spouse, a marker of their value: 86.1% of survey respondents reported having been taught this.

> I did go back and read my old children's Bible, for pre-teens. It was one of the pink, 'just for girls' Bibles and they had little extra things that they had written in little bubbles like, 'Should I kiss while I'm dating, before I'm married?' and all this stuff, and I'm like, would I ever expose my daughter to something like this? (Valerie, USA)

Tessi Muskrat Rickabaugh (USA) is an academic at the University of Missouri studying the outcomes of purity culture. She tells me about the impact of prepubescent purity culture messaging: 'By the time girls are old enough to be sexually active, the shame is already engrained: their bodies are dangerous stumbling blocks to boys and men. From childhood, they are already objectified by adult men.'

Laura (USA) tells me about her own and her parents' experience:

> My parents got pregnant with my older brother before they had gotten married. They both attended that church, but it was my mum who was publicly brought in front of the entire church and shamed. She had to say all sorts of things. She had to listen to people come up in front of other people and talk to her. One of the really frustrating pieces was

that my father was sitting in the pew the whole time and none of that was given to him. I think that's very clear marking of how we put that responsibility on women entirely and rob men of that.

I very much felt as her daughter those things were also being applied to me directly, but not to my brother, not to my male youth group friends. The boys were given *Every Young Man's Battle*, so they had their versions of things, but they weren't brought in front of the entire church like the girls were. It was a ceremony and we made pledges and took vows.

Some 19.3% of respondents stated that they had signed a purity pledge or worn a purity ring, markers of a commitment to sexual abstinence until marriage. Less than one in seven of those were men. Most people signed pledges or started wearing rings around the age of 12–14: just becoming interested in sex, not old enough to understand what they are committing to. What surprised me was that while some came under parental pressure to wear a ring or take a pledge, many of those I spoke to had chosen this for themselves (although with encouragement from youth leaders or peers). The practice did not exist pre-True Love Waits, and parents often had not experienced this in their own youth. Nina (UK) tells me:

I must have been 14, 13, young teenage. I bought my own purity ring. Like, I went and *bought myself* a purity ring! The funny story about my purity ring is that at a friend's 18th birthday I had got quite drunk and was making out with someone on the trampoline. There was a little stream that went through the garden, and we stumbled into a boat and ended up falling out into the stream. I remember he asked me to go to his car and I was like, 'No, no way am I doing that.' But the next morning, I wake up and my purity ring is gone and I've lost it in the river. I felt so much shame, 'Oh my gosh, that's it, I've lost my purity ring, I've sinned.' I remember feeling so dirty and that it was so symbolic that I'd lost my purity ring in the river because I've been fooling around with this guy.

Holly (UK) laughs as she recalls her purity ring, given to her when she spent a year working in Texas after leaving school:

How embarrassing! I had a Texan boyfriend for a while and he bought me a purity ring. You just would wear it with such pride, especially in Texas. To be honest, if you didn't wear one, it was a bit strange. I got embarrassed to wear it and I moved it onto the other hand, and some of the girls were like, 'Why have you moved your ring?' So there was definitely pressure there, and I felt real pressure when I came home from Texas that if I was going to a be true Christian, I should still wear it, it doesn't matter if I'm in England and no one else is wearing one. It didn't last very long because I just felt so embarrassed, but obviously then felt guilty for taking it off and tried to justify in my head why I was taking it off, but I was still a good Christian.

Austin (USA) was one of the few men to take a purity pledge:

We had a sex ed class in high school, and it wasn't helpful at all. It was basically just somebody telling us the reasons why we should be abstinent. I don't remember any actual education about anything. They passed around a form and they were like, 'We want everyone to sign this form and promise that they will be abstinent.' So I signed it. I wanted to be accepted, it just made sense: your teachers are telling you this, your parents are telling you this. I had to raise my hand and ask, 'What does abstinence mean?'

For those who went against the rules, the sky didn't fall in:

I agonized over the whole thing of sex before marriage, I thought I'd have a mental breakdown, because it was so forbidden. It seemed to have such enormous importance. Then when I did have sex before marriage, it was kind of like, what was all the fuss about? So that was one of those watershed moments. But then there were painful aspects of that because of condemnation from my sister. She likened it to David's sin with Bathsheba, and how God's blessing could never really fall on your life again after that. (Sally, UK)

Several of those who did keep the rules, now parents, told me that they would not expect the same of their own children. Julie (UK) is one of them:

I don't know how I'm going to help navigate my children through teen-age years, but I definitely won't encourage them not to have sex before marriage. I think that was massively damaging and I really regret not having sex before marriage. That sort of 'save yourself for your hus-band and you'll have amazing sex just because you've done that': what a farce, who believes that? And totally contrary to that, I remember my wedding night just being the biggest disappointment, thinking, 'God, is this what I was waiting for?'

I do feel angry about how coercive that was really, the guilt it put on people. I do think it destroyed the faith of quite a few people.

Violence

I don't recall ever hearing the word 'consent' used in a Christian context, and only 6.8% of survey respondents reported having heard a positive message about it. For Joy (USA), the lack of teaching about consent and the demand for submission were a dangerous combination:

> When you've already submitted what is supposed to be the most valuable thing – your soul, and your child's soul when you bring your child to church – then you've already taught your child that they don't get a choice, that consent is not valuable, that all you get to do is trust in authorities.
>
> Bodily autonomy, any kind of ownership or consent was not even something I was aware of. I walked into situations that led to nonconsensual encounters because I didn't have that concept of consent. I thought they were just going to happen and that I couldn't change it.

All sexual 'sin' is seen as equally bad (sin levelling), so mutually consensual pre-marital sex is viewed on a par with sexual assault. The sinister outcomes of these teachings can be seen in the levels of sexual assault in evangelical contexts and how these are handled by leadership. When men's sexual 'needs' and inability to control themselves are seen as inevitable, perpetrators are excused. Sheila Wray Gregoire writes:

> The *Act of Marriage* describes a husband who raped his wife while she was 'kicking and screaming' on their wedding night as 'equally unhappy' as his rape victim … [In] *Every Man's Battle* … a youth group volunteer who was married with three kids rapes a 15-year-old girl and is portrayed sympathetically, since his lust overwhelmed him.
>
> When abuse scandals like Ravi Zacharias or sex scandals like Carl Lentz are exposed, we should stop being surprised. These men acted out exactly what so many evangelical resources taught them: Men need physical release; they can't control themselves without women's help; if they don't get help, they could easily become predators. And this is all presented as God's design. (Gregoire, 2021)

More and more abuse scandals are being exposed, particularly since the explosion of #*ChurchToo*. For those who assault or abuse, their (female) victim is often blamed despite men having the power in a hierarchical, 'complementarian' setting (shades of Adam blaming Eve for his bite of the fruit). A girl in Abi's (USA) youth group became pregnant by an older youth group leader, the power dynamic grossly unequal: 'They stand her up in front of the whole church to confess her sin, and then it's this beautiful, loving thing where we embrace her. But he's nowhere to be found. He doesn't have to do that.'

Holly (UK) recounts what happened in her church:

My best friend and I grew up in church together. When she was 14, she was abused in our church. I was 19, and I sort of knew what was going on. She told us that she was having these contacts and communications with this person, he was 25. I viewed it at the time as sin and temptation and I tried to help her by praying for her. Then she went off to uni, spoke to non-Christians and realized it was abuse. We all had to wrestle with the fact that we all played a part in that, I suppose. So then I left the church, because I just couldn't be there anymore. He still went there.

My friend is very, very gracious, and she was very forgiving of her friends who played a part in it. We went through a year and a half process with the police and going through the court process. I was already wrestling with a lot of theologies, but church was everything, so they didn't seem as important. But then I realized how, when my friend went to the police, the church weren't supportive. They were very defensive, very self-preserving. So much pressure on us to forgive, for her to forgive, and there was no accountability from the church put on him to apologize or be held accountable or face consequences.

I was 19, so I should have known better and I could have helped my friend a lot quicker, but also I'm aware that I was being indoctrinated and I was therefore doing it to my younger friend. So I've had to really come to terms with that. It makes it even harder when you go through that and then stand in court as a witness and be honest about that. And then seeing that the church so successfully just preserves itself rather than being open to that accountability and change, I think that's really where all the bitterness lies now.

The stuff that is permitted to go on in churches, that level of control, and you're just expected it to go along with it. When I reflect back, I think it's really scary. With what happened to my friend, at the time of her being 14 it was brought to the attention of the pastor and the pastor just had a word with the 25-year-old and just said, 'Stop it.' It's that power on one pastor who is leading a church, and that control he has that he's just like, 'I've dealt with it, I've had a word with him', and it led to years of her being silent, abused.

The court case was two years ago, and we went back to the church. My friend really wanted to go to be like, 'Look, I still exist. It's easy for you to write me off when I'm not here, but this is me in person.' My mum came, and one of the women from the church said to my mum,

'Why didn't you just deal with this in church?' That's still the belief that they have, that safeguarding doesn't exist, and it can all be dealt with in the church. It's the arrogance within a lot of churches that we have the right way and we can deal with everything because we've got God on our side. The harm that causes is huge.

When churches and ministries deal with sexual violence within the paradigm of 'purity', survivors deal with additional shaming. Mia (Costa Rica/USA) tells me she was sexually abused as a child:

A lot of my religious trauma stems from trusting people with my own trauma and then having that either be invalidated or being told that there was something that I had done to provoke it or some lasting effect that the abuse was going to have in my life. I was told multiple times that I had a soul tie with the person that abused me.

I have PTSD, so it continues to affect me in a very real way, but I felt so guilty about it because they tell you so many times, 'Just set it at the foot of the cross, the one that he has set free is set free indeed.' So I felt guilty every time I had a flashback or nightmare because I was trying so hard to give this up, and I wanted so badly to be free of the guilt and the shame. They were telling me, 'This is what you need to do', and it didn't sit right with me, but I was going along with it because I wanted so, so badly to not be that sad, scared little girl anymore. I wanted to be whoever God wanted me to be. That was a repeated pattern: people praying that God would heal my hymen so that I would be a pure virgin for my husband on our wedding night. Because clearly that's the most important part of being a woman is being a pure virgin for your husband. Nothing else.

I was told that there were demons that entered me when I was abused, that I was incapable of forming healthy relationships and that I would not be able to be a good, submissive wife for my husband if I didn't have these demons cast out of me. I was told that potentially my children could be abused if I didn't deal with this because it would be a generational curse. Just one thing after another, and I ended up doing the deliverance ministry thing because I was basically told I had to as part of this church.

Courting

I am 23, and have been seeing someone for a few months. I am certain God has said that this is The One. I express some affection. 'Guard your heart,' he responds. 'Don't get too attached before marriage.' I've heard the same teaching a few times, so I try to stop myself falling for him until we're married. The One dumps me a few months later and my sense of failure is huge. I don't go on another date for ten years.

I was talking to a friend this weekend and she had bumped into a boy that she went to school with. He was laughing and saying he'd asked her to prom when they were 16, and he still had the message that she'd replied, saying, 'Thank you, but I'm actually focused on God right now.' (Holly, UK)

The first time a boy phoned me, my dad called me in for a chat to ask me whether this boy was a Christian and say, 'It's very important that we're not unequally yoked.' Needless to say, that relationship didn't go anywhere. I was maybe 14 or 15. That was probably my one shot at teenage love. Never got over that.

How are you ever going to develop a healthy approach to building relationships with the opposite sex or any gender at that age, if that's what you're given to work with? There's an expectation that if you started dating somebody, then you were inevitably going to get married, so that put a lot of pressure on. People were hyper-careful about who they decided to go out with just in case they had to marry them. There was no sense of freedom or fun or enjoyment. (Laura, UK)

Josh Harris's book *I Kissed Dating Goodbye* was published in 1997, when Harris himself was 21, and became a standard text for young evangelicals for the next 20 years. It pushed the idea of 'courtship' rather than mainstream dating. It also suggested that, on your wedding day, it wouldn't just be your spouse standing in front of you at the altar but also all the other people he/she had had any sexual contact with, including kissing – those pesky soul ties again. In my survey, 29% of people had been taught that being attracted to someone was wrong, and 59% of people reported having learned that they shouldn't date (or court) anyone unless they already knew they could potentially marry them. I certainly followed this advice, treating first dates as pre-marriage. Hope (USA) was one of a few women who told me that it put them off altogether:

I remember talks in our youth group about courtship and how dating is the way of the world and is practice for divorce. It makes it so that we don't actually know how to have really rich, healthy dating experiences.

The idea that you can have a dating relationship that can be beautiful and successful and not end in marriage is a mind-blowing concept to me because it was like, 'Oh, no, dating is for the purpose of marriage and that's it, so you better not date unless you know you're going to marry them.' Which also makes dating really difficult because of the pressure put on those kind of interactions. It's so stressful that I don't even want to do that.

For some, however, Harris's book was a form of liberation. Tessi (USA) says:

When I met Josh, I was 14, he was 17, and he was trying out talks about dating and courtship at homeschool conventions. In that context, his message was pretty liberal because several teachers that were really popular at the time were like, 'Your parents should choose your spouse because they have all this wisdom that you don't have. And also patriarchy. You should never even try to be friends with members of the opposite sex. You should never be alone with them, should never be within six inches of them, should never touch them.' So then Josh comes out with this book that's like, 'Actually, friendships could be great, and guys should also do the thing that girls should do and we should all be trying to be pure.' It's interesting how your reality impacts your experience.

Tessi started a chastity and pro-life organization when she was 16, saying, 'We really believed that this is the way to end up with a stable relationship and a healthy family in your future.' Her comment about a stable relationship resonates with me. I remember being told that if you have sex before marriage your whole relationship will just be based on sex. Dating a non-Christian is out of the question because they only want to use you for sex. Holly (UK) is thoughtful for a while:

I think I'm still undoing a lot of the harm that that causes. In terms of being able to talk about sex or trying to date in a non-Christian world, I felt like I was catching up. I was 27 and I hadn't done anything that all my friends have done when we were 17, 18. And the shame around things and just feeling totally out of touch with myself. There was so much harm in that value, but it was done in a very subtle way. I even remember when we were in a youth group, we had these people come and talk to us about relationships and they didn't talk about anything educational, just about how to avoid lust. The man literally said when he's on public transport, he looks at his feet to avoid lust. What that makes you believe about yourself, especially as a woman.

Those who pray together, stay together

You haven't made it unless you're married. Singleness is very much only for the pious. You're still a child if you're not married, almost. We got married when I was 20 and my wife was 21. I basically saw it as a signifier of belonging to the Christian community. (Neil, UK)

There was so much pressure because you desperately wanted to find a husband, and so you obviously wanted to be desirable, but in a very pure way, and that balance was on your mind all the time. There's just so much pressure to be a desirable Christian woman in the right, modest kind of way, like wife material when you were 20 years old. (Holly, UK)

The goal of all of this purity is heterosexual marriage to another evangelical, preferably with a 'quiverfull' of children to show for it: the pinnacle of achievement, especially for women. Girls are primed for this from a young age and given activities to keep the mind focused:

From when I was 15, I started writing these letters to my future husband about saving myself for him. But then I'd have boyfriends, and I'd feel really guilty because this is a person who I felt like I was almost betraying or cheating on. (Catherine, UK)

It seems contradictory that fantasies about boys are sinful, but girls are effectively writing to a fantasy husband. (I didn't find any men who had been asked to do this but, like purity pledgers, they may be out there.)

For those who don't find a spouse by their mid-20s, the constant questions about why they aren't married, instruction to be patient, admonishment for any expression of loneliness (because a spouse won't fill the Jesus-shaped hole in your heart and your relationship with Jesus should be sufficient) or congratulations on their 'gift of singleness' can become grating, to say the least. Given the gender imbalance in the Church – far more women than men – this is the experience of plenty of women. Unmarried in my 30s, I was told by a few people to 'just find a friend and settle down', as though I were being too picky (although the pressure to marry surely leads to a lower bar being set) and that 'any Christian should be able to make marriage to any Christian work'.

I quietly prayed that God wouldn't make me marry someone I wasn't attracted to. As Tamsin (UK) points out:

> Men were the minority in churches, so if you are with someone you could potentially marry, stick with them regardless of behaviour as they might get away. At 35 it's a very different set of conversations about sex and sexuality than it is when you're 15 and when you're 23.

Bridget (New Zealand) has been thinking this through as well:

> At 46, I am still not married and am now thinking that there is a good chance that I never will be. This causes a lot of rethinking of what I have been taught. No one has anything to say about it at this point. The idea of taking one's virginity to the altar is one thing – taking it to the grave is another!

Marriage to a non-Christian is strongly discouraged, with over 92% of survey participants having been taught that they should not be 'unequally yoked', snatched out of context from 2 Corinthians 6.14. (A quick search online comes up with some delightful attitudes concerning this passage: Focus on the Family acknowledges that this verse was not written about marriage, but then applies it anyway and claims, 'An unbeliever doesn't follow the Lord – doesn't worship the one true God – so everything else in their life is an idol. Including their spouse' (Focus on the Family, 2020).) I can think of several couples I've met who are both Christians but are 'unequally yoked' in other ways which cause all kinds of issues.

Julie (UK) tells me her experience of unequal yoking: 'I had been pray-ing for a man that was tall, dark and spoke French: really specific. This guy came along, he was Plymouth Brethren, and he was tall, dark and spoke French. I was like, "My prayers are answered."' He invited her to help lead a Brethren youth camp:

> He was sussing me out as wife material, as they do. Naively, I thought I'd be actually interacting with young people and spiritually contribut-ing. But no, I was side-lined into a Portacabin with the breastfeeding women, as a 20-year-old, and it was terrifying. But the pressure I felt from other Christian friends, because he was a Christian, was immense. If I'd married him, I'd be in a Portacabin, breastfeeding a multitude of children that I'm producing to help maintain the size of the church. I've always been quite strong-minded, and I don't know how anyone thought I was happy in that situation, but because he ticked the box, they'd be happy to push me into that.

I met my husband on the first day of my new job. He's not a Christian, still isn't after 16 years, and he would never be interested in anything spiritual. I was in a church, but I'd gone from a situation where I was often asked to speak and was viewed as potential leadership material, then I started this relationship and very quickly I felt very second class because I'd sold out, you know, 'don't be yoked with an unbeliever'. I felt incredible guilt and it took me a long time to overcome that.

They welcomed him, they tried to befriend him and convert him, but obviously he wasn't interested. I was never offered any sort of leadership. I was never even asked to pray for people. I was often put on public-facing things because I was quite a PR-friendly person, but then when it comes to the spiritual stuff, very much second class.

As students in the youth mission organization I worked for, we 'girls' were taught about waiting for our spouse. I was given the same message as a friend in a different location, although her group were given this in written form on pink, frilly edged paper. In what is presented as a letter from God, we are told that only when we are completely satisfied by our relationship with God alone will we 'be capable of the perfect human relationship that I have planned for you' and our mate (yes, 'mate') will be miraculously provided, the resultant marriage a fairy-tale image of perfection. 'God' signs off, 'Believe it and be satisfied.'

This makes God look like a controlling, narcissistic partner: you cannot have anyone else until you love only me entirely, and even then I will choose who you get. And what exactly is 'the perfect human relationship'? It also sets up the gendered expectation that good Christian women are simply to wait passively until God brings them a 'mate', and the tacit shaming that if God doesn't bring the perfect human relationship, it is the woman's fault for not being 'ready' or perhaps for using her own agency.

Enticingly, young people are also taught that if they wait until marriage, God will 'reward' them with 'mind-blowing sex' (more objectification: no person should ever be another person's 'reward'). Having taught that sex before marriage makes the marriage all about sex, this 'reward' does exactly that. Additionally, youth are taught that marital sex will be less satisfying if they have been sexually active before marriage, and that sex is better for Christians than non-Christians. It doesn't always work out that way. Austin (USA) recalls the early days of his marriage:

Definitely, once you get married, everything is going to be good and your sex life is going to be amazing. But when you spend most of your life feeling like you're battling or trying to suppress your own desire, or you're feeling immense shame for your sexual desires, you have this deep sense that your sexuality is deeply sinful or deeply problematic. That doesn't go away once you get married. It just doesn't.

I've been married for almost seven years now, but I was shocked at how much shame I had around my sexuality, how much it felt so deeply wrong, even having sex with my wife. It wasn't something I could even explain. It was more like this visceral, 'I'm not supposed to be doing this. I don't feel comfortable. I don't feel good about this. I don't feel safe.' It was like my whole body was recoiling in a sense. I just felt so much shame. People don't really talk about that. I never heard anything like that growing up, ever. I was always told, 'Yeah, you get married and it's going to be great and it's going to be like Song of Songs or whatever.'

For women, the pressure continues after marriage vows are said, just in the opposite direction. Having been told they must not have sex at all before marriage, now they are to have perhaps more sex than they want: once again, agency is taken from them: Nina (UK) told me about a conversation she had with the minister's wife: 'She came back from a pastors' wives conference and said, "It was amazing. They taught us how to love our husbands more and help support them in their ministry by having more sex with them." Just horrible.'

The physical fallout of purity culture is inevitable, even in otherwise healthy, happy relationships: if someone spends her formative years being taught that sex is to be avoided at all costs, that boys and men cannot control themselves and effectively view her body as prey, that virginity is where her value lies, is it any wonder that her body continues to interpret sexual contact as 'unsafe', even in the 'appropriate' setting of marriage? After years of repressing all desire and arousal, how can anyone magically become a sexually available siren on their wedding night? Abi (USA) tells me about how this marred the early period of her marriage:

We were not allowed to date in high school. You were supposed to guard your heart, which basically meant that you weren't even supposed to have crushes or anything. I started dating my husband when we were in college. We messed around, and we didn't have penis-in-vagina intercourse, but it was awful. I was so ashamed. At least once a week, I would have a hyperventilating cry about it. And so then, of course, we got married super young because we wanted to have sex, but also I was terrified of having sex.

We totally did love each other, we're still married and he's great. But it changed for me from, 'I get to have sex' to, 'I have to have sex.' I was very scared leading up to it, and then it was awful and remained awful for a while. I was very traumatized by our wedding night and honeymoon. My body knew I was scared and was not ready. I dealt with the fallout for a long time, but also I was like, 'God is punishing me', and was confused and angry and resentful that he didn't seem to be punishing my husband, just me.

I rarely knew if I actually wanted to have sex. That was another purity culture holdover, because there's so much pressure to do it to maintain the relationship and to keep your husband from cheating, basically. There is so much duty tied to it that I was like, 'Most of the time, I don't know if I want to.'

I read all the books, you know? I read, *I Kissed Dating Goodbye*, *Passion and Purity*. A lot of stuff, though, really messed with me, and did the opposite of what it promised. Absolutely the exact opposite.

The body of research that points to damage done by purity culture is growing. Sheila Wray Gregoire's book (Gregoire et al., 2021) and *Bare Marriage Podcast* (one of the few times that female sexual pleasure is even mentioned in Christian resources), address the parallel trauma symptoms experienced by both sexual abuse survivors and women affected by purity messages. For both abuse survivors and purity culture adherents, the individual's sexual agency and autonomy is taken from them. Her survey of 20,000 Christian women in North America points to double the levels of vaginismus in evangelical women as in women who have not had purity teachings. Other studies on severe dyspareunia (painful vaginal penetration and contact) in women without a history of sexual abuse also make the link to the purity movement (Happel-Parkins et al., 2020).

Nina (UK) also mentions this:

I had vaginismus when I got married and I didn't know what that was until two years ago. At the time, I thought, 'There's something wrong with my body, I need to go see a doctor and they need to sort me out somehow because I'm not made properly, or there's something wrong with my character.' So, my response to that experience wasn't, 'Oh, something's wrong, let's try and get help.' It was, 'There's something wrong with me. It's my fault.'

Gender hierarchy continues into marriage, with teachings of complementarianism and male headship almost unavoidable, as outlined in the previous chapter. 84% of survey respondents had been taught that the husband is the head of the household: the most intimate relationship most people will have is based on power differentials, with a husband having the final say in any disagreement. By extension, if wives must submit, their only recourse to unacceptable or abusive behaviour from their husband is to change themselves and pray that God will change their husband. I suspect that the teaching, heard by 50% of respondents, that in marriage 'women need love and men need respect' does nothing to help here. Several studies (e.g. Heise and Kotsadam, 2015) find that male authority over women is predictive of domestic abuse: abuse is enabled by the system and survivors dismissed or silenced.

Reinforcing this dynamic, 25% of participants had been taught that wives must have sex whenever their husband wants it to protect him from infidelity or porn use, for which she is implicitly to blame for not having enough sex or for not keeping herself looking good (only 3% had heard the same rule applied to husbands). Even more sinister, 13% had been taught that marital rape does not exist: a man has a right to have sex with his wife (combined with the lack of teaching about consent, this figure is effectively far higher). If you have no space to say 'no' to sex and bodily autonomy has been consistently undermined, especially where theologies of male headship are present, is 'yes' ever truly consent?

Between gender hierarchies, 'purity' and unrealistic promises, it seems that evangelical marriages are almost designed to be hard. Of course, there are plenty of examples of happy marriages. However, once married, the message switches fast to a continual narrative about how hard marriage is and the importance of enduring this, normalizing or even sanctifying unhappiness. Any admission of marital misery, or even abuse, can be greeted with a dismissive, 'marriage is about holiness, not happiness' (and where there is a power differential, this can only serve the person with the most power).

Church leaders are not necessarily willing or equipped to tackle spousal abuse. Instead, forgiveness and submission are emphasized, scripture (mis)quoted and unhappy spouses told that 'God hates divorce', as though God is comparatively fine with human misery or uncaring, coercive or abusive behaviour. 74% had been taught that divorce is a sin, and 15% had been taught that even domestic abuse is not a reason for divorce: the couple must try to reconcile. A 'successful' marriage is a lifelong marriage, regardless of the wellbeing of those inside it. Christine (USA) followed the rules, and discovered the cost:

I was probably 12 or 13. At camp, I braided these little bracelets all with white thread. I wore this white bracelet around my wrist like a sign of purity, and I gave it to my first husband on our wedding day.

One of the biggest regrets I have is that I was not physically attracted to my husband, and I thought, 'Oh, this is so great that I don't have any desire to be impure.' Then somehow that didn't switch when I got married.

In marriage the message was that you just have to satisfy your husband's needs because that's your role as the wife, and so in many ways, the whole idea of consent in marriage was not a thing because that's your duty as a wife, right? So, it set up all kinds of dysfunction. As a woman, sexuality is particularly shameful. Even in marriage, it becomes difficult to be a sexual being because you've been taught this whole time, 'That's shameful, that's shameful, that's shameful.'

I married a man who had a deep history of abuse himself and came from a family who had a lot of drug abuse and gangs, a lot of violence. But they had found God, and now everything was fine, they're saved. Religion for me was a lot of just powering through and not acknowledging the truth of what's there.

We ended up becoming missionaries in Turkey, and, long story short, there was a lot of violence and abuse and he was a substance user. I tried to come forward and say the truth of things, and I was always told, 'God will fix it. If you just trust God and if you're a good enough wife, it'll be OK.' There wasn't a recognition of abuse. You just stay with someone. Divorce is never an option.

In order to give myself permission to leave my first marriage, I also had to question my faith and my faith community. When we left, my kids and I were in hiding for a little while. It was a really fearful time. The church came at 11 at night, knocked on the door. I was terrified. They just handed me this big packet, and the title was 'Why it is never OK to divorce'. I just fell on the ground and I felt like, 'OK, it's just me and God now.'

A year after I left my first husband he died by suicide. I ultimately lost my whole church that I was really involved in, especially after I left my husband. People didn't understand, they didn't know the dynamics of what went on, and so they blamed me for leaving and for his death.

The same combination of purity and complementarian teaching left Marie (Australia) ill-equipped to even recognize the abuse she faced:

I'd absorbed this narrative that I shouldn't question things if something's wrong. It's just my job to look for how to fix it. Some of the messages were quite powerful and disempowering to me as a young woman who didn't really have mentors or leaders that spoke another narrative to her.

I was married for seven years before that broke down. It took me a few years after that to realize that some of the things I accepted were so psychologically abusive and neglectful, and I had a right to question those, and I should have questioned those. I don't believe Jesus thinks that you need to be a good wife and be beyond reproach and not question.

We revere marriage and married people and don't talk about singleness, and we don't talk about post-marriage experience for those who go through divorce, even though I think times have moved on from where they once were. I haven't felt openly discriminated against, but a lot of women, and some men too, do a lot of questioning about how is this going to be perceived in my faith community?

While I have known more than one friend to be forced out of church for leaving an abusive husband (while the husbands stayed and declared themselves 'healed'), it is not solely women who face judgement. The male headship model backfired on Josh (USA) when his wife filed for divorce:

Our ministry leader took that headship model and said that as a husband, that was my failure, and that I wasn't fit to lead anymore. They asked me to step down out of the ministry that I had helped start. And of course, the community I was a part of had no idea what to do because nobody had any vocabulary for handling those kinds of situations.

Ronnie (USA) is a minister whose experience has informed how he raises his own children:

One of my fiery preacher uncles showed up at my house after I divorced and said, 'You need to turn in your ordination papers. It's over for you.'

Because of the severe restrictions in intimate and sexual relationships that were required of young adults, I had rushed into marriage when that was just unnecessary. There was just no way to explore your sexuality or to explore intimacy in any way, apart from putting the ring on the finger. Purity culture drives people into relationships for the sake of intimacy and sex when that's unnecessary. You're forcing that role on men and women.

I've remarried a wonderful woman and we're raising boys. Their relationships with their significant others are radically different than the relationships that I had, because the same severe expectations have not been put on them. We talk very frankly.

Individual responses to divorce vary widely: I have had a range of kindness, judgement and vanishing acts from Christians through my own divorce. But the idolatry of marriage is perhaps no better illustrated than in attitudes that put human health, safety and thriving below the 'sanctity' of an institution that purportedly reflects the relationship of Christ to his bride, the Church.

Purity culture also fails to address the experience of those who lose a spouse. Liz (UK) was widowed young:

> I'm right there at the moment, because I've been married my entire life, really. I've been in a healthy sexual relationship for 17 years, and now I'm single again. And then I think about a chewed piece of gum: what does that make me now?

After Tessi's (USA) teenage years of abstinence activism, her own road to a happy marriage was a winding one:

> I was committed to staying under my father's 'umbrella of protection' – that is a term that we used: his 'headship' – until I got married. That was the plan. My plan as much or more than his plan.
>
> I moved out of my parents' house when I was 24. I justified that – and I had to justify it – I figured even though I wasn't moving into a marriage relationship, if I could find a pastor to practise headship, and because I was moving out for the purpose of serving God in ministry, that it would be OK. I really had to do these mental gymnastics to allow myself to give up on, 'this is the way that you're supposed to do relationships', because nobody showed up on my little rural goat farm to come and marry me.
>
> It's actually not entirely true. My husband did show up, but I kept saying no. We were married ten years later, but I met him and fell in love with him when I was 19, 20 and told him no, because God wouldn't let me marry someone who had been divorced, and God wouldn't let me marry someone who had grown up in the Latter Day Saints Church. So he went and married somebody else.
>
> There are some degrees to which it's great that we went away and did our growing and came back together, but also we lost ten years of being together, and we both really wanted it. He'd come over and do ministry stuff with us and then we'd have lunch, be very careful not to touch each other and to have other people with us and side-hug before we left. And then I would go home and cry myself to sleep because everything in my body and my mind and my heart wanted him to touch me. I just wanted to put his hand on my face. I was having dreams at night of him reaching out and putting his hand on my cheek – that was all I was able to even imagine.

I had kind of, sort of dated one other person who never made me feel like my husband made me feel. The guy was a wonderful person who had a great job, was very stable, was very healthy, but I knew what it felt like to have been around my husband and he just couldn't do anything like that. I pursued this relationship in my mid-20s because he checked all the boxes and I was like, 'Well, I can fall in love after we're married.' He knew better. He very gently went away and did something else.

By the time the chance for a relationship with my husband came around again, I was at a point where I was like, 'I know what the Bible says about this and also I can't say no to this relationship again. I won't say no to it again.' I really had to defend it to my ministry team members, to my family, to my church. I was kicked out of the church. I mean, I was always 'welcome to come back to the church' – and removed from all my ministry positions. But I wasn't about to not say 'Yes' this time, because I knew, I knew the first time, and here I am knowing again.

Tessi's doctoral research reveals a wider picture of long-term harm, even among those who still support purity messaging:

One of the first questions on my interview list is, 'In what ways was purity culture positive or beneficial to you?' Most answers for those people is, 'I was protected from …' and then there's the list of things that purity culture taught you that you would be protected from if you followed it: you didn't get an STD, didn't have a broken heart, didn't … OK, but we can't really count as benefits hypothetical bad things not happening.

I've done 47 interviews at this point. My first set of 17 interviews I set out to try to balance people who responded in their surveys that they had had mostly positive purity culture experiences with people who had had negative experiences. I was unable to come up with eight people to interview. I might be able to pull a few more now, but I'm not sure and I've received over 800 surveys. So I did maybe four or five interviews. Within those interviews, very clearly, there's either an overwhelming amount of sexual shame or sexual fear very present. Among people who said, 'Yes, purity culture worked great for me', their story is full of, 'Well, it took me two years to be willing to date this guy because I was so afraid of the idea of having sex. But this person from my church and this person from my church and this book and this book got me to the point that I felt like maybe after I got married, I could have sex.' Or, 'It was great. And also I was terrified to take my clothes off with him.' I don't interpret that as purity culture working great for you.

All of this purity culture teaching that we've had, none of it has worked out the way it was supposed to for anybody. None of it. For nobody. Even the people who are happy with it, they're happy in spite of, or they're happy after they worked through.

Healing

It's February 2021, and the UK is in lockdown. We are allowed to meet another person outdoors but it is freezing, so Annie and I have parked our cars next to one another and are chatting through open windows as we drink coffee. Annie has designated herself my adoptive mother. She smokes as I tell her about purity culture. When I tell her that my husband and I didn't have sex before we married, she takes the cigarette out of her mouth and stares at me in disbelief. 'Fucking hell', she says slowly. It is the most validating thing someone has said to me about purity culture.

I feel like I was told so much about how a relationship should be, like, 'You have to get married, you have to do things this way', and it's been so hard for me to sort through do I actually believe that or not? Or is there a different way to do things?

There's also dissociation. Over the past couple months of trauma therapy I have been able to feel things in my body, because I was just told all the time that your body is inherently sinful and you shouldn't trust your body. It didn't affect just my sexuality, it affected the way that I live in my body. Like just me by myself. It's been really hard because now it feels like there's all of this sensation all at once. Things are almost painful to the touch because my body was just shut down for so many years. (Valerie, USA)

Penny (UK), an Anglican minister, calls me, laughing loudly: 'Look what I found!' She holds her purity pledge card up to the screen. 'Do you want it? I don't need it anymore!' So I am writing this with Penny's obsolete pledge card propped up on my desk.

In 2018, Josh Harris fully retracted the message of *I Kissed Dating Goodbye*[1] and pulled it from publication. In 2019, he stated on his Instagram account that his own marriage was ending and, a week later,

---

1 From Harris's statement (now deleted) on his website regarding *I Kissed Dating Goodbye*:

While I stand by my book's call to sincerely love others, my thinking has changed significantly in the past twenty years. I no longer agree with its central idea that dating should be avoided. I now think dating can be a healthy part of

that he was no longer a Christian. Harris is one of only a handful of high-profile evangelical leaders to have listened to voices speaking about the harm his work has done and apologized: plenty of others still teach purity messaging.

People have found a variety of ways to heal from purity culture, from the shaming, from being so cut off from their bodies that, like Valerie, they shut down and found it hard to feel. Many mentioned therapy, specifically trauma therapy and those including embodied practices. Others have found solidarity and answers for their lack of sexual or physical knowledge by following online sex educators or joining online recovery groups (or starting one, in MJ's (USA) case). Some help women heal as part of their career: Christine (USA), above, has become a therapist and Elisabeth (UK) is a physiotherapist:

> I find it weird that I'm helping people in ways that I feel like I've experienced. I see people that aren't able to have sex. The biggest population is people who've grown up strict Christians or strict Orthodox Jews or other strict religions. My whole life I've been, 'Control, don't let anyone …' and now I'm, 'You need to release. Get to know your genitals and the pelvic floor, sex is great.' So that's a dichotomy for me.
>
> I just wish that it had been a bit different for me. I've got a lot of friends and we were all virgins before we got married. I see it as a privilege that now I'm learning about the pelvic floor and about sex so that I can help other women, but a lot of my friends just take what their experiences are, they're like, 'Yeah, well, this is it', not realizing that there's more. Then the whole thing about masturbation and self-pleasure being wrong for so long. I try to encourage a bit more openness and discussion with my friends, but particularly if they are still in church circles, it's quite hard. But it's like a defining thing, isn't it, for many Christian teenagers? That would have been my identity as well: I'm a virgin and I'm proud of it.

My own 'embodied practice' involves swimming year-round in a nearby river, even when there is snow on the ground. My surroundings are

---

a person developing relationally and learning the qualities that matter most in a partner …

To those who read my book and were misdirected or unhelpfully influenced by it, I am sincerely sorry. I never intended to hurt you. I know this apology doesn't change anything for you and it's coming too late, but I want you to hear that I regret any way that my ideas restricted you, hurt you, or gave you a less-than-biblical view of yourself, your sexuality, your relationships, and God. (Harris, 2018) beautiful as well as challenging. When I walk into the water, I have to be utterly present: I am incapable of focusing on anything else but the physical sensation of icy water and how my body is responding, staying safe among slippery rocks and possibly a current or the blast of a waterfall. It's the lack of inhibition needed. It grounds me in my body in a way little else can. Some people say it is mind over matter, but for me it must be matter over mind: my mind tells me to stay warm and dry, but I allow my body to feel – really feel – what the water, the weather, my surroundings, my emotional state are all doing to me physically. And then I get out and drink tea and laugh with friends.

Nina (UK) found a renewed connection to herself in dance classes, which fed into her deconstruction more broadly:

At the end of the class I just felt so joyful and light and that my heart was open and things were going to be OK. I remember walking back to my house from the dance class through the park and really noticing the light and the colours and the flowers and the wind as if I was there for the first time – I walk through it every day on the school run. I think that was the first thing I noticed: how I felt afterwards.

We didn't just dance in the class, there were elements of yoga as well and at the end she would do a meditation. She would get us to say something that we love about ourself, or something that we're really thankful for, and just think about it for a while. It was my first experience of somebody leading me through something like that, and I remember finding the 'think of something that you love about yourself' being quite a new idea and being really moving. Something happens when you become aware of your bodily sensations and connecting with your body in that way.

I asked Laura (USA) what had helped her healing process:

My capacity to heal has only happened in as much as I feel safety within my own body, outside of sexuality. There's so much that comes from my body, and it's all hinging on my connection to her.

I am very grateful that I had children. For many reasons, but the birth process, pregnancy process, nursing, using my body to bring physical life, to nurture, to be present with, was a game-changer for me. I started being able to see my body as a good thing that not only physically brought life, but also there's so much in parenting that feels easier to address with my body. Like when my toddler gets hurt, I could stand five feet away and talk at them and say, 'Oh, you're OK', or even, 'I see that you got really hurt.' That's all good and fine, but I have loved the ability to just pick up my child and hold them. That has created a way to find some safety and goodness in my body.

Far from people deconstructing because they just wanted to have sex, purity culture is a widespread and major area of unhealthiness and even trauma: it destroys people's relationships with partners and with themselves. It is supposed to protect people from sexual and relational harm and vulnerability, but instead creates it, whether through lack of education about relationships, sex and consent or through promoting repression and shame. At best, it offers the gift of sex (within heterosexual marriage), but then reduces it to a formula and unrealistic expectations. At worst, it forms part of a palette of control by evangelical authorities: if you can control people's bodies, if you can persuade them to try to control their own thoughts and physiological processes, and shame them when they can't, then you can control them completely. A basic component of a sense of safety is bodily autonomy, and purity culture effectively removes this, especially for anyone who is not heterosexual and a cis man. In the name of protecting young people, purity culture leaves them more vulnerable, and in the name of valuing 'biblical marriage', purity culture's messaging condemns its followers to legalistic rules as a substitute for a healthy sexual and relational ethic.

Following divorce, and now in a new relationship, Josias (Denmark/ Finland) sums it up when he tells me, 'With relationships specifically, I was someone who did all the right things and didn't get what I was promised. I had to leave it all to get what I was promised.'

Perfect Design

I am 32, sitting in a staff meeting. About 25 of us sit in a circle around the room as my friend gets to their feet and stands in the centre. They are half crying as they 'confess' to 'same-sex attraction'. I don't remember anyone else ever having to publicly confess their sin in a staff meeting. When they finish speaking, three of us stand and hug them. Everyone else stays sitting, silent. Months later, I ask if they did that voluntarily. I already suspect what the answer will be: 'No. The leadership team told me I had to.'

I am 37, attending a Christians in politics meeting. The UK Government is debating a bill to legalize same-sex marriage. In our meeting, there have been some vociferous opinions against this. 'What's actually wrong with it?' I ask. 'Who is it harming?'
'It's just not God's highest,' comes the reply.

We've been taught that the Bible says to love the sinner, hate the sin. What does that actually mean? (Elisabeth, UK)

The groundwork of my deconstruction had been laid in evangelical churches. Being in an evangelical church, you have to preach against the gays, because we have nothing better to do. I remember being a queer person, sitting in those congregations, listening to the sermons going, 'Oh my God. That's me.' I think that fed into my radical zealot phase as well, trying to redeem myself, I suppose.

I had questions that nobody could answer: 'Do I have to pray the gay away? If I don't, what's going to happen to me? Does God still love me in spite of everything?'

My biggest pressure was to pray the gay away. Some of that was coming from the church, but a lot of that was coming from myself because of what I had been taught and what I had absorbed from church. (Katie, USA)

Being anything-other-than-straight is a major factor in people's deconstruction, whether it affects them directly or not: those I interviewed and surveyed were disgusted by how they see churches treating those who are LGBTQ+.

Attitudes I have come across vary from complete dismissal ('gay people don't exist, but some people think they experience same-sex attraction/ are deceived by Satan and choose that lifestyle'), to repressive ('it's not a sin to be gay, but to act on it is, so gay people must be celibate or get healed'). Some of the teaching reaches levels of nonsensical hysteria:

> I had a high school teacher who was going off on some rant about how if gay people get married, it erodes the sanctity of marriage. He held up a pencil and said, 'If you can just love whoever you want, then why can't I marry this pencil?' There're so many crazy, dehumanizing things where I think about these now and I just get angry. (Austin, USA)

So-called 'gay conversion therapy' comes in many guises, from the explicit and violent to the gentle but insistent pressure to 'pray the gay away', or softly patronizing phrases about this not being 'God's perfect design'. Jemma (UK) experienced the soft-sell:

> I remember going to a seminar at Soul Survivor where this guy basic-ally said that he was gay, but he had prayed enough and now he was married to a woman. I just remember sitting there thinking, 'Why can't he just be gay?' It was such a shock. He was not explicitly saying, 'Kids, do conversion therapy', but there was a clear, implicit message there.

The fact that no one could point to any harm caused by the existence of LGBTQ+ people and relationships was one of the earliest factors in my own deconstruction. Later, studying New Testament Greek and realizing that the Bible does not, in fact, 'clearly say', was only confirmation of this. If there's a range of scholarly views on this, why don't churches choose the kindest, most inclusive option?

Sam (UK) tells me what he thinks about church policies:

> Churches often make decisions two or three steps removed from the individual. The routes by which the church has come to policy decisions I think are quite flawed, and they're based on a particular view of the Bible. It has forced what's essentially a two-tier system, which isn't sustainable.
>
> If gay people know that that's the church's position, they don't join the church, so the church doesn't have to face up to 'this is a real person who is being discriminated against'.

The phrase Elisabeth (UK) used, 'love the sinner, hate the sin', is almost exclusively applied to people who do not fit the heteronormative boxes laid out in church (a meme reading 'love the believer, hate the belief' received some serious backlash). As Greg (USA) put it, 'To be gay, it's like the worst. But if it's just sin, why is that so much worse than jealousy? Why is that worse than pride? Come on! Evangelical churches absolutely deal with pride, and that's in the list, too.'

Eva (USA) and I discuss the fact that churches treat ideology as more important than people's humanity or safety:

> We are literally holding a Bible over a person's humanity. We're saying, 'These words in this book that I've interpreted the way that I think is somehow the only interpretation: that is more important than you being a human being.'
>
> I started to see how homophobic everybody was, and I thought, 'How can I go to a church like this when I have friends that are gay? How can I ethically do that?'

Things are not getting better with time. Tamsin (UK) tells me about the change she saw over the years she worked for a church:

> When I was interviewed for the post as a children's and families' minister, nobody asked my opinion about sexuality. By the time I left, every single person who has any position on the staff was being asked their perspective on sexuality, including the person who was caretaking and an assistant to the children's team.
>
> Then there were a series of sermons that were preached about sexuality and one about transgender as well. There was no other perspective offered. I know group leaders who I really respected left the church, because in their small group they're being asked to toe the party line on those issues, and they said, 'We can't', so they left.

In Canada, Margaret has also seen the creep of conservatism at a denominational level:

> I've moved to a place of affirmation, which is not our church's official stance. The official stance is that it's not sinful to be gay, but it is sinful to engage in LGBTQ sexual relationships, at least same-sex marriage.
>
> The Synod commissioned a study group a number of years ago to revisit the original report, which came out in 1973, called the Human Sexuality Report. The report came out last year, and it almost doubles down harder than the '73 report. They're trying to say it's a salvation

issue, rather than the '73 report which kept it more open, didn't allow for ordination, but also didn't draw the hard line that it was a salvation issue.

It's hundreds of pages long, so most people are just reading the summary, which makes it sound really nice and educated because there's professor this and professor that. But our campus ministers got together and they all read it with a fine-tooth comb. There's a diversity of opinion among them, but they all hate the report. They all agree that the sciences quoted are pathetic. One is a scholar and he's quite traditional, and he said, 'If this was one of my students, I would fail it, and I would like to know what our seminary is turning out.'

So that has really angered me. I can quietly deconstruct my thoughts on atonement theology and all these other theologies. My local congregation is lovely. We have a female pastor. We're not this crazy, nutty group, so I was comfortable staying, even if I don't like some of the music and I don't like some of the theology, you know, I've been there a long time. We have good friends. They're all pretty easy-going around these things. But this really disturbs me, the Human Sexuality Report. I get what it's like to have the old view, but I also understand for the people coming out, there's so much at risk in terms of their safety, emotional and physical.

In terms of the denomination, whether it approves the report or not, we are going to lose members either way. If they approve it, I may stay a member of my local congregation, but I'm going to withdraw my official membership from the denomination. I don't want to be counted as a member of that.

Perhaps more pernicious are the churches who are simply not upfront about their stance: search the website, sit through a few sermons, and you might get the impression that this church has no problem with diverse sexuality. Vivian (Netherlands) attended a branch of Hillsong before switching to her current, more traditional church. She says of her previous church:

They tried very hard not to be offensive to anybody, which meant they never really stood for anything. But I had gay friends there, and they were on stage but they were not out. That was never going to happen. The people who were out could not be on stage, but there was no talk about it, and that felt like if we don't talk about it, it doesn't exist. But 'everybody is welcome'.

They're also very aware of popular culture and the culture wars, so they don't want to appear racist, homophobic. I find that with my current church and the previous church, it's completely opposite in some ways. My current church is a very modern, open message in a conservative jacket, whereas the other one is a very conservative message in a very modern jacket.

Evangelical teaching tells us repeatedly that being LGBTQ+, and LGBTQ+ relationships, are 'not God's highest' (at the very least). Yet surely the thing that is 'not God's highest' is the damage that the Church does? The stories of those who came out (or were outed) in church contexts could fill books. Plenty of people had been kicked out. I lost count of the parents who told me how relieved they were that they became affirming before their children came out, and of their anger at seeing their children ostracized in church. Robert (USA) told me of the years he spent hiding:

I was drafted into the US Army during Vietnam in March of '69, and fortunately ended up in Germany for two years. I got involved in Christianity through Army Chaplaincy. When I got out of the Army, I'd become a Lutheran. In America, there are different Lutheran denominations. I ended up in the more conservative one because I was indoctrinated in this literalism of the Bible.

I spent the next 25 years as a pastor, all as a closeted gay man, in denial and struggling with that and covering up: 'I'm in this conservative group, how can I be gay?' Secretly, though, I'm praying to God, 'Cure me.' It's very conflicted psychology here. In fact, that's one of the motivations that led me into ministry: I figured if I became a pastor, God was going to reward me by curing me. Which didn't happen. After I finally realized that I was born gay and it was not going to change, I began to question this belief system I had joined.

In my third parish, the pressure was getting too great. I started a hidden relationship with a professor of music. I was with him for 12 and a half years, a good part of that in secret while I was still pastoring. Things came to a head at my church, and I challenged them about their conservatism and in regards to they were anti-gay. I never came out to them, but being a single man, they probably suspected. I think there were rumours flying. I was given the option of either resigning or being kicked out, so I resigned.

Even though I didn't really like the ministry I was in, because I'd been in it for so long, my identity was there, so that was traumatic. I was coming out and at the same time I was unemployed, I was living off savings, I had lost my medical coverage. I left the church with my pension intact. They couldn't take that from me, so I'm pensioned off and I'm on Social Security now and I have another partner who lives with me. To have left all that was like a burden was lifted from me, even with the conflict of leaving a job and all that went along with it. I became involved in a gay activist group, because you need community and that's where I found it.

I'm 73, and there's a lot of anti-gay old people out there. They're going to have to die off. The new generation is replacing them and they're not anti-gay. That's the only way it's going to happen, although I'm afraid that they have managed to indoctrinate some of their young people.

I try not to stereotype all denominations. There are some denominations out there that I would consider open, progressive and trying to make change. But those in the middle, they better get off the fence. Decide what you are, you know?

You would hope that things had changed in the years since Robert entered ministry. Mia (Costa Rica/USA) is in her 20s, though:

I had questioned my sexuality a little bit throughout high school, but the environment was so conservative and so oppressive that I was like, 'This is a problem for later. I'm not even going to engage with it right now. I think I like girls, but I also like boys. So hopefully I'll just get lucky and find a nice boy and not have to deal with this.'

At this point in our interview, I hear a voice from off-screen: 'Spoiler alert: she didn't end up getting a guy.'

Mia smiles. 'My wife's over there in the corner.'

That's when I meet Freya (USA), who adds, 'Oh, "get lucky"? Yeah, you did.'

Mia responds, 'Not the way I was thinking, but I'm very glad that it turned out this way.' Freya joins her on-screen, and she continues:

Jesus never said anything about homosexuality, so I started really diving into certain verses in context and ended up deciding that it probably was OK that I liked girls and it probably was OK if I ended up being with one. I met my wife and had a good amount of turmoil from that, but the reaction that was really hard to deal with was the reaction of people in the church, because at that point I was still involved.

When I ended up going to some of the leaders in the church I got a range of reactions that all fell in the negative side. The person who was the director of the prophetic ministry that I was under said she didn't think it was biblical, but that she still loved me and would support me and that she cared most about my relationship with Jesus. So she was like a neutral negative: 'I don't like this, but I'm not going to shun you for it.' In the moment, I was content with that reaction because I was expecting to be fully shunned. As I've gone on, that actually is really hard for me to think about, because she was somebody who I had trusted so much and done so much work with and shared so much deep personal things with, that to have her say, like, 'This whole thing about you is wrong, but I guess I still love you, and I guess we can still continue talking to each other', in the moment it was a relief, but actually it's very hurtful.

When I went to the lead pastor, because of course you have to talk to the pastor about these things, he said, 'There's nothing wrong with you for being gay, but you can never act on this. This is openly rebelling against God. This is sinful. This is disgusting. This is not what God meant for you or for your life.'

With my mentor, there was a little bit of an undertone of, 'Are you sure you don't need to address your trauma more? Isn't this part of the reason why you're gay?' But there was a lot of that sense of, 'There's something wrong with you, how will you ever please God and have this ministry in which you're a loving servant wife if you're openly rebelling against it?' Just all that bullshit. They told me directly that this was a matter of my salvation and my girlfriend's salvation, and that if I truly loved her, I should break up with her so that we could both take time apart, re-focus on the Lord and then maintain a path of sanctification. I had been convinced for so long that they were right and I was wrong that even when they said things that were very explicitly hurtful, I was still inclined to believe them and doubt myself and my own sanity.

After that, I very much stepped back from church. I tried to go into the building a couple of times because they didn't explicitly say, 'You can't come here.' They just reprimanded me and just shy of told me I was going to hell if I didn't change my lifestyle. I was no longer allowed to be part of any leadership that I had held previously. I stopped being invited to things. I literally went from sharing my testimony in front of 500 people and all these prayer meetings, leadership meetings, and coming up with different curriculum, like I was up there doing shit, and then I was allowed to come sit in the back, was the demotion.

When I came to church, I came up the stairs into the balcony area, where a lot of the college students would sit. I went up and nobody, not one person, spoke to me. I walked up to a circle of people that were talking in the intermission, when people are getting coffee. Everybody stopped speaking immediately. One person who I was friends with from school talked to me, everybody else just looked at me like I was the scum of the Earth and did not even deserve their acknowledgement.

So I didn't go back after that, because I was like, 'You're telling me that I'm welcome here, but clearly that's not the case.'

I think the biggest thing it did was it made me realize how unwelcome I had been to an extent all along, because I had worked so hard to make myself a good Christian who had this horrible past but had been redeemed and made whole and Jesus had saved and now I was going to do all these things for God and that was going to be a witness to his glory and his love and yada, yada. I had worked so, so hard. Ultimately, my sexuality has always been a part of me, but it didn't matter how hard I tried or how much I worked to be this pure, redeemed, godly woman, I was never going to be enough and I was never going to be wanted in that space.

My mum already thinks I'm going to hell because I'm gay, and she's told me that multiple times. She actually refused to come to my wedding for the longest time, and then ended up coming, standing way in the back with sunglasses and dressed like she was going to a funeral, and sobbed the whole time and then gave me a hug and left. Just so dramatic.

Mia hands over to Freya, who tells me her own story:

I was that conservative ass in high school that totally judged everybody. People would come up with discussions, and I'd be like, 'No, the Bible says this, so it's wrong.' But then I started coming out to myself, and that was terrible, and I didn't think I could come out to anybody, because I went to a Christian high school and they would talk about anything bad you've done, God can make you clean. I remember crying because my sexuality was not something that could be forgiven in the past: it was just a part of me. So, I do that whole 'pray the gay away' thing, and I felt like every time I prayed, I just got gayer and gayer.

I didn't end up coming out to my parents until I had a panic attack and I ended up yelling it at them. I had attempted suicide twice at that point. My dad would always be like, 'Well, God put you in my life for a reason, and I think it's so that I can convince you to be straight.' But I was convinced that I failed at suicide because God was doing miracles to keep me alive, like, 'OK, so God does love me despite this, so the best I can do is live for him.'

I'm gluten intolerant, and my pastor was like, 'Hey, I noticed that you haven't been taking communion. That's because you're gay, right?' I'm like, 'Well, no.' Then he was like, 'I think that you and your mentor and I need to talk about whether or not you can take communion at our church.'

In high school, I came out to my brother first because he was the safest, but he ended up saying there was a special place in hell for gay people. Fast-forward to our wedding, I was like, 'Will you be my best man?' and he said, 'Oh, I'm not coming.'

I would talk to my parents about each Bible verse, and it just wouldn't make any sense to them, but then they did a Bible-in-one-year study and they're like, 'You know, we've just not felt convicted about this whole gay thing going through the Bible. So, maybe this isn't a big thing.' Then they met Mia, and they're just like, 'Oh my gosh, we love Mia. She's great.' That's when they got 100% supportive, and then we ended up having the wedding in their backyard.

That bittersweet mixture of happiness and remaining non-affirmation from loved ones was present in quite a few stories: a number of parents also told me of siblings who have been split apart when one comes out, with newly affirming parents trying to hold the family together.

Gordon (UK) deconstructed before he came out, and managed a happy re-arrangement:

Homosexuality was illegal before I was 24. I came out as gay in my late 30s, and my wife has been so supportive. We have separate bedrooms and she's got a wonderful boyfriend. Not being a Christian did mean that when I did begin to accept my sexuality, I didn't have that dreadful homophobic pressure. Going through leaving the faith was very similar to coming out of the closet in some ways.

The homophobic pressure Gordon mentions has a broad impact, beyond those who already know they identify as LGBTQ+. Even being affirming can be silenced: I remember arguing in favour of same-sex marriage, using my basic grasp of Greek, only to be told I was 'being all heart and no head', despite my interlocuters' lack of Bible knowledge in either Greek or English. Helen (UK) had a similar run-in:

We had this Bible study and it was 'Blessed are those who are persecuted', and somehow my friends managed to move this conversation to, 'Well, we're not even allowed to say that we think homosexuality is wrong anymore, and there's going to be a time when the Church is going to be punished for not performing gay marriages', essentially saying, 'We are being persecuted for being homophobes.'

I was so angry and trying to not allow myself to be completely rumbled for being affirming. I didn't think it was a space that I could safely say, 'Actually, I think gay people should be allowed to be married and the Church should marry them.'

I don't know at the time if I was even questioning, but since then my journey to becoming affirming continued into a journey of, 'Oh, actually, I'm bisexual and I can't believe it's taken me until I'm 35 to figure that out.' But if I can't be myself in terms of talking about what I believe, I definitely can't be myself in terms of being out.

Helen's story was part of a pattern: I was astonished by the high number of women who told me that they had no idea that they were queer until their late 20s, 30s, 40s, due to the combination of heteronormativity and purity culture repression. Many simply thought they were really good at purity rules. MJ (USA) puts it well:

I was told that you were straight or you were going to hell, so that gay little part of me just went and hid so deep inside that I didn't even know. I was 39 years old when I realized that I liked girls. Looking back, I see so many clues, but my whole entire world, everywhere I turned, there was Christianity.

Jemma (UK) also found a disconnection from herself:

The problem is not so much working out what my sexual orientation is, but more a connection with sexuality in the broadest sense, and previously not feeling in any way connected to it or knowing how to interact with that part of myself. It's such an unlearning, isn't it, to see these things in a totally different way?

I've really been thrown in the deep end because my partner is polyamorous as well as queer and non-binary, so I've gone whole-hog into the most non-heteronormative, non-conforming relationship possible, and trying to think that a relationship can be positive and healthy and have meaning and be worthwhile, even if it doesn't end in Christian marriage, recognizing that that's OK.

The key word being *end* in Christian marriage! Churches are doing people no favours by forcing people's sexuality underground: realizing this later has profound implications. Laura (UK) came out as bi a few years ago:

This is not new. This has just been buried. Trying to allow these parts of myself to emerge into the light, to try and figure out what that means and how you start to build a new identity in the context that you find yourself as a married woman with children, it's quite a challenge.

Angela (USA) defied everything she knew to build that new identity:

> My father was a minister. In my home there were Bibles everywhere and we prayed over everything. I was completely immersed in that culture as a child. Getting married, I had just turned 18 and I started having babies when I was 20. I have both sides of the spectrum of grief and guilt, of being brought up in it and then also bringing children up in it. Thankfully, as I've deconstructed, my grown children have been watching.
>
> I had a platonic friend. I would go to her house after work and we would sit on the couch and watch TV. And she was a lesbian. I felt right at home in a way that I'd never felt safe and at home, ever. In 2017, she had a break-up, and she was like, 'I need to get myself back out there, but I'm scared to death.' I said, 'I'll take you on a date.' Evidently, I planned a damn good date.

Angela's world was further rocked when she read Linda Kay Klein's book *Pure* (Klein, 2018), and recognized herself in the stories of purity culture:

> Deconstructing helped give me the strength to leave an unhealthy situation. The way I was brought up, you marry a man, you have his babies, you stay till you die, the end. I was dying on the inside for quite some time. I left religion and God first, and as I broke those things down and pushed them away, I was able to see myself as just myself.
>
> I call it my giant, flying, fucking leap I took in early 2019 when I packed my shit, and it's been a wild ride. I moved out on my own for the first time in my entire life and got my own apartment when I was 48 years old. I didn't even know what my favourite colour was. It's astounding, the depersonalization of religion.
>
> If you had said to me in 2017 that I would be living in a house with my wife and our two dogs, I would have laughed and said, 'What alternate universe are you speaking about?' I proposed because this was my choice, which was important to me with my history. I feel healthier, happier and more whole than I could have ever imagined.

The other side of this is the people who knew they were queer, but whose churches pushed them into straight marriages. The fallout hits whole families. Anne's (USA) story haunts me:

> My husband and I didn't like each other or have anything in common but married quickly on a 'prophetic word' that everyone celebrated. My husband was attracted to men and had many frightening 'deliverance'

sessions to remove that. He was encouraged to marry a woman and would therefore find healing if he was a holy and godly person. He told me this after the prophetic word, and my heart welled with such compassion for him. I was so excited to be used by God for his freedom. Spiritual leaders encouraged me, telling me this was an honour most women don't get. But on our wedding night my husband started convulsively crying that he couldn't have sex.

It's been 16 years of really low self-esteem and anxiety, because until now I thought I had failed or messed up God's plan. Now I see how it was all a stupid plan. They all listened to my descriptions of emotional abuse for years and said I was letting fear steal my joy. I was severely gaslighted. The hardest part now is seeing that I kept going for help and advice to the exact group of people who led me into the terrible life. It's so maddening.

A lot of spiritual leaders said things about how they did counselling for married couples and they saw that after a couple of years or so, people would fall out of love or the honeymoon is over. They kept telling us that we would never have to go through that because we were starting just from faith and God chose us for each other. They really thought that we would have the best marriage and have less pain than anyone else.

Last week in a heartfelt talk I started sobbing that I'm so angry my chance for real marriage was stolen. My husband is kind-hearted, and didn't do it in a mean way, but him and the leaders trapped me into this pain and I'm reeling with anger and sorrow. I wish I could marry someone who loves me. I never dated, so I've never known a guy to have feelings for me and I've never kissed someone who liked kissing me.

A model for the Church

So many of us were promised abundant life, community and our true identity in Christ (the evangelical version, at least). Yet so many of us found these things when we *left*. This was perhaps most clear for those who are LGBTQ+. KP (USA) speaks about where she finds herself now:

I keep waiting for God to be like, 'Hey, you're not supposed to be doing any of this stuff or thinking about any of this stuff.' And that's not how I feel, so I guess I'll just keep ploughing on.

I definitely feel like I'm a fuller version of myself. The conservative evangelical Christian, cis heterosexual version of myself was not me, and I think I always knew that there was a version of me far out there who was fuller than the me that I was living. So there's a more empowered me, there is something more grounded about the way that I'm living now, more of a trust of myself. I know that I can participate in the flow of the divine, and it doesn't always look like these rules or these things that I have to do.

The kind of relationship that I want is a lot of times the kind of romantic relationship that is modelled in queer communities, where there is a lot of equality and companionship and intimacy without the roles, and being more inclusive of other perspectives, less fear, less exclusion.

Becoming a fuller, more authentic version of ourselves is such a core part of people's deconstruction. It stands to reason that, for some, deconstruction and coming out or becoming affirming are part of the same process. Fran (UK) says:

It took me a long time to get over the same-sex relationships teaching that I had. I bent over backwards to try and soften it because I think I knew it was wrong, but I thought I had to accept it because I was taught that what is most important is 'this is what the Bible says, therefore'.

It was a combination of hearing people explain ways the Bible could be read in a more inclusive way, but also a bit of letting go of the Bible being the only and final authority. The Bible had to take its seat among other sources of input, along with empathy for people and just, logically, is this reasonable to hold this stance?

You see the fruit of anti-LGBT theology: it's cruel. And yes, even the people who soften it. I'm trying to remember who I was: there are times when I get really angry at anti-LGBTQ stuff that comes out, but having the humility to realize I'm not that many years removed from when that was me and I'm very grateful for the people who were patient enough to talk about it with me, knowing that I probably have said some pretty hurtful and offensive things. But people did speak to me and took the time and created resources that I used.

I remind Fran that when they filled in the survey, they wrote about seeing parallels between the Early Church and the queer community today. Fran laughs:

Maybe my last sermon at church I will go out with a bang and tell them that! Wasn't that what the Early Church was? A lot of the people in the Early Church would have converted and not brought their families with them. I think that's one of the reasons why they were so keen on calling each other brother and sister. The first jobs in the Church were deacons, providing for widows who didn't have anyone else to take care of them. The closest parallel in our society is how the LGBT community has built chosen families around people who love and care for them, reaffirming that the human need for family is more powerful than biological families, that where we can't find it in the people who are related to us, we build it for ourselves. The place where that's happening is not in the Church at the moment.

Fran's point reminds me of Gordon (UK) and others who liken deconstruction to coming out. So often we lose our church community and find our chosen community among others who have also deconstructed. Jude's (Australia) experience combined both communities:

When I was fired as a pastor, when it was deeply traumatic in the early weeks, the people that turned up for us were our gay friends, gay Christian friends, my gay pastor friend who knew what it was like to be excommunicated. Instead of saying, 'Praying for you' – eff that, how do you even know what to pray for me? How do you even presume that that's good? – they were the ones that said, 'Let's go out to dinner', and they sat there and entered into the anger and pain because they had already experienced it for themselves and weren't afraid of it. Over Thai food at a local restaurant, that was communion. They didn't talk about love: they showed me love, and they continue to show me love, and that means I just can't tolerate a whole lot of theology that used to make sense.

The ways that has reshaped me, entering into the pain of my friends' sexuality and their Christianity, their faith intermeshing and how difficult that is. Just as they let my pain touch them, I let theirs touch mine.

What I can't understand is that when everybody is not welcome, how could anybody want to be there? Because I feel excluded, but I know that as a straight Christian I've got some freedoms to give up. I'm seeing my straight Christian privilege.

White Jesus

I am 24, living in South Africa while I work for a ministry that seeks to incorporate different cultures into its identity and way of working. As a white Brit who has not had this depth of exposure to other cultures, living and working alongside people from those cultures is a revelation. The ministry's appreciation for and inclusion of non-western cultures is revolutionary in the evangelical mission world of the late 1990s. What I have heard about things from other cultures being 'demonic' is blown away and I start to realize how much ethnocentricity we add to the gospel. My African colleagues seem to be having the same realization: I hear my Tanzanian colleague freely playing the drums he was once taught were demonic due to their association with ancestor worship. For the first time, I hear Africans tell me about the harm white people have done to their continent and peoples. I'm learning and growing, but I receive pushback from other white Christians, concerned that I'm involved with something 'dodgy'.

It is 20 years later, and I look back and understand that even as we researched how those cultures view the divine, even as we pointed to which elements we (in our wisdom and discernment) recognized as 'God's revelation of himself in those cultures', we – even those who are Black and brown – still centred the white, western, evangelical God we knew and tried to 'redeem' those cultures towards that image. Often our allowance for the expression of those cultures and their faiths extended only to the aesthetic and artistic expression, and not a more profound understanding of their deities and what we could have learned from very different expressions of the divine. It's a tangle of good and bad; a positive step along the way and something that remains deeply problematic.

Decolonizing and deconstructing have to happen at the same time. (Tiffany, USA)

My husband is from India. He has really struggled with how excluded he's felt in UK churches. We have a few people who are openly racist and it can be hard to call that out in a church context because it's always minimized. (Louisa, UK)

I have questioned a lot the mixture between what is mission and what is colonialism. I've completely deconstructed the concept of evangelism and how you interact with a religion that you're not from. It feels very awkward. (Laura, UK)

Decolonization and race were mentioned numerous times as key elements in deconstruction. For some people this was a historic overview of how white theology and Christian action have impacted the world and been complicit in imperialism and slavery, while others said that events of the past few years such as rising white supremacist, anti-immigrant and anti-refugee rhetoric, the death of George Floyd and others and the response (or not) of churches to current events was the final straw for them. Eva (USA) tells me:

When Trump was elected, that really blew open the doors of white churches, we started to see like, 'Oh no, this is bad. We've been sleeping on this', because there are so many very passionate Trump supporters, especially in my church.

I was starting to deconstruct, and Charlottesville, Virginia, had a big white supremacist rally in August of 2017. A man drove through a crowd of people, killed a woman. I was there for that, and I saw how little my church cared. I started to notice things, like a lot of our worship songs had military themes, like 'God is going to fight for us, and those people that don't agree with us, we're going to make everybody worship him.' I started to notice how much colonization and white supremacy was in the way we taught the Bible. In my church it was only white men that were straight and married and had kids that could be in charge. That's the most powerful demographic in our country, if not the world, and we're letting those people interpret scripture and teach it to everybody else. We cannot be more wrong.

This is an issue that was mentioned by participants globally with reference to their own countries. Talk of 'taking cities/countries/etc. for Jesus' is explicitly colonizing. More insidious is the exportation of white evangelical culture and ways of 'doing church' and theology. So much of deconstruction is about seeing through the power and control inherent in evangelical churches and theology, of which we have been a part and complicit, so seeing through other power structures becomes – you'd hope – interwoven with that. But it is also the case that the participants in this book (and in deconstruction spaces online) are almost entirely white.

I have no definite answers as to why this is: perhaps for those who have not benefited from those power structures, questioning them is obvious? When I ask Veneda (USA) about this, she tells me:

We've been the only Black people in church for the whole time that we've been here. So I have no idea what's going on with other Black people, but I think it's more of a spiritual thing and maybe not a thing with Blacks and whites. I do think in Black society it's easier to say no and go your own way because there's not always this covering of 'the way it's supposed to be'. It's never the way it's supposed to be for us.

Joshua (UK) adds:

The whole philosophical history of deconstruction is all based in white western thought as well. Maybe 'decolonizing' would be more appropriate or would be more inclusive of people who aren't white.

Whatever the reasons, we cannot escape the fact that those who are Black and brown in white evangelical spaces are often treated very differently from white church members, and/or expected to fit into the white culture of churches and mission agencies, even where there appears to be diversity. Some of the stories included in this chapter were very, very hard to hear, and come with a strong trigger warning. But they are stories that need to be told, and which have often been dismissed and ignored in Christian spaces.

Veneda (USA) continues:

We were always the only Black people. We didn't know we were being treated differently. We were also very poor during those church times, and we didn't know that they thought, 'Well, of course they are. They're Black.' We had no idea why they wouldn't help, why they wanted to open up our books and make sure that we were being faithful with our money. We were so full of shame for being poor, for struggling.

Also we didn't really realize the stress we put ourselves under about having to be perfect at all times so that they wouldn't yell at us for being not perfect at all times. My husband sings really well, and so do I, so we were talented, we cooked, we kept the social life going. All that was very, 'OK, that's what Black people do', and when we stopped, people got upset that we weren't helping enough because we were dying due to the crushing poverty. We didn't understand any of this until we were out, until we started actually seeing the racism, the classism. In America, it's a huge thing about whether you have money or not. God likes you, that's why you have money, and if you don't, God doesn't like you, and you must be sinning somewhere.

They called me 'Mamma', and I never even got that either. And we called it 'the bosom anointing': people would come and lay their head on my bosom for comfort. I tell you how blind and stupid I was, and when I figured this stuff out, I went, 'Oh my Lord. No wonder I have bad images of myself as a woman.' All the guys called me 'Mamma', so that they don't have to deal with any kind of sexual anything that they might feel, in the process making me feel dowdy and ugly and Aunt Jemima-like. It took me years to let all that shed off.

I comment to Veneda that even I, with limited knowledge of American history, can see the blatant historical tropes, and I'm shocked that her church friends didn't. Veneda continues:

They never have to think about it. They're not racist: they like me! Finally, on Facebook, I just put, 'Don't try to think you all are OK just because you like me. Don't use me as your "I'm not racist" card.' They just don't get it. I'm done. My husband says I'm being a little mean, but right now I'm done.

I doubt if I'll ever go back to church again. I think we've been burned enough.

As horrifying as Veneda's story is, in some ways it doesn't surprise me, given what I have heard from others. Ronnie (USA) tells me about an experience he had in 1986. This comes with a strong trigger warning:

My upbringing is conservative and fundamentalist, and where I grew up was extremely racist. When I was 15 years old, I stood on the church porch in a circle of people – and a couple of these people were my family members – on the Sunday night before the first Martin Luther King national holiday. Someone in that circle said, 'What do you think about us taking this King's Day off from work tomorrow?' And another person – in that circle going into the church – said, 'I think it's great. We should kill six more n-word and take a whole week off.'

Far more recently, Mia (Costa Rica/USA) found that her church – her employer at the time – did not appear to care when she faced this kind of violence:

One of the biggest things that led me to deconstructing was the election in 2016. I was living in the most diverse building on campus. After the election was announced, people started chanting, 'Build a wall around X Hall', where I lived. Some of my classmates were getting death threats, people are getting called the n-word, people are getting spit at, people are getting harassed. The school sent all minority students an email telling us not to go outside by ourselves. We had to have campus police stationed in our basement and outside. They were monitoring who came in and who came out. It was absolutely awful.

I remember texting all the church leaders, because I was really close with them, and talking to them about what was going on. They were all like, 'That's terrible, I can't believe that's happening, I don't understand why people could do that.' They all voted for Trump. When I tried to talk about how I was afraid, it was like, 'Oh, that's too bad, we'll pray about it', with no desire whatsoever to take action or advocacy, or even in the pulpit say, 'This isn't OK. We're not going to stand with people who are racist, this is ungodly.' Nothing. It was just, 'I'm sorry that's happening. That must be scary. Moving on.'

This doesn't stop with individual church members. Even those with apparent authority in church are not immune from racism. Anselm (USA) recalls of his denomination:

This is something that I don't think I fully realized until I was deep into the church. I was a minister there, and I think that the way Christianity was taught, the interpretational framework of the Bible, is very white-centric. It centres white theologians and it centres an interpretation that has been used very insidiously to advance the ideas of white supremacy and colonization and racism.

On a micro scale, there was a personality that came to be put forward as the ideal way to be a man, the ideal way to be a ministry leader, the ideal way to be a disciple of Jesus. A lot of the characteristics that were pushed forward are very much valued and even idealized in white American culture: being the loudest person in the room or being strong in the sense of holding onto your values no matter what and bending people to that while also being humble. I found that the white men who were at my level on staff and who exemplified these qualities were promoted and advanced far more than the Black men like myself. But then if I, as a Black man, exhibited some of the qualities that I saw other white men around me exhibiting I was labelled as prideful, disobedient, problematic, and I saw other Black people get the same exact treatment.

The denomination prides itself on its diversity, and it is a diverse space as far as the different ethnicities that are represented there, but as far as who's making the decisions, as far as the culture that we're all forced to take on, I would say it's very Eurocentric and white-centric. I would be in meetings where we're going through the list of the people in the ministry, like who's healthy, who's struggling, and I noticed that the Black and brown members of our ministry were oftentimes considered to be weak because of, 'This person thinks very independently', or, 'This person is not able to commit as much to attending the meetings of the body because they're working these jobs to take care of a sick parent, but Jesus comes first', or whatever.

I haven't shared a whole lot about what I did to other people that even today I'm still working through. I've talked to a lot of them. I've done as much apologizing and listening as I could for some people; for others, I just have to sit with what it is that I've done. As the Black minister, I was often called in to quiet down or to influence towards conformity a lot of the Black people within our ministry, even people who were not in the ministry I was overseeing. I'd get phone calls like, 'Hey, this brother is at it again. Can you talk some sense into him?'

I have been a lot more outspoken lately about the complicity that Christianity has in white supremacy. In slavery, there were Black people who were given a little bit of power, but they were told to use that power to keep their fellow people in line. I realized that that was what I had become. I think we all want our lives to matter in some way, and for me, the taste that I got of that by being given this little bit of power, the ability to influence: I came to want to protect that no matter the cost. I think that's how this particular interpretational framework of the Bible is utilized to keep the people who have power, in power, and to keep the people who are oppressed, oppressed.

Lucas (UK) has also been reflecting on the historic structures that keep oppression in place. He remains a church minister:

I was reflecting with all the George Floyd stuff about how I was unable as a teenager to articulate any of my experience in the church growing up. I would be having all kinds of social and political and theological conversations, but I couldn't talk about race and ethnicity at all. We did talk about it a fair bit at home. A big part of this was you cannot talk about these things without at least implicitly shaming everybody you know and love, especially all the middle-class white people around me.

My family history is a story of the British Empire on both sides, so I can't understand myself apart from that story. I led a discussion on white supremacy, Babylon and the Church. It was a kind of theological, historical, biblical journey looking at my understanding of the origin of white supremacy and empire, and white supremacy being an inevitable outcome of economic injustice and slavery. It's really damaging to the human soul to be perpetrating injustice and it's easier to do that psychologically if you come up with some sort of justification as to why these people are worthy of your mistreatment. So the Church was fully participating in this imperial stuff and completely accepting of and participating in the justifications and the frameworks for understanding the world. It's a systemic failing of Christian theology and practice and the Church has never yet wrestled with that. In Protestant churches we have not got a sufficient historical memory. Our whole history is consumed within the imperial project.

Lucas's point makes me think about ways churches continue to uphold white supremacy, perhaps unwittingly. When I worked for another, more theologically diverse, mission agency, a colleague sent me a description of how a Thai Buddhist would understand John 3.16, which is very different to how we in the West are taught to read it (and it doesn't come out like 'good news'). I mentioned this in a Bible study. There was silence, then someone said, 'Let's move on, shall we?' Nothing other than the white version was allowed.

When I speak to Isabel (UK), whose husband is of Indian heritage, she sheds more light on this interpretational framework:

> It's the microaggressions that are common. In church he felt uncomfortable, and especially in missions, because there's quite a lot of tokenism, even if it's not intentional, and the feeling that you're a bit of a project. A lot of the unspoken racism, which is still so strong, probably has shaped a lot of our experience.
>
> The books of Ezra and Nehemiah talk about intermarriage between the Israelites and the people of the surrounding nations. It made me think about how entrenched in the Judeo-Christian cultural heritage and tradition is this idea of racial purity, and then that gets me thinking about what people think about mixed-race marriage.

This plays out in the stance some churches take on global politics:

> A message I did hear a lot in my Dutch church was against the people in a multicultural society. Then one of the things that sped up the deconstruction process is when they started talking about supporting Israel. It's as if they can deny 1948, Bible in hand, 'This is what it says.' That made my skin crawl and that was definitely a catalyst. You're waving around a 2,000-year-old book and you forget to mention what happened 60 years ago that we were all part of. (Vivian, Netherlands)

Over in New Zealand, Josh has seen the creep of right-wing politics in church:

> In New Zealand, of course, we've got the Māori, who, through colonization, have been given a really raw, difficult hand in life. There is a legacy of many decades of disadvantage and passive racism towards our Pacific Island or Māori communities.
>
> There are a lot of people in church who resonate with the more fundamentalist Christians that have been quite vocal in the States. That has been a component of established Christianity that I found difficult. This idea of entitlement as well, like people just need to work harder, this neo-liberalist idea that everyone's been given chances and if they've stuffed it up, then obviously they've done something wrong rather than it being a systemic problem.
>
> I struggle with that from the perspective of it being racist or discriminatory, in particular towards Māori. I mean, I am now the beneficiary of the exploitation of this country and the Māori being disowned. I struggle with that right-leaning undercurrent in many church circles, this Luddite way of looking at things, like things are better in the past.

Ronnie (USA), who sees these attitudes all around him, gives me his outlook for the future:

> The evangelical church in the United States is collapsing no matter what they may say about it. The joke here in the South is a dying mule kicks the hardest, and I believe that's exactly what's going on. Just pure demographics are on the side of diversity in this country.
>
> One of my sons is an African-American young man. He's been my greatest teacher and having him as a son has been a massive piece of my deconstruction about white supremacy, about privilege, my role as a white, middle-class, middle-aged man, how power works. He's engaged to a Latina dreamer who was brought here when she was two years old. She's not a US citizen. So when those issues come up, people start talking about the border and all this stuff, and I say, 'What do you want me to say? I have a brown son from a heritage of people that we attempted to destroy and he is in love with an illegal immigrant, and those will become my grandchildren that they produce. Where do you think I'm going to stand?' I mean, I'm going to stand where there are loving and compassionate and unifying solutions. Not in these polemic, hardcore certainty pieces that are false.

There are subtler ways that churches enforce whiteness: ways that took me years to see were just ethnocentrism dressed up as spirituality. My mother and – amazingly for the start of the twentieth century – my grand-mother both travelled extensively and worked overseas, and our house was a clutter of things they had collected. I grew up conflicted, seeing beautiful and fascinating items but hearing from church that they contained evil spirits. Romilly (UK) grew up with the same thinking:

> My mum had some beautiful things, like a mah-jong set. She was like, 'I've got to get rid of it all.' And chopsticks, anything with kanji characters on it. You've done a good deed in burning it, not giving it to the charity shops, so no one else can be affected by it. It's this really fragile, one-dimensional way of viewing the world.

Non-western medicine was another huge area: diagnosing my bad back as spiritual oppression was apparently fine, but something like acupuncture was definitely not, so I was confused to find that some of my Christian, South Korean colleagues were using traditional Korean medicine and didn't seem to be demon-possessed by it.

Panicking about a chopstick is the thin end of the wedge. What Tiffany (USA) experienced was the total erasure of their identity:

> I was so oblivious, I had no idea that that was what was happening. I had a concept of racism and it wasn't happening around me, and so it's only in a new understanding, looking back, that I can really identify that. The churches that I was involved in were charismatic evangelical, very enthusiastic about Christian work. I don't even know how young I was the first time I saw a slideshow of Black and brown people doing their traditional things and heard it framed as, 'This is the absence of God.'
>
> The way that my dad framed things, he used religion as a reason for racism. My mum is Cherokee and our last name is a Cherokee name, but we were so cut off from any concept of ourselves as indigenous, and it's a small part of our story, but it's one we had no access to whatsoever because Native religions are demon worship and woo-woo. You might as well be getting a pentagram tattooed on your soul. When we did our American History year in school and we tried to study different Native nations and tribes and people, we did our reports in front of our parents, and there was scorn any time there was a positive word being said about indigenous practices and traditions. Because he had this capacity to say, 'That makes us vulnerable to spiritual warfare, and those practices are not based on the Bible', there was that pathway to internalization.

My journey into deconstructing racism and colonialism within my faith and within my capitalist self and my American self has actually been a path to go, 'Oh, shit. The genocide of indigenous people in the Americas is continuing in my story.' I was boarding schooled in a way: I was taken away from my mum's family for spiritual reasons and incorporated entirely into my dad's European-heritage, white family, and that was the only goodness that I was allowed to have access to.

In New Zealand, Josh sees this continuing in church:

We've seen a revival of Māori culture in New Zealand. They've had more rights awarded and since the 70s and 80s they've found their voice in terms of their political leaders as well, and there's been a lot more focus on bringing the Māori language back, which I think is amazing.

Church is a generation behind. Part of the Māori renaissance relates to their cultural identity and spiritual journey, and a lot of pākehā, the white-predominant churches, find that a struggle because it brings all those taboo subjects of spirituality outside the Bible to the forefront. So there's a lot of passive resistance to allowing Māori a say in the churches.

Lynn (Canada/Ireland) explains how this has woven its way into evangelism:

Understanding how white privilege worked within my theology, in my psyche, my worldview. How it operated without you even knowing. I mean, that's the whole premise of white privilege: you're privileged because you don't even know you're privileged. It was this idea that you were bringing Christ to the indigenous people as opposed to looking where Christ already was there. The hubris of that is beyond cringe-worthy, but you don't realize just how deeply embedded it is. So much of this – and particularly I speak for Canada – this idea of the indigenous people being essentially savages and unsophisticated, not civilized people. I thought that I didn't have that within me, only to find that it shows up in different ways that you never expected: you think of some indigenous people that seem to be successful and totally integrated into Canadian life. Then you think, 'Why can't they all be like that?' What I was doing without realizing was, 'Why can't they be like us white people?' Their own way of doing things, their own spirituality, didn't have validity.

Lynn's point about 'bringing Christ to people' in other cultures brings us to the issues of missions. I am not denying that real compassion and sacrificial service exists, but it is too often muddied by colonization, denial of agency, thinking we know what is best for others. (I am also not denying that secular aid and development agencies don't also suffer at times from being patronizing, white saviour-ist, ethnocentric, ignorant of local culture and even exploitative at times, but they don't do it in the name of God.) It is a complex area: I know former colleagues who spent decades as members of communities far from their 'sending' country, quietly working for local leaders; I know several African and Asian missionaries who have come to the UK (the power dynamic inherent in this is simply not the same as white people going to Africa, Asia, etc.). I've also seen shocking insensitivity, incompetence, and colonizing attitudes and behaviour: the marketing photos of young blonde women 'ministering' to Black and brown people. The short-term teams visiting 'orphanages' (or setting them up) and sending unskilled young people to do skilled work that takes paid jobs out of the local economy (or has to be re-done when the keen young things have gone home). The offensive acts of 'spiritual warfare': Wendy (USA) tells me, 'We trekked the wrong direction around a holy mountain in Tibet as a prophetic act.' Yet, as Sophie (UK) found when she joined a mission organization, 'There was a boundary in the level that I could question people's approaches, like, "But if you're following God's calling, then it's OK."'

The other area where racial disparity exists is in who is seen as 'missionary'. When I worked for a mission agency here in the UK I noticed a pattern: when those going overseas were not white it took far longer for them to find churches willing to support them financially, regardless of the fact that they were often highly qualified, endorsed by the agency and already knew the language and culture of the place they were going.

Of those surveyed, 15% said they had, in the past, been involved in long-term overseas missions, and over 61% had been involved in short-term missions: these short-term trips are often an unquestioned part of church activity, especially for young people. The first short-term mission trip I did was to newly ex-Communist Eastern Europe when I was 16. This led to more trips, including several to Ukraine. The aim was to build relationships with churches there in case they faced a repeat of the persecution they had lived through under the Soviet Union. I am aware that the relationships our team leader created have lasted, and that 30 years later, through those relationships, she is closely involved in helping refugees within and leaving Ukraine. I'm not so sure the rest of us were so helpful, although it was certainly a learning experience. Tamsin (UK) tells me about what she did as a young person:

I went to Bulgaria for a short-term mission with children from orphanages, I guess is the term. We took them to the coast and had a holiday camp with them, and we also did some kind of building work. We cared well for the children and the children had an opportunity to develop and learn and play. But there was always a background agenda that we were evangelizing. Even more locally, community projects, we are offering an opportunity so that you will listen to our agenda, which is telling you about Jesus in the way that we think about it and hoping that you will say a prayer that we think you should be saying, so that Jesus can be your friend. I am sorrowful that at the time there wasn't a wider understanding for me, and probably for those running it: maybe we could have just given the good stuff without the agenda underneath.

A significant majority of the children we worked with were from Romani backgrounds. Honestly, what did I – a white, middle-class, British girl – really think? There is a real load of white privilege in there, isn't there? I can swan in for a period of time, give everybody a nice time and then leave again, and in between the arriving and the going impart some of my values, from my culture, to these children who have little ability to discern anything different. And through a translator: there's not even any easy conversation, there's no ability to engage with the ideas that are presented to them.

Even in the UK: university mission weeks and community projects and kids' camps. There's an interesting imbalance of power in some of it: the children are having a great time and they probably do look up to their leaders, but it's not exactly an environment that genuine questioning can happen. And people who need a community project to come and help them practically: again, there's an interesting power balance, isn't there?

I don't like some of the stuff I probably did and said, and you can't undo it, but it doesn't sit comfortably.

We talk about how normal it was to do this kind of thing: it's a staple of so many churches, particularly for young people who have not yet learned to question. Charles (USA) came across this normalization and pressure, which later led to him spending several years in missions:

We would go on these mission trips every summer, very much with the understanding that there was a saved and a lost. The way that was framed to us was our youth pastor would say, 'You can't give me one unselfish reason why you couldn't go spend a couple of years as a missionary.'

Christine (UK) was involved with a group that did street evangelism when she experienced this simplistic attitude to someone with multiple layers of disadvantage:

We did outreaches in Trafalgar Square. One day I saw this homeless guy sitting there. After the session was over, people got together to share testimonies and somebody said, 'We talked to this homeless guy and he became a Christian and it was wonderful.' I was back there the next week to go to the art gallery, and I saw him so I sat down with him and said, 'There was a group here last week and I was part of them', and he was so enthusiastic. He was a refugee from Sri Lanka and he'd been an artist and now he was just doing chalk drawings on Trafalgar Square. He didn't have asylum.

I went back to visit him quite a few times over the coming months, and that initial enthusiasm very quickly turned sour. He just seemed to get worse and worse in terms of his alcoholism, his self-harm. He'd lost all his family in Sri Lanka and he was just devastated. To start with, I was like, 'Let's pray together', and after a few months, I thought, 'I can't offer to pray for him because he doesn't need God to miraculously break in and sort his life out. The things that make me have a very stable job and a roof over my head hasn't come because of my belief. That's just my privilege that I've got a British passport so I can get a job. He is going to the Home Office every week and he can't get a job. He can't even start to turn his life around, and a prayer is not going to fix that.'

That was a very stark moment for me. Of course, because we like to believe in miracles, we pray for people on the street and we hear lots of testimony about things being good, but what we were offering him when we preached to him was, 'Accept Jesus into your life and everything will be great now.' That just wasn't the reality on the ground, it didn't make a material change in his life, and what use is it if I could say, 'Don't worry about all your suffering in this life, because when you die, you get to heaven'? It just felt very shallow, very trite.

Elise's (UK) diocese nearly fired her for setting up a successful community project with her local government authority:

It's so ingrained in us that we feel a divine right to own stuff, to manage stuff, to decide stuff, to get to be right. It filters through every element of how we do church and yet we have no self-awareness about it.

In community development work, they've learnt that looking at what's in your community and engaging with the people that you're connected to is the best way to develop community work. Yet in the Church, we've still got this top-down approach: here's our building, this is who we are. You're going to need to come to us. And it's just colonialism. People are uncomfortable with that: we don't want to be 'done to'. We want to be empowered. And yet the models that we rely on in much of how we do church are dependent upon doing to.

I mention to Elise that the giver, however well intentioned, is always in the position of power relative to the 'beneficiary'. She responds:

We're working against a culture of our church considering themselves to be benefactors of these poor people. That is the dynamic that has historically always existed, and it can be quite hard to eradicate that. And it is power, isn't it? It's a desire to be in control.

I agree with Elise: once again it comes down to power and control. I ask myself now where the balance is between being an ally and being a white saviour. For those of us primed all our lives to be saviours it's a tricky line to walk.

The inverse of white saviourism, still predicated on privilege, is the assumption that we are 'blessed' when we are, in fact, just privileged, and a blindness to the needs of others:

It's important to me that my faith brings more joy than suffering. So much of what was turning me off Christianity was the arrogant whiteness of the women saying, 'I prayed for a parking space and God opened a parking space.' I've literally heard people say stuff like that while other women were being raped and murdered. Praying for things like that was couched in a whole mindset that if you're living a good life, God's going to answer your prayers. God became a genie in a bottle, and this disconnect between the suffering of other people in the world and my privileged existence galled me. (Kathy, USA)

Ronnie (USA) reflects on how we got here, and where we could go:

So much of this is about how we've construed power, and a lot of white people are realizing that our theology for 500 years, it has just been about conquest and colonialism. I think we are at this seismic change, and it's dangerous because it can go in any direction, but I do think we're at a seismic change where we must realize that theology cannot be structured on conquest any longer. That's all we've had since the Reformation.

Prayed For: Preyed On

I am 23, 28, 34, 39 … and yet another person has told me that they 'just really feel' that God wants to heal my mother, who was left with severe physical disabilities following an accident. Increasingly my questions are building: if God wants to, then why isn't she healed? And, while well intentioned, is this more about what the speaker thinks would be good than anything God may or may not want? Those people were remarkably quiet after my mother died.

I am 40, meeting a friend's new wife for the first time. She says, 'If your church isn't seeing healings in every service, it's not a true Christian church.' I have a failure of manners.

> I've tried getting back to the Bible and thinking, 'I'll just focus on the teachings of Jesus.' So I started reading Mark, which is probably the worst thing to start with because it's like an action film: B'dang! Jesus is doing this, saying that, healing people, kicking demons out! I would love that to happen today, but I've lost so many friends to cancer and other diseases. God seems to be very selective: good at healing migraines but not the life-threatening things like cancer. So what's that about? (Geoff, UK)

> My wife has ADD, and a lot of the way that that played out prior to diagnosis was generalized anxiety and panic disorder. She's had experiences where she had a panic attack and a group of people then attempted to cast out demons, which is unbelievably fucked up. (Tim, Canada)

Healing is one of the most complex areas of faith. It gets to the very core of human suffering and loss. I've heard so many stories from people whose understanding of the divine and of church have changed out of all recognition, but who still have no idea what to make of an experience involving apparent healing: why was this person healed, why did that one die, why did someone's condition improve but not go away completely?

One thing is clear: how evangelicals have treated and mistreated 'healing' feeds directly into people's deconstruction. Too often 'healing' is treated like a magic trick which, when it doesn't work, is used to blame desperate people: they didn't have enough faith, there is sin in their life, they need to pray more.

The word 'healing' is used in the narrow sense of 'cure', as a quick fix for a specific problem, rather than a broader, more holistic sense; perhaps acceptance or comfort, or a new perspective. And, separating 'us' from 'them' once again, it is too often treated as the property of the evangelical church: 'proof' that our God is the real one and blesses us, not them, when in fact unexplained healings and cures are reported in many faiths, and by people who have no faith at all.

I have no doubt that most of those who pray for others to be healed have good intentions: a genuine desire to see human wellness in particular ways. But this does not mean that good intention cannot also harm, cannot also be mixed with a desire to prove something or to see dramatic 'signs', and cannot also be predatory, targeting people made desperate by illness or loss, or those who have not consented but who the pray-er deems in need of healing (a particular experience of those with visible disabilities). Tim (Canada) tells me what happened to his wife when she broke her ankle:

> She went to a conference and she had a cast. So many people were like, 'I want to practise my faith, and so I'm going to go and pray for her', and she's a really confident person and she's willing to push back and say, 'Why are you singling me out, what do you hope happens, do you actually feel that God wants you to pray for me? Or do you feel uncomfortable, is this something for you?' She is comfortable asking those questions. Not many people are, though.
>
> You want something so bad that you're willing to harm in order to get that. We're involved in the special needs community. My wife works as a respite care worker and occupational therapist. There's one family that she works with where they've had to tell people to stop praying for their kids because the assumption in that theology is that God desires to heal, we're the vessels for healing, therefore, we push until there's breakthrough. That's internalized by these kids as either 'there's something wrong with me that God doesn't want to heal me' or 'God hates me and so this is why I'm not receiving healing'.
>
> With the culture of healing, it can be altruistic: you desire wholeness or you desire the best for another person. But the other side of that is that it creates cultures of shame and pressure and expectations when things don't go the way that we expect that they ought to. There's not a category of openness for what diverges from wholeness in terms of the norm of a white ableist community.

Church culture is saturated in this ableism: healing culture gives the message that those with disabilities are not enough as they are, and the lack of leadership figures with disabilities compounds the attitude that those with disabilities or chronic illnesses must receive rather than give ministry.

What does it say about welcome and inclusion when churches are inaccessible for certain people: when people are made to feel disabled by how churches respond or cater to their needs, whether that is steps to the door, lack of sign language or anything else? Even at a stylistic level, evangelical church services and practices are pushed as a 'one size fits all' when they do not, in fact, suit quite a number of people. My own frequent sensory overwhelm at the level of sound, light, crowds and hands-on prayer gave me empathy for Katya's (UK) experience:

> We ended up in the Baptist Church in my early teens, and I put my foot down about joining the youth movement because I am autistic, and I really struggled with the social aspects of Sunday school. So I ended up sitting in the pews for the main service, with sermons that went on for about 45 minutes and were really hard-line, fundamentalist right-wing evangelical stuff. I got through it by going into my head, and I just hunkered down for a while. I refused to get baptized. Partly it was the social aspects of the full immersion dunking, being the centre of attention. I think, honestly, my social anxiety probably saved me from a lot of the testimony stuff.
>
> At 16, I managed to win a scholarship to a boarding school that is very high Anglo-Catholic. I joined the choir and it was incense and sung everything, but I was like, 'This is amazing, this moves me spiritually.' The sermons were ten minutes because it was preaching to a bunch of schoolchildren, but the whole experience was just mind-blowing and I was like, 'Why have I been turned against these other expressions of Christianity that don't involve crying, shouting and demonstrative stuff?'
>
> It was just such a relief; it was like waking up after being in a bad nightmare and realizing there was a way to be a Christian that didn't involve the kinds of touchy-feely stuff that I found very coercive, and still do.

Several parents told me of the response of churches to their children's needs, and the faith questions this raised for them. It led Lis (New Zealand) to deeper exploration:

We went to a community church for 20 years. We raised our family there. It was through that whole experience, growing and maturing, you rub up against experiences that make your faith tested. We have a child with an intellectual disability, and with a range of other experiences, I realized that what I experienced in church was very superficial, and where I was going internally was quite different. There's a lot of dissonance. I couldn't find those places to talk about it or find the answers in the church experience.

The point is, where is God in suffering? We were in this community church, which wasn't prosperity gospel, but it was very much 'you do the right things and God will look after you', and I was thinking, 'No, this is not our experience.' It's not that we had a bad life in any other way, but I would look at our son, and his life is difficult and it's always going to be. How do you deal with God in those situations? They were all busy worrying about who's going to be in this home group and which church building shall we build first. It all seemed completely upside down.

Evie (Australia) was also forced to confront her beliefs more broadly through experiences with her son and others who sought healing:

I was very curious about that experiential part of knowing God, and so we got very involved with that. We were involved with a church plant – I think they used to say it was evangelical teaching with charismatic gifting – and in those early days, it was so beautiful. There was a lot of care for each other.

Our youngest son is severely autistic, and I had this belief that Jesus is going to heal Liam or the second coming would happen, and people were praying for his healing, so that was always in the background. My other son is also on the spectrum, but higher functioning, but Liam was profoundly difficult and needed a lot of care and support.

When Liam was around 21 his mental health was starting to deteriorate quite significantly. Around that time, the Toronto Blessing came. It just started to sour, I don't know how to explain it. The emphasis on healing changed tack somehow; there was a lot of pressure. And not only was Liam getting worse, but he was quite tormented mentally. So we pulled back on leadership, I pulled back on the worship team to give Liam more time and care and myself more time and care. But I started to notice when we stopped doing and being, and the messier life started to become, people didn't know how to handle that. It was so much of this victory talk and healing talk and yet our reality was going down the gurgler, really, and I started to feel a distancing. People started to say things like, 'Oh, if you did more, if you did this, if you did that', kind of putting blame on us for Liam's deterioration.

There was talk of God's favour, and our daughter is quite high achieving and she's a beautiful person, but people were saying things like, 'God's favour is on her', and I'm thinking, 'So, on her, but not my boys, in particular not on Liam? What does that mean? Where does Jesus use that sort of language, that favouritism?'

It all came to a head when Liam had a psychotic episode. That really affected me and I had a breakdown, and I felt completely abandoned and isolated and just cast adrift. So I started to really have a look at what I actually believed and deconstruct why I believed certain things, where did that belief come from?

I had just given up on God, really. Probably Richard Rohr's stuff saved us from completely giving up. I felt that the faith structure that I had just had no content to it, it didn't have a framework that could hold pain and suffering and darkness. I think the teaching that we were experiencing was, 'There's something wrong with you.' But that's a very white, western, middle-class view, isn't it?

We had to relinquish care of Liam and then I had this breakdown, and the dominoes started to fall because of that experience. But no one checked, you know? I stopped being a useful commodity, I think.

It was almost like people set up camp at the experience thing, when we were going home to this very difficult child who started to be violent. I was thinking, 'Liam's not going to get healed. So what does that mean when we've been told that he will?' It caused me to have a look at the whole deal. That whole sinner's prayer thing: Liam would never have the cognitive ability to pray. What does that mean for him? I started to think about not just people with disabilities but people in far-flung countries and, like, is God that cruel? What have we done to this faith journey?

Also just being so quick to make promises about healing: one of my daughter's friends, her mother was dying of a neurological disorder, and someone actually said, 'Tonight your mother is healed.' She was reprimanded for her lack of faith if she didn't believe. There's just some abusive things going on. A friend of ours on renal dialysis went and someone told him that if he continued with dialysis, he would never get healed. He died. He was a young father and was believing for healing.

Our church started a healing room where anyone can go in off the street, but it ended up being a lot of Christians from other churches coming in, and they do the old leg-growing thing, and my husband, he's a doctor, he said, 'That's not how you measure leg length anyway.'

Because of Liam, we started to become very aware of people who had slipped through the system. So we started to visit this caravan park where people ended up, like people coming out of prison and out of mental health institutions, people who couldn't afford rent or were blacklisted. A lot of people with addiction or mental health issues. We ended up going for about 12 years, taking meals. This fella that we met there got saved and his life was turned around, he didn't want to use speed, and he didn't want to smoke, he didn't want to drink. He went to the healing room because he had a shoulder injury, he'd been beaten up or something. They started to measure his legs and he goes, 'I'm not here for my legs!' He'd been abused as a child, too, and when they started touching him without asking permission, he just took off. It's this assumption we have that you treat people in a certain way.

As hard as it has been with Liam, I think it's because of having Liam that we've had to really think outside the box, and we've met a more diverse group of people. Sometimes churches get so incestuous, they become so polarized.

I had experiences that I cannot deny happened, but that's not the goal, is it? It's what you do with that. But in church that was the goal, and that means you had a good meeting, almost like you skip everything else to get to that part of the service. I think those things happen, signs and wonders, but that's not where it begins and ends.

A clear theme from Evie's story, and so many others, is the lack of a theology around suffering, pain and loss. Yet these are experiences integral to life. Instead, churches too often offer either a toxic positivity in place of genuine wrestling with reality, labelling it 'hope', or place blame on those who suffer, or try to use it as a 'teachable moment'. Emma (UK) and her husband saw the full range of these theologies across different ends of the evangelical spectrum:

We started trying for children when I was 24 and ran into a lot of problems. By the time we joined this evangelical church in 2014 we'd been trying for a number of years and were about to embark on IVF treatment. Coming out of the Pentecostal environment, we had a lot of, quote, 'prophecies' about God was going to heal me and I was going to have kids. It began to really erode my relationship with God because I constantly felt disappointed.

That culture is very much driven by the miraculous side of Christianity and I know people where crazy things have happened and healings – whatever you want to say – have happened and they seem remarkably blessed. So you're constantly comparing yourself to these miracles, and when it doesn't happen, you feel utterly crushed and you think, 'Does God hate me, have I done something wrong? Is there some sort of sin in my life that's preventing God from …' you know, all the questions.

Coming into this much calmer evangelical environment where prophecy didn't happen at all was a bit of a tonic. The first couple of years in that church were really good, just supportive, loving people who are genuine.

In 2019, after treatment and surgeries, Emma became pregnant, but an early scan revealed that the pregnancy was ectopic. She and her husband were devastated. After a couple of months, they ventured back to church:

On the day we walked back in, the pastor was preaching from Corinthians, about the thorn in the side. He's being very aggressive, saying that any difficulty in your life is God-ordained and God will jam those difficulties in further, like a thorn, to get your attention, to make you grow. They knew what we'd been through. As a couple, they had had fertility struggles, so they knew to some degree what we were going through. But of all the things to say!

We sat there in the middle of it, and my husband and I looked at each other. My husband was absolutely livid and he was like, 'We are leaving now.' I was like, 'No, don't draw attention.' Then we let the sermon finish, and we slipped out.

The pastor's wife messaged me after. She's a lovely person, but she said, 'What happened to you?' I said, 'I'm sorry, but you know we've just been through all of this, and the day we get the courage to walk back into church, your husband says this. I cannot be part of a church that holds a theology that says that my ectopic pregnancy was ordained by God. He might not be the Pentecostal God of blessing that owes me a baby, but he definitely says he's a God of love, and I just cannot buy in to a God that would ordain, after ten years of trying, an ectopic.'

The judgemental misunderstandings of illness are harshly applied to those with mental illnesses. Freya (USA) has faced this since her teens:

In middle school, I got really depressed and I would try to talk to my parents about it. My dad is a doctor, and he said, 'There's something wrong between you and God that you need to work on and then you'll be happy with your life.' So I stopped talking to them about things.

In middle school what kept me from attempting suicide was I thought that people who committed suicide went to hell because they wouldn't have a chance to ask for forgiveness afterwards. After I first attempted suicide in senior year, people would be like, 'God will not tempt you beyond what you can bear, but when you are tempted, he will give you a way out so you can endure it.' Really, is suicide his way out?

Sharon (UK) also struggled with depression and anxiety:

People tell me I shouldn't suffer anxiety because God says, 'Don't fear, I am with you, don't be anxious.' People are using the Bible to suit what they believe.

I've had some of those comments as well, 'Do you think you're holding unforgiveness towards people and that's why God isn't healing you, or is there some sin that you need to confess?' The Church really damages people when it puts these things on them. But when you hear that phrase, 'We're not perfect, are we?' that's such a cop-out. Saying we treat each other badly because we're not perfect, that's just not acceptable to me.

I spent two weeks in a crisis house for women with poor mental health. It was incredible, it felt so much like the Christian community that I've longed for. There were only four of us and the staff; very different backgrounds to me. But the vulnerability and the genuine care for each other was so powerful for me.

It might sound a strange thing to say, but I had such a lovely time there, even though the reason I went was because I was really unwell. It felt like church to me. When I tell people from church, they look at me like I'm a little bit mad.

Things are changing in evangelical approaches to mental health, not least after high-profile figures such as Rick Warren, pastor of megachurch Saddleback Church, and Frank Page, former president of the Southern Baptist Convention, spoke out publicly about their own children's deaths by suicide. Yet both Freya and Sharon's experiences are recent, and there is still a long way to go.

When I speak to Liz (UK), she reflects on how her approach to healing has changed across the losses she has faced:

When I was in my early 20s, my family informally adopted an asylum seeker, an unaccompanied minor. He had come from Congo, and, very sadly, he got refugee status but he then got stomach cancer and died when he was 21. That really forced my niggles into the open, because up to then my life had been so lovely and straightforward, and the formula worked: you do the right stuff that God expects of you and then God will keep you safe. And then this 21-year-old, who had been through so much hardship, who was really committed to God and had so many people praying for him, died. I was really confronted with the evidence that being good and doing the right things and praying doesn't mean that God will keep you safe. So what's the point?

I was wrestling because there was so much about God and about faith that was so compelling to me. I didn't want to throw it out, but it didn't hold together for me anymore. That led to us leaving that church. It was so positive all the time, talking about the great things that God's doing, and then, when you're in a place where you're feeling desolate and bereft, it feels that there's not a place for you, that it's not OK to be not OK, particularly as we were leaders, and if you're a leader, you're supposed to be together and positive. It was difficult to do that in the midst of grief and doubt. They just didn't have a language or framework for talking about it. It was swept under the carpet and it still is now: people are very sympathetic because my husband died, but nobody knows what to say in terms of theology.

Liz and I discuss the idea that the higher number of people who pray for someone, the more likely they are to be healed, almost as though we need a certain number of names on a petition before God will be persuaded to act. Liz says, 'The idea that, if you're famous, then you can harness more people to pray and therefore you've got a better chance of being healed: that's horrific. That can't be how God works.' It certainly contradicts the concept of a God who cares for the most vulnerable.

We talk for a while about the denial that the constant emphasis on healing can bring. Liz agrees:

I have a friend whose husband died, and he absolutely did not believe that he was going to die. He believed that he was going to be healed, so he didn't confront it at all and he didn't talk to his kids about it. And then people at the funeral prayed for him to be raised. If my kids had gone through that, I would be concerned about how damaging that would be.

Romilly (UK) had a similar experience when she was growing up and her mother became sick:

Dad was told that, as the head of the house, he needed to pray more and it was down to him, and I think he felt a lot of guilt about that. She had breast cancer, and it was only a couple of weeks before she died that they finally accepted it. They hadn't really considered that she would die. We weren't prepared for it at all. She didn't talk to us about what she might want for us or anything about the future. It was all just about getting better and avoiding death, which is understandable, but as a parent now, I would be thinking about my kids and what they might need.

There was a lot of focus on the spiritual warfare side of it. I think it all distracted from what was really going on and what would have been a healthy way to deal with it.

Facing reality

Hope does not lie in dishonest theology, in empty promises or unverified reports of healing. When the promises and 'prophesies' don't work out, any short-term comfort they initially gave is dwarfed by the devastation and disillusionment. The constant emphasis on miracles can itself undermine the faith of those who do not experience them in the way that is expected.

Given that, in some senses, churches are supposed to be preparing people for death, and given the role that community plays in wellbeing, churches should be – and in some cases are – excellent contexts for facing up to the hard realities of life. Instead, too many evangelical churches serve up an ableist cocktail of glossy wellness and triumphalism, garnished with denial and toxic positivity, and with a chaser of judgementalism and shaming.

Some of those I spoke to told me about the ways they are moving forward in their practices around health, healing, diversity, from the personal to the professional. For Ruth (Canada), it impacts her daily life:

I feel better about knowing why things make me anxious or what can trigger me, as opposed to being in a place where I felt like anxiety was sin or because I wasn't trusting God enough. It's knowing I can relax and go, 'Oh, I'm anxious right now. What should I do about that? Maybe I'll take a breather.'

After seeing the toxic side of ministry, Bridget (New Zealand) changed how things were done when she moved churches:

I developed a determination that I wasn't going to be an ignorant do-gooder in my ministries. I led a ministry that was working with vulnerable people. Right from the start, I was determined to follow best practice. We had policies to make sure that people were safe. The people that we approved to pray for people were people that we trusted, who knew about the risks of praying for healing and around working with vulnerable people.

I still believe that God can work in whatever way he chooses to work, but I'm sick of the naivety.

Surely it wouldn't take that much for more churches to have specific policies – beyond a generic, legally required safeguarding policy – in place?

For Kit (UK/Thailand), deconstruction led to healing as a way of life and a profession:

As a child, the Spirit-filled stuff didn't feel too strained or pressured. It made me feel really alive. My memories of the Holy Spirit are liberating, exciting, healing.

Now I practise reiki every day, I teach reiki. One of the strongest common threads that I have with my life back then is the Holy Spirit, because I think the Holy Spirit, as it acts in Christianity, is the same source or essence as that which acts in other religions and spirituality like reiki. So when I first met the Holy Spirit outside of Christianity, it was a wonderful moment because I felt like I'd lost so much, and that was like a reconnection for me.

In reiki, the practitioner is told not to try to make anything happen, so no expectations, and it's very gentle compared to charismatic Christian healing, where it's pretty high pressure. With reiki, you don't expect radical change instantly. Sometimes people do get healed from cancer and stuff, but it's much lower key and it's more open. It's kind of like, 'where two or three are gathered': you get two people coming together for some healing and maybe something good happens. Maybe they just go away feeling relaxed because they were laying down for an hour. That's OK as well.

In terms of what causes the healing, most reiki practitioners say it's a universal source of energy, which the practitioner channels through their hands. Other people just say it's the body's own natural healing, and reiki stimulates it. I would say it's the Holy Spirit.

We will never stop needing to face the fact of human suffering. An over-focus on apparently miraculous cures leaves less space for simply accepting and being with all people on the inevitable road to death.

Liz (UK) tells me about the church she attends now:

The thing that I like about it, in contrast to the church where I was before, is that every Sunday, somebody will say from the stage, 'For some of you, everything isn't OK, or sometimes things don't work out, or some of you might be grieving.' It has felt possible for me to be there throughout this time of losing my husband and grieving.

Following deconstruction, Zoe (UK) became a minister: 'Jesus talked and he healed, and we might not be healing somebody with a heart attack of the heart attack, but we might be enabling people to deal with the things they face.'

At the church I attended in London for a while around 2010, the vicar used the sermon time one week to talk about his own experience of depression. Then his wife joined him to discuss her experience of severe post-natal depression. There was no over-spiritualizing, no miracle cure. It was simply a message to let others know that they could bring that part of themselves into the community. It gave me far more hope than a thousand empty promises.

Heretic

I am 39, sitting in a Bible study. I mention a theology book I'm reading, but I've barely finished my sentence before the group leader says, 'You shouldn't study theology. It might make you question your faith.' It's not the first time I've heard this, and it turns out they're right.

It's last year. I read the etymology of the word 'heretic': from the Greek 'hairetikos', meaning 'able to choose'. I decide that's a label I can live with.

Welcome to church. Check your brain in at the door. (Margaret, UK)

We're not asking these questions for the first time. These are ancient questions that have been wrestled with, and one side wins and therefore they get to write doctrine for the next 200 years. (Ed, UK)

What are the consequences of recognizing that people have thought differently and that we don't necessarily have the answer nailed down? It seems like that goes back to fear and vulnerability. We can't acknowledge that we might not have the black and white answer for this or that issue. (Marie, Australia)

The evangelical church is often accused of being theology-light, preferring to focus on things like sexual purity or same-sex relationships. When I tell Margaret (UK), who has just completed her PhD in theology, that I was told not to study theology, she says, 'I've heard that too! I've been asked whether I'm a Christian now, can I stay in community, am I dangerous? "You keep your eye on the cross, Margaret, keep your eye on the cross."'

George (Australia/UK) also heard this: 'It's certainties without having done the theological work. I ran into, "Theology deadens the spirit."' Yes, heard that one. Instead of depth of theology, we had apologetics: a set of arguments by which to defend our doctrines. Sam (UK) excelled at this:

It really fed my need to be right. I realized so much of it is rooted in fear and superiority. Looking back on it, the only way that you can use the scriptures or the arguments that you're making in defence of your position is by taking such a convoluted or twisted interpretation of them, which only works if you start from the conclusion that you want to make.

When I look back, I realize it's just poor scholarship to start from a conclusion and work backwards through the 'evidence'. The way that doctrine is defended and justified through apologetics perhaps reflects the essence of evangelicalism: controlling the narrative, foredrawn conclusions, categories and binaries. Like most people, too, I was taught that what I was learning *is* theology, and not that it was, in fact, evangelical, white, straight, male doctrine. All other theologies needed a qualifier (if they were referred to at all): liberation theology, womanist theology etc., effectively centring the doctrine we were taught and preventing exploration.

There are a few core doctrinal issues that have come up for a lot of people in their deconstruction: biblical inerrancy or infallibility; penal substitutionary atonement; original sin; hell and the Rapture (and a few more niche Creationists). Michael (UK) is a Baptist minister who sums up some of the things I have also learned over the last decade:

> Some of these theologies are not traditional at all. Penal substitutionary atonement theory is not the traditional understanding of the Church. Eastern Orthodox and most Catholics would not recognize that theory, and yet we present it as if it's verbatim doctrine of the Church. It's not. It's only more recently that we've made it into this primary theory, in the last 400 years of a Church that's existed for 2,000 years. Rapture theology: from the Plymouth Brethren 150 years ago. The infallibility of scripture: no Orthodox person believes in the infallibility of scripture.

For those deconstructing, much of this again centres around the lack of space for other theologies or broader discussion. As Josias (Denmark/Finland) puts it:

> What people have thought the Bible meant has changed so much throughout history, and that's something I was never taught. That scares me a little bit, just how closed to information I was. It makes me think how scary it is for any community, political or religious or whatever, to choose where you can get information and where you can't, and who is the person or the people who decide where you can get your information? They have such power.

Probably why we were told not to study theology, then.

The Bible clearly says

> If God were evangelical, there would be one clear text, even in the Greek or the Hebrew, which there isn't. As far as I can understand, our recognition of the scriptures comes down to the fact that we recognize the scriptures. (Lucas, UK)

> Even within denominations, if you want to start a fight, ask about the version of the Bible that is the correct version. I was told that I was going to hell because I read *The Message*. (Katie, USA)

Realizing that the Bible never claims to be the Word of God started me wondering what else we read into – or out of – the Bible (it says that Christ is the Word: the fact that the Bible gets substituted for Christ is surely idolatry?). Gordon (UK) tells me what happened when he started studying it:

> The missing ending of Mark was the most shocking thing, because if this really was the Word of God and God wanted to use the Bible to communicate, then he needed to look after the book. You can't let people lose the ends of the thing. It can't get lost if God is looking after it, so it seemed he wasn't looking after it. And if it is the Word of God, it would be absolutely clear in any language to anybody, at any time, ever. And it wasn't.

Lynn (Canada/Ireland) is undertaking a PhD in theology. She tells me about her journey with the Bible:

> We were extremely privileged to have a professor from one of the Bible colleges in our church. We were talking about the Trinity one Sunday, and Ron was saying that there's nothing in scripture that refers to the Trinity and I said, 'Yes, there is, in 1 John.' He says, 'Actually no, that verse is a late addition.' The skies opened for me and I said, 'Wait a minute, are you telling me there's an error in my Bible?' and he says, 'I think it's time that we do a textual criticism class', and that was the beginning of opening it all for me.
>
> On the other side of the 'inerrant Word of God' is now a greater appreciation for scripture, but also understanding that it is humanity's grappling with trying to understand their God. I think that the Church Fathers did the best job they could, as did the rabbis, in putting together the Canon, and they had good reasons for what was included and what wasn't, and it was over hundreds of years of deciding which books had

the most impact on the faith of people. But that doesn't mean that anything that wasn't included in the Canon doesn't have something to tell us about God, and so with that expanded Canon, or acknowledgement of other writings that speak and can teach us about God, then that again just deepens my appreciation for the Holy Spirit's inspiration in people writing down their experience of God.

If you're going to say 'scripture', let's look at all scripture. I mean, the evangelicals will say that it's a living Word of God, but they don't actually let it live, do they?

These different versions of the Bible, different collections of writings through different times with different interpretations, were something many people mentioned as an awakening after being taught a very flat, unnuanced perspective: that the Bible has a cohesive message without contradictions, that it is a complete system that explains itself. To get away from this literality, Neil (UK) started to look at the Bible through different perspectives which still held the Bible as authentic and authoritative to some degree:

Of course it was supporting my new perspective because I was reading my perspective into it, same as I was before. That was very destabilizing: if it'll just say what you want it to say, what authenticity does it have? The Bible then crumbles as a divinely inspired and authoritative piece, and not holding it to such a high standard meant that the humanity was able to come through more. It became something that was just some people's thoughts on God. That was kind of the end, to some degree, of my Christian faith, in that if the Bible had very little to make it authoritative, what was the rest of it based on?

The other major problem many people raised with the Bible was the violence. I do remember owning a children's pop-up version of the Moses story, in which I could pull various tabs to make the Red Sea drown the Egyptians, or a soldier behead someone in battle. Laura (UK) went a step further:

Me and my dad and my sister would act out some of the Old Testament stories, like the guy who threw darts in the back of Absolom when Absolom's hair was tied up in a tree. That was always a popular one because I had long hair. I ended up being Absolom dangling by my hair from the tree, with my sister gleefully miming throwing darts into my back as my dad narrated. There was a childish enjoyment of the stories, but at the same time, there's an awful lot of violence in there that's just uncritically accepted, like the ecocide that's inherent in the story of Noah. It's like, 'But it's just a nice story about animals hopping onto an ark, floating off, having a nice little cruise.'

Lynn (Canada/Ireland) again:

The Levite concubine is one of the worst. Why are we not talking about the fact that the Levite is not being told off by God for just giving his concubine to be gang-raped? Why is it not even mentioned that that's a bad thing to do? There's no way you can tell me that that was God-inspired writing. The story of David, the rape of Bathsheba and the murder of Uriah: you want to say this is the Word of God?

For Kathy (USA), it was precisely this kind of thing that led to her decon-struction:

It finally started falling apart for me as I got deeply into reading the Bible. I just couldn't look at the genocide and believe in that God as the God I intuitively felt I was seeking.

It encouraged me to let go of that anger that the Bible was perfect. That was what was tying me in fear, because I've been taught to equate the Bible with God. Once I decided the Bible was a book written within a historical context by people, I didn't have to justify all those things that made me crazy about it, so I could let go of a lot of doctrines that never satisfied me.

Fran (UK) also found freedom in letting go:

Part of the deconstruction process is letting other things have their say, including hearing stories and empathizing with people and letting that shape your worldview as much as whatever some person thinks this passage of scripture says.

In the survey, I asked about people's view of the Bible today. 47% checked 'inspired by God but written by men. Sometimes but not always directly applicable to modern daily life.' 17% chose 'written solely by humans, with mixed relevance to modern life', 6% went for 'irrelevant to today, or even toxic' and less than 2% 'the Word of God, inerrant and directly applicable to modern daily life'. The rest all chose their own options, with quite a few 'I don't knows' among them. Anselm (USA) wrote:

A collection of writings by a people who sought to reconcile their history, culture, and experience with their evolving understanding of their deity. This wrestling reflects the same grappling endemic to the human experience, which is why it stills speaks to so many people today.

When we speak, he explains more:

We connect with the very human experience of trying to understand what's happened to us, our heritage, what can we hope for in the future, how do we understand the world around us? And then you bring into that our complex relationship with our spirituality. If you approach the Bible that way, it's so much more interesting and engaging than trying to use it like a rule book.

When I studied New Testament Greek, our teacher, an Oxford University ancient historian, introduced herself as 'an atheist Persian Jew'. She told us she didn't mind what we believed; that she was here to teach us language and culture. It freed me up (a little) to have a broader perspective on the Bible, to see a set of anthropological records of struggle, joy, violence, life, death and mystery. It's far more compelling than trying to make it fit neatly into my life.

My friend was an Orthodox Jew, and when I decided to become a Christian, he said, 'Just remember that more than half of that book is ours. And just remember that the Jews were big storytellers, and that we like a good big fish story. If you remember that, it will serve you well.' (Steve B., UK)

All have sinned

Adam and Eve, in pretty much ignorance, chose to eat a piece of fruit, therefore they moved from a state of being immortal to a state of being mortal and suddenly being subject to death. It seems an awful big consequence for an awfully small decision.

As an Adventist I was involved in an Adventist–Muslim relations group, and hearing Muslims say, 'Why couldn't God just forgive people? Why does he have to go through all this process of it has to be his son, substitutionary atonement?' The more I thought about the basic justice of God, the more it didn't seem like justice. (Andrew, Australia)

Original sin and penal substitutionary atonement are more of those things we have been taught to read into the Bible. They are so fundamental that, for many of us, discovering alternatives unravels an awful lot more of our theological framework. KP (USA) explains what this did for her:

> I've poked holes in so many aspects of theology that are so massive that at this point, I don't know if I could craft a cohesive story again. One of the first ones is atonement theory, which matters for everything. The first time I read about scapegoat atonement theory and a more communal approach instead of individualistic approach to atonement theory, I was like, 'Oh, this changes everything. This has a ripple effect to everything about the way that I read scripture, the way that I look at who God is, and now I don't know what to do with that.'
>
> I really don't know what I think about hell anymore. I don't know what I think about evangelism and our responsibility with that anymore. Whatever: I don't even show up like that anymore.

I learned that Adam and Eve sinned and God cursed them and therefore we are all sinners who need Jesus to 'reverse the curse'. But then someone pointed out that God cursed the Earth and the snake, not Adam and Eve, and that 'original sin' has more to do with Augustine than the Bible. Margaret's (Canada) experience parallels mine:

> I thought the basic fundamentals were the same throughout. All my time working in Christian organizations, and I didn't realize that not everybody did original sin. I don't read scripture right now because I still have too much of the old lens there.
>
> I came to the conclusion something's infected and brought evil and sin or whatever you want to call it into the human experience. But I really trust my intuition that we don't start out as rotten, undeserving, horrific piles of shit, quite frankly. No, I don't believe that, because you can't say that and then say we're made in the image of God.

Original sin is antithetical to any kind of self-esteem: we learn that any good in me is not me, it's God, and any evil or failure is me. Women, in particular, mentioned the impact this had had on them:

> In my first marriage, when I would be abused for whatever was perceived as an imperfection, I thought that's what I deserve. Being the self-sacrificing one was seen as a sign of being righteous or good, so I've had to learn a lot about what healthy boundaries are. Now I'll drive by churches and they'll say, 'Love God and love other people', and I think

'But you're missing self: it's so important! Love your neighbour as you love yourself!'

That wasn't the message that I got. It was more like, 'Love others significantly more than you love yourself. Don't even love yourself.' Now I really get that I am the most highly equipped to love this person that is in my own body and when I do that, when I take care of myself, I have so much more capacity to genuinely give from overflow to other people. (Christine, USA)

Laura (UK) is trying not to pass this down to the next generation:

I've only now been realizing how little I trust myself and my own instinct, my own body. I'm having to relearn all of that in my 40s. It's all stuff that should have been modelled to me as I grew up. I've got two girls, and I'm trying to model for them how to listen to their bodies. You can see how difficult it is to have a good sense of self and a good sense of trust in yourself when you are told how worthless you are, and that God had to come and rescue you because you're just so terrible. How do you construct a sense of self on that that's healthy? You can't really, and that keeps you in that state of fear and shame, which is just prime controlling territory, isn't it?

I have to wonder if the more we understand about trauma and the impact that has on our behaviour, the more the understanding of 'sin' will shift, or if those who preach it are so wedded to this idea, for whatever reason, that they will hold to it no matter what. Perhaps, too, a more trauma-informed perspective would move theology on from the retributive view of the cross – someone needs to be punished – to a more restorative view. The study of criminal justice systems makes clear that retributive justice leads to high re-offending rates, but restorative systems lead to recovery and reintegration into community.

Lucas (UK), a minister, tells me what happened in church when he tried to question penal substitution:

I'm a pacifist and totally up for non-violence and would see that as central to what Jesus is doing on the cross. I tried to name contemporary idolatry in the life of the Church, which didn't go down very well, strangely enough. But what if one of those idolatries was militarism: that we have faith in the Government to provide protection by means of lethal violence, and this gives us comfort and security?

Our understandings of violence are rooted in our atonement understandings: I could comfortably commit myself to self-sacrificial giving in a non-violent way, because I understand that to be what Jesus was doing, and the congregation had a bedrock for their support of lethal violence because they understand that to be what God the Father was doing on the cross. And that was a conversation that we couldn't have. I knew if I were to open a theological conversation, it'd be the end of my ministry in the church. They wouldn't fire me – they're too afraid of not getting another minister to fire me – but useful conversation, trust would be gone because they couldn't entertain another way of understanding it. I found that agonizing, because I love these people here, they're not bad people. But at the centre of their faith is something that I can only see as abhorrent.

I comment to Lucas that this ties into society's casual attitude to violence against bodies. He responds, 'And the way we relate to the environment. The way we relate to poverty and structures of injustice.' Sam (UK) is another who sees original sin and penal substitution as the opposite of love:

God killed Jesus in order that we could be reunited with God, but who of us as a parent could ever imagine demanding a sacrifice in order to forgive our own child? That model is so against our own experience of love. Fundamentally underpinning that very idea is that God requires a payment for sin in order to forgive, which makes God subject to the power of sin.

It's not actually forgiveness at all: it's Jesus paying a debt. Those are not the same thing. For Karen (UK), understanding forgiveness like this was an early component of her deconstruction:

One of the questions I had was that we say the gospel is Jesus dying for your sins, but what was the gospel message that Jesus was preaching when he was living? He's not telling people that. All he said to them was, 'Your faith has healed you.' It wasn't like, 'OK, pay the debt and I'll forgive you.' He just freely did it.

Penny's (UK) experience of studying other atonement theories led to a reversal of the 'original sin' effect on her self-esteem:

The teacher went through Christus Victor, and I remember being like, 'But in that one, God *really* loves me.' It suddenly clicked. I'd had this experience at 15 when I nearly tried to top myself and felt the voice of God being like, 'No, I love you, you're loved.' That was an emotional pull out of the gutter, but it took another six years for my head to catch up: there is a way of understanding the story of Jesus that doesn't make me a pile of crap. It was like I'd heard God say he loved me, but there were still conditions because he had to hate me because of my sin. And then it started to be, 'If I'm worthwhile, I don't need to be treated like I'm being treated in my job. Actually, I'm worthy of respect.'

Hope (USA) also found this a transformative shift:

To be given a new idea that love can just forgive wrong, it doesn't need vengeance, that was where all the reconstruction started: how do I re-build a picture of God and these Jesus stories through a lens where God doesn't need a mechanism to forgive, God just forgives?

It transformed my relationship to certainty and feeling like I don't have to be certain to be safe, and I don't have to be certain to be loved. It's completely opened up my world, and it's allowed me to be so much more generous with people. It's totally transformed my relationship with love in general, the idea that that God never punishes anyone for anything. I mean, that messes with everyone's sense of justice because, well, there's always some group of people that we want God to punish. It's expanded my definition of what it means to love and of who belongs. This has been so fruitful that how on Earth could you say that the Holy Spirit isn't in the middle of all of this?

Part of deconstruction is often reassessing what, then, we think of the concept of 'sin'. I ask Evan (UK) what he thinks now: 'Don't be a dick. That's the definition of sin.'

Fear factor

How can I really believe that an all-loving, powerful being who knew us when he fitted us together in our mother's womb and all those nice cushy verses that are great if you're a Christian, how can I really, deep-down believe that he would send people to conscious eternal torment in hell forever for some sins that are done in a finite amount of time? (Harry, UK)

I think hell was the first thing to go for me. Hell is of our own creation. We can make hell now; you can live in a prison of your own mind. Mental illness is essentially hellish because you're estranged from your-self and from others and from the compassion that you need. And I've been there, so frankly, I'm not worried about what else is out there after being mentally ill. I just don't believe in any kind of eternal torment.

I find heaven harder to square with the kids because they're asking about what happens when we die, and it just feels disingenuous to keep talking about going to heaven up there. But I don't have a better set of stories to allow them something to hook onto for now. (Katya, UK)

In the survey, 65% of people reported regularly hearing teaching on hell, damnation, salvation, Satan/demons, the Rapture/Jesus' return. 60% seriously worried those they loved would go to hell, and 45% about God's judgement or that they would go to hell:

I remember as a child watching these videos that were terrifying of people being burned alive. You know: the kid is drinking at a party and then dies in a car accident on the way home and now is in hell. The fear that it puts in you.

When I get curious about why can't I leave this abusive marriage, or why can't I say no? Well, because ultimately it leads to this, and there's a childlike part of me that feels terrified. (Christine, USA)

For those who grew up in North America, in particular, these theologies were reinforced in 'fun' ways. Ruth (USA) recounts her teen years:

We had a Hell House. My brother and me and two or three other teens helped the pastor build the set in this old warehouse downtown, and then I was an actor in it. It was like a haunted house; you could walk through the rooms. Then we had *Heaven's Gates and Hell's Flames*, that play. It was various scenes like we're going to drive to church and then we're going to crash, and since we're on our way to church, obviously we were Christians so then you go to heaven. And then I'm talking about how I had sex last night, so I must not be a Christian. I die and go to hell.

Everything was fear-based, and I look back, I had nightmares all the time. My biggest fear was being left behind, being left alone.

Laura (UK) also mentioned those childhood experiences:

It was a very strong teaching that either you go to hell or you go to heaven, and you need to pray the prayer, you need to give your life to Jesus. I remember some really quite terrifying stories people at the kid's clubs used, to almost scare you into becoming a Christian. I don't want to pass that fear on to my kids.

She is one of many (including me) who credit Rob Bell's book, *Love Wins*, with changing their beliefs on hell. For others, like Christine (UK), it was that things just didn't add up:

> I thought, 'If this is true, how dare my parents knowingly bring me into this world and risk me spending eternity in hell?' I started to think about how the Christians I know actually act, and recognizing that I don't think they actually believe it, because if you really believe that every person who wasn't part of your group was going to hell, how could you sleep at night?

Wendy (USA) wondered why God wasn't doing more:

> I started questioning the things that I was told to not ask, like if it's true that people are going to be tortured for eternity if they don't do certain things or say certain words, then if I were a loving God, I would make it super-clear what those words are, and in scripture, there's like four different ways you're supposed to be saved. I wouldn't make it ambiguous at all, like, do you need to be baptized? Do you not?
>
> I would write it in the sky every day. I would have every single dog, cat, everything, walk up to their person every day and be like, 'Please repeat after me.' I would make it the default that you were saved unless you opted out. If I were really loving, I would make it like breathing. The things that we need to do in order to live, our bodies naturally do it and they make a lot of noises to us if we are not getting it, there's panic, there's survival instinct. But it seems extremely easy to go to hell.

Hell is such a core doctrine in evangelical teaching. Elisabeth (UK) tells me, 'It is a big thing, isn't it, to say, "I'm not sure I believe in hell anymore" when you've had that thrown down your throat for your whole life?' When people do start to deconstruct what they have been taught about hell, it has a far broader impact than intellectual assent to one theological belief. Kay (UK) was one of several people who told me that losing a belief in hell had stopped the pressure to evangelize:

> Working in a hospice and having people want to discuss things like where do I go after I die, I began to see that doctrine from the perspective of somebody that wasn't a Christian, and I couldn't reconcile a loving God and a God that would send someone for eternal torment. So I spent six months to a year just going through the theology and the different scriptures, and it just didn't hold water theologically, that evangelical perspective.

The tradition I come from is very much you're in or you're out, and if you've prayed a prayer, you're part of God's special club and if you haven't, you're not. But actually, people that wouldn't call themselves Christians were having these experiences of God, and they were connected with God through nature or other spiritual experiences. It was like God was just reaching out to everybody in whatever way they were open to him, and somehow I'd confined God to this box, and I was quite surprised to find out he exists outside of it.

So things like that started to challenge the way I saw things, and the whole thing of evangelism as well: the more I started to understand about Jesus standing for non-violence, the more it almost felt like a form of violence to be trying to put my opinion on somebody else or tell them there was one way, and actually part of my work as a chaplain is to get alongside people from their perspective and beliefs. It's given me a whole different viewpoint.

Caro (Australia), a pastor, also found that it changed how she works and lives:

I remember when I first found out that eternal conscious torment wasn't the only possible theory you could believe in as a Christian, and this feeling of just being absolutely gobsmacked and so irritated that I was 30-odd years old and no one had told me that there were options of faithful belief within the spectrum of Christianity.

That realization has informed so much of my Christianity, maybe my leadership, certainly my preaching. I've totally stopped saying that anything is the only way to believe something, because it's not true. As soon as you start realizing it, you realize this diversity of belief and opinion on nearly everything within the Christian faith throughout history. It's like fashion that comes and goes. It's not that my faith fell apart; it opened up because I was like, 'Oh wow, there is so much to explore. If I ask these questions, what else am I asking?'

For Fran (UK), losing hell meant finding freedom:

One of the big moments of deconstruction was when I let go of the more fear-based theologies, so hell and judgement and damnation. I don't remember that being a big, conscious turning point, but subconsciously it frees you up a lot when you don't think that whether you're a Christian, whether you've said the sinners' prayer, is the difference between heaven and hell for the rest of eternity. There's less at stake and you can start to focus more on the aspects of faith that apply to everyday life: is this bringing you meaning? Is it making you a more caring person or are you happy? Do you have a story that roots you in a sense of who you are?

Andrew (Australia) didn't have to worry about eternal conscious torment, but has other issues with what he was taught:

> Adventists don't believe in eternal burning hell, but they do believe in annihilationism, that when the Bible talks about the destruction of the wicked, it's a fiery destruction.
>
> Some of the turn-offs for me are more specifically Adventist ones in terms of the preoccupation with end time issues. Every news headline is scrutinized for how it might fit into the signs of the end, and in particular what the Catholic Church might be doing, what the Pope might be saying. Conversely, things like climate change and species extinction and natural disasters, they're greeted with a little bit of excitement: this is a sign, this gives us urgency that Jesus is coming and this means that we need to get out there and tell people they need to get their hearts right.

His point about climate change reminds me of something I could never quite square with the parts of the evangelical church that do not believe in it: the end of the world is coming in terms of the Rapture, but there is complete denial about the thing that might very well end it. No matter: the Rapture is another great way to scare people into staying within the fold. While some mention still working through this fear as adults, David (Puerto Rico/Netherlands) is able to laugh about it now:

> I remember being about six or seven years old and having these nightmares of hell or the Rapture: if you are good, the Lord takes you, otherwise you are left behind. One day I woke up and no one was home and I panicked, 'Now I'm all by myself. I knew I didn't have to take that cookie!'

For Traynor (USA), this kind of incident continued for much longer:

> I grew up very much afraid of missing the Rapture. I remember being 20 or 21, and I was supposed to lead music at my church one Sunday morning. It was the day of the time change when the clocks go back, but I didn't know that, so I showed up and there's nobody there. This is before cell phones, and I walked around this place for an hour thinking I missed the Rapture. There was no other explanation for me.

The belief has concrete consequences for some. Gary (Canada) explains his career choice: 'My parents thought Jesus was going to come back soon, so there was no real pressure to do anything with my life. Why go to university where I'm going to learn secular ideas? So I became a missionary at 18.'

A new framework

All these areas come down to fear-based theologies, rather than love or grace (even biblical inerrancy/infallibility/literalism: any deviation or uncertainty may also have eternal consequences). So many people told me of their childhood terror: any other situation where children live in constant fear of death and torture would be viewed as unacceptable cruelty, and yet in churches this is normal.

It's a tough one to let go of, though: things that implant deep, existential fear often are. I woke in a 2 a.m. hell-panic a few months ago, and I'm not the only one: 'There's always that thing that pulls you back that's like, "What if I'm wrong and now I'm going to hell?"' (KP, USA). But if we are only holding to a belief out of fear, is that a God worth following?

Lucas (UK) tells me what happened when he let go:

I became a massive, obsessive, argumentative, trapping-people-in-logic-puzzles of a Calvinist, in a really horrible way. A question would lead to a question that would lead to a carefully selected Bible verse.

Realizing this thing that presented itself as a complete system wasn't a complete system helped me relax into the wholeness of the Church, that there isn't one narrow stream that is close to God's heart, and everyone else has vanished off into a wilderness of error and heresy, but there's actually deep strengths in all of the traditions and deep weaknesses in all of the traditions.

One thing that shifts for everyone who deconstructs is their view of the divine, usually far more than just 'God is a bit nicer now' – whether someone retains a belief in divinity or not. What Dr Margaret Metcalfe (UK) had to say certainly challenges orthodox theology and power structures. She is a British Sign Language interpreter in her church and initially studied theology to improve her interpreting. When we spoke, she had just completed her PhD (Metcalfe, 2020):

It was based on exclusion in church communities and seeing how words to and for the divine influence our behaviour, and if the words we use have any correlation to the exclusions going on. What do we mean by the divine? Who is this 'God' that we talk about? 'God' is not even a proper name.

Ideologies are expressed and maintained in words, so as we use words, we keep the ideology going. Ideologies constitute us in the words we use: even before we're born, we're talked about in words that give us identities: girl, sister, daughter, and then teacher or cleaner or doctor. We become who we are within the dominant ideologies that produce the language.

I used psycholinguistics, the processing of language and how we understand and use language. As we hear a word, we have a set of associations activated. For example, when we're in a conversation where we know the topic, we don't have to work hard, whereas if we're in a situation where we're hearing new theory or words used in ways we are not familiar with, we have to work much harder to be making the associations forming semantic networks.

I comment to Margaret that this says so much about feeling comfortable in church and dismissing different theologies as 'heretical': they make us work.

If there's an association with a word, it becomes automatic unless we are conscious of it. But you can't do language consciously all the time. 'God our Father' is going to stay in our semantic networks, whether we use it or not, and so that links back into how the dominant ideology uses words. It's successful because of the way language operates.

We have this representational view of language where we say, 'cup': the word is linked to the object. 'God the Father: the word is linked, that tells us who God is.' No, that's how we use it. Let's be careful where we are using words of patriarchy – whoever is in power, because patriarchy is generalized out to just men, but it's about power over, really. So that relates to the disabled, people who are neurodivergent, people of other faiths, there's a classist element, a big sexist and hetero-sexist element. Wherever there's power over and words for the divine are profoundly hierarchical, heterosexist, they will be influencing our behaviour in different ways, depending on who we are.

So, if we're women in a church context, we receive words of submission, and they form who we are. If we're men in a church context, we receive words of power and authority. Because in most churches God is only 'he', the relationship between men and the divine and women and the divine is different because we're constituted in language and our words form us in identities, which also have a link to our relationship with the divine. It also affects our relationships to each other and how we respond to others in power over us or what our behaviours are.

All those things are leading us to the social practices of the ideology, in which God is embedded. Who's in, who's out? Who does what in terms of behaviours to each other, in terms of the hierarchy? When we challenge that, what happens? But because ideologies are expressed and maintained in words, if you change the words, you show up the fault line in the ideology. So there's hope in changing the words. It's not just a politically correct thing to do; you change the words to get change.

Once you say 'Who is the divine?' and start to be iconoclastic about 'Father' and 'Lord' and 'Son', and you say 'Sister' and 'Friend' and 'Lover' and 'Sparrow' and 'Raindrop' and 'Mountain' – why can't we investigate God as 'Drag Queen'? – then that throws into question Christology, trinitarian stuff, pneumatology. It throws into question our theological anthropology and ecclesiology, possibly our eschatology. So the whole thing is up for grabs now, and I think that's one of the reasons that people don't like to talk about language because there's something in us that knows it's significant.

I ask Margaret how this has gone down in her church:

There are two reactions. One is, 'Interesting, Margaret, jolly good.' It's like, 'I didn't really want to engage with this, this is too hard.' And the other is, 'But it's my choice to speak about God as father.' Yes, it is, but that's not informed, and you don't actually want to be informed, so there's pushback or general disinterest.

I am still part of a church, and I am still interpreting services. Although not what the vicar says.

Wherever we end up theologically during deconstruction, we do not just deconstruct specific beliefs: unpicking that narrow mode of thinking is part of the work, so that we don't just end up doing the same thing with a different narrative. That's partly what makes it so hard to deconstruct. I tell Laura (UK) about a theological argument I got into a short time ago, when I realized that throwing Bible verses back and forth simply wasn't working for me anymore; that's just not a framework I have now. She says:

It doesn't interest me anymore to debate one side or the other, because that's still quite dualistic, isn't it? I guess it's moving away from the 'it's this or it's that' mindset to, 'it could be a combination of all of those or nothing at all'. It's a very different way of seeing.

When thealogian Liselotte (Denmark) and I speak, we discuss what the Church misses by not having the Jewish tradition of *midrash*, where scripture is wrestled with, disagreed over, allowed to live:

> Jewish thinking takes so much more seriously that we're here to co-create with God. Whereas it seems to me that especially in evangelical theology, you can just sit back and be bloody grateful that God did something because we were so hopeless.

If only more churches allowed this diversity of belief that Caro (Australia) is aiming for:

> Each month we take one Bible passage and then across three weeks we preach it through different lenses. So a feminist perspective, an indigenous perspective, a Middle Eastern perspective. There is a whole world out there of different ways to see the same thing and come to beautiful conclusions. It's OK if they're different, it's OK if there's tension and it's OK to wrestle with things that are hard to understand. I was never given that in church. It was always, 'just believe this and you'll be right' and it didn't serve me well.
>
> I'd like to think that in still leading a church, somehow the people who are with me, and certainly all the kids and youth, are growing up with something different than what I received. Time will tell, I guess.

PART 3

Slippery Slope

Pilgrimage

It is February 2020. For some time, I have been looking at my bookcase and feeling visceral revulsion at some of the Christian books there. I take almost all to the recycling, including six Bibles in three languages. I keep the gold-edged one I was given as a baby and the Russian one given to me by a woman whose house I stayed in shortly after the end of the Soviet Union. She'd kept it through years of pressured faith and I couldn't part with it. But the highlighted, page-marked, note-filled one I've had for years has to go: my earnest scribbles have added too much certainty and cognitive dissonance to its pages. Out go all the old journals filled with self-disgust and striving. I feel like when a snake outgrows its old, dead, itchy skin and sheds it to reveal what is fresh and healthy beneath.

The ground slipped out from underneath my feet. All of the certainty and all of the assumptions I had about Christianity suddenly went and it was very destabilizing. But it definitely felt like something that God was doing, something that happened to me, not that I intellectually took this path and decided to start doubting things. (Helen, UK)

Where it started for us was a willingness to admit a discomfort with an idea. It wasn't like we woke up one day and said, 'I don't believe this: I believe *this* now, and I have this tight theological argument.' It was more, 'I grew up with this little set of doctrines that everyone said we can be sure that we believe because these are solid facts. And I'm willing to question that, I'm willing to hold that loosely.' (Charles, USA)

If the lid's come off the box you can't put it back on again, you just don't fit anymore. Those in the Church look at you as if you're heretics who've lost the plot. (Malcolm, UK)

One of the criticisms you get is that people church-shop and they're trying to find something that fits all their needs, but I think it's different from that. For a long time, church has never felt completely secure and safe for me. I don't think it's people being inflexible or needy or wanting church to meet their every need. It's core stuff. (Marie, Australia)

It's been a very gradual peeling. When I look back it's like, did I really believe that? It's surreal. It's almost like someone else was living through me. (Elisabeth, UK)

No one who responded to the survey, no one I interviewed, no one I have interacted with online or in person tells me that they took a conscious choice to deconstruct their faith. Whether it was triggered by trauma, curiosity, tragedy or cognitive dissonance, everyone expressed in some measure that they could not ignore this process and keep their integrity and authenticity. Karen (UK), for instance, was simply doing what she thought was right when she met a non-Christian: as their friendship developed, she shared her faith. Her new friend asked questions:

She made me do a lot of research just from asking those questions and that's what started my deconstruction. I feel like the journey has been led by God, not by anything else. I've gone through this journey in a prayerful way. When I first started having conversations with my friend, in my mind it was, 'God's using me in her life.' Actually, it's been the complete opposite: it's been him using her in my life.

The all-encompassing nature of faith and church life means that when someone's entire worldview shifts, their identity shifts and their sense of belonging is often taken away, either by leaving or by being forced out of a community. It shakes people to their core and rocks many of the relationships around them, particularly with those who feel threatened or concerned by Christians whose faith changes, who believe differently. For me, deconstruction is a mixture of awakening, liberation, grief and guilt; a letting go and a picking up, anger and gratitude. It's something I see as a lifelong process – there is always more to uncover and discover.

The stories

I could fill a library with deconstruction stories. These are just a few of those that were shared with me. For a minority, like Sonia (UK), deconstruction has been a gentle, natural process as they themselves evolve:

I know for a lot of people, they've been in churches and it's been incredibly toxic and they feel that deconstructing has been something that's been really frowned upon. That hasn't been my experience, and I know that's very unusual. A huge part of my practice professionally has always been reflective practice in which you accept that your views are going to change, potentially. They should do, really. So I find it quite hard when I see people, particularly in the church world, where that isn't necessarily the way.

Major life events were a starting point for quite a few: perhaps a personal loss, perhaps something more external. A number of Americans echoed Nathan's (USA) thoughts: 'Really, it comes down to I just can't be around the politics of these evangelical churches and I don't want my kids in those environments.'

Nick (UK) had an experience less clear-cut, more personal:

I can't put my finger on exactly when things started to shift and the door started to blow off. It certainly started to creak years before I finally left the church. It's hard to unpick the deconstruction journey from some quite deep emotional periods. I experienced depression for some time, and real deep questions about the job I was doing and fundamental things being challenged about me and my understanding of God. God in depression is a very different God to God in an upbeat, 10 o'clock Sunday experience. I couldn't reconcile the two.

I realized it wasn't a blip; this was actually a new stage and this wasn't going to change. I wasn't going to go back and rediscover my faith: I had actually discovered something that was different and I needed to explore what that was. It felt like taking off an ill-fitting coat, like a straitjacket. I didn't know if what was left would just be a pillar of salt or there would be a new something that would emerge from it. I felt like if I completely walk away from faith at least I do it with integrity.

In terms of deconstruction, there's also a sense of trusting my heart if it's telling me, 'this doesn't feel right, this feels right'. Being willing to go with that, not looking for the Bible verse to prove or disprove it or how do I interpret that within this structure? It's just, 'how do I interpret that?' Not always having an external reference point against which to judge things.

That learning to listen to yourself, or to hear the divine above what leaders claim God is saying, is a key part of deconstruction for so many of us – certainly it has been for me – after a lifetime of being told that our hearts are 'deceitful', that our leaders know better. It's a pattern that is repeated throughout these stories. It takes practice and courage to rediscover intuition, especially when there has been church abuse and control.

Sadly, although unsurprisingly, too many people found their deconstruction was prompted by the actions of those in leadership in churches or mission agencies they had loved and served. Harry (UK) explains:

You may have been hurt by the Church and by people who purport to be Christlike or chosen by God, and then behave in ways that aren't. When people aren't repentant and they don't say sorry, they do so much damage to your faith. It's hypocrisy. It is the power dynamic. My repulsion towards the Church is a power thing. I'm not trying to be difficult. It pains me that it feels like people are playing the game, that people are too plugged into the matrix to see what's really going on.

I can't look at the church leader and completely demonize him. In lots of ways, he's a very good man. He's been very encouraging and kind to me. I know that no one's perfect and all the rest of it, and nobody expected them to be, but some of these abuses go much deeper than just someone being a bit of a tool. It's a dangerous thing to work for the church you love. Like finding out what they put in sausages.

Phoebe (USA) was forced out of her job at church, and bullied in the process, leading to deeper changes in her faith:

I had tremendous anxiety for the first time in my life. I couldn't face crowds and people. I couldn't play dress-up anymore, and I couldn't do all the things that felt so superficial and ridiculous and pointless. It caused tension between my husband and I because he really felt that we had a responsibility to be in church and that it looked bad. I didn't love the whole Sunday morning gathering, but it was bigger than that: I didn't love the machine, the institution of Church.

I'm sick of people saying I have to spend time in the Word. I felt like if I keep spending time in this Word, I'm throwing this Word and burning this Word and never, ever wanting anything to do with this Word again. I was sick of being forced into things that I really didn't want to do.

Ever since that dark season, which started in 2015, we started reading different books instead of reading the ones that the evangelical world were publishing and everyone in our church was buying and reading and loving. I was so sick of all that fluff, that junk, and I threw a lot of those books away and started buying books by Rachel Held Evans and Sarah Bessey and Peter Enns and Brad Jersak, and I felt like it was time for me to see the world through a different set of eyes, to see Christianity through a different set of eyes, to see God through a different set of eyes.

I wish it hadn't taken me so long to start feeling free. Mostly, I just felt a lot of guilt. I felt a lot of fear that I was being misled and that I was going to fall away from God and never come back. I felt like, 'I don't want to cross that line. But if that's where I'm headed, I want to be honest about it.'

Some of our evangelical friends are hearing about deconstruction and questioning and untangling things and they're like, 'Yeah, everybody goes through that.' But I don't think they understand that it means every single aspect of my faith life, which is a really big part of who I am as a person, it's pretty much crumbled and it isn't rebuilding yet. There is a solid foundation that still stands, at least for now. Will I get to a place where I eventually let go of God? I don't know. I sure hope not. But I'm still open to the fact that deconstruction, I don't think, is something that you can predict how it's going to end.

For Matt (Australia) and his family, working in overseas mission had a similar effect. I'm well aware from my own experience that when things go sour and you're far from home with a mission organization, you can be terribly isolated: the organization can be your whole world, with very few 'outside' friends nearby:

The organization turned out to be a pretty toxic place. None of the old things worked, like prayer, reading the Bible. Those things were more triggers now for spiritual anxiety. Going through that spiritual trauma made me question, like, these people that are in power, people saying this is how it is, they're not operating in a way that is good. It's actually hurting a lot of people, so how can I trust people that are in power to tell me what God is saying or not saying? So finding God within and actually trusting in my own interpretation of things, my own self, then not being worried if I do think something different to the others around me.

Matt and his family resigned from the organization, prompting further areas to deconstruct:

Working for the mission organization I had a real sense of purpose and call. To have that totally taken away was really hard. To not be sure what I was doing. I was a music teacher before I went overseas, and then coming back, I found another job as a music teacher and was like, 'Is this what I'm meant to be doing? Who am I?' So that's been really hard in the process as well. Those existential questions become more real.

Charles (USA) also returned from the 'mission field':

I wrestled for a long time with a lot of anger and resentment that I gave my prime years to missions. I'm like 2% of energy and skill on social services. Why the hell did I think I could be a missionary? I'm just not cut out for this at all. I'm 95% mathematical analysis, financial systems. What a misuse of my wiring and my skills.

Shame on mission organizations if they're meeting with a 25-year-old kid. You need to tell them, 'Here's the reality: you might be giving up your prime years, your critical career-building years. Don't do it because we said you should or your parents said you should or your church said you should. This is not your identity. This is not how you get God to love you. Do it if you're passionate about it.' They don't say that because they have to mobilize people, because if they don't, financially, they go under.

I felt like I was the trophy that people liked to put on their shelves and say, 'Look who we sent out. We're so proud of them because they're doing what God's called them to do.' Meanwhile, I'm just like, 'What am I doing? I'm not a good missionary, I'm miserable, but it's what everybody, myself included, maybe even God says I should be doing.' As the spell broke when we transitioned home, it was like, 'I don't know what to do because I have a college degree but I spent the last seven years, in terms of a resumé, doing nothing.'

While Charles has found fulfilling work now, that grief, that sense of having been robbed – perhaps of career or relationships or emotional health – was widespread.

No one I spoke to has stayed in overseas mission following deconstruction, but there were several church leaders who have remained in position. They have had to completely deconstruct the basis of what church is. Amanda (USA) says:

This is really what they said to me: 'You're here to keep the front door open and the back door closed.' That opened my eyes to see, like, what are we doing? Are we connecting people to God? Or are we connecting them to the church? And who is benefiting? If the Church ceased to exist as we know it, like the institution, what would people's faith look like?

I'd been giving myself to this church for almost three years, and when we left, we retained two friends. That doesn't look like Christianity to me.

George (Australia/UK) has experienced both mission and church leadership. I ask him what his deconstruction triggers were:

One of them was the move from the youth mission organization I'd been part of into the Anglican system. My kids are the same age as we were when we were in missions and I'm replaying the stuff that was either told or implied or pushed at us. There's no way I would push my kids in that direction.

So there was that shift away from crazy, spiritualized, almost occultic charismatic practices, which I didn't realize they were until I found myself in a more academic environment where I actually had to think. My first year at Bible college was confronting all the assumptions that I'd made about what church was like and what faith was about. Critical thinking came in.

The second big shift was when we church planted, but that ended with me having a breakdown, so suddenly, any sense of positivism, any sense of 'follow these spiritual laws and you'll have success' wasn't there.

I've been trying to work out whether I can disconnect church from God. My deconstruction isn't so much epistemological but about church. It used to be deeply in me that I longed for the Church of England to come back to life and be filled with the Spirit, but now I walk around and go, 'What if this place burned to the ground?' That might be the right thing. We may be worthy of being burned to the ground. I don't think it's fixable through programme or bureaucracy. If you try and fix it through bureaucracy, you'll just hurt someone else.

The faith that I hold to, I hold to for experiential reasons fathomed in the depths of breakdown. So I don't let go of them loosely, but I don't impose them. At the same time, I know what it's like to be in the place of unknowing.

Caro (Australia) has managed to lead her church through a process of deconstruction, but that doesn't mean that everyone has been on board at all times:

Having to lead a church at the same time is undoubtedly the hardest thing. My husband has been deconstructing alongside me but he's had heaps more permission to give up on things or chuck them out or simply stop and not care. Because of my role and the fact that I'm wanting to love the people that I lead who are very different to me and need a different thing, I haven't had as much permission to just go, 'Stuff the whole thing, I'm not reading my Bible again for five years.' I have had to preach even if I'm not really reading it and I don't know if I believe this thing today. It's a loneliness in the church world. I look around and I wonder who else is doing this.

I haven't really read the Bible for a very long time, apart from preaching from it, and I have not preached out of the Old Testament for at least six years and I'm not sure if anyone's noticed. I have had to work it so that the only things I preach on are things that I can preach on, so we've spent a heck of a lot of time in the Gospels.

It's hard work to repattern your brain when you thought one way for a very long time. I totally understand people who just say it's too hard, I can't do it, I'm done. Sometimes people need to do that, they need to get out, they need to let go of God. But that hasn't been my path. I've chosen, for whatever reason, the road of trying to find a more beautiful faith.

Actually, you know what else has been hard? The levels of rage in me towards other Christians who aren't deconstructing, who still believe the old things or don't even ask questions or who want to tell me I'm wrong. That has been hard to manage. I don't know if that reveals something of my own immaturity!

Yes, me too, at times, and I have to remind myself of where I was not so long ago. It is also an indicator – a projection, perhaps – of my anger at myself for having believed things for so long. For Ronnie (USA), also a pastor, it points to something else:

The times when I've been angry or, 'How could they have done that to me?' or, 'Why are these people still so retrograde in believing this way?' What I'm actually dealing with is grief, the loss of relationships and friendships. I thought they were stronger and deeper than that. I thought they were based on love for one another and what you realize is those were all transactional.

For others in leadership, deconstruction has cost them their livelihood. Jude (Australia) asked questions about the status quo:

It's been devastating and freeing. It's hard to untangle both. I think the trauma, from being excommunicated and fired unjustly and the spiritual betrayal, led to a dismantling and fragmentation of everything. This was my community. This was my job. I invested years of study. I'm still unemployed.

The hardest part was losing a sense of God. No longer living in a God-soaked universe. There's a short little snippet in Jeremiah, 'You have deceived me and I allowed myself to be deceived', and it was a fierce wrestle with this sense of, 'Who even are you? If you are mother and father, what sort of mother are you that you would allow this to happen? What is the nature of divine protection and unanswerable questions?' And following the mystics, the way of unknowing, becoming wordless, losing prayer, and then the giving over and being found by moments of grace, sunlight through the trees and a glistening spider web. It's a vaster, safer, more confusing and unsafe kind of universe, but this is where I am. Sometimes I wish I could go back to something neater. I'm tired of it being so hard.

Liselotte (Denmark) tells me about her career:

I studied theology and I still love theology. I eat theology for breakfast. The only thing you can do with a degree like that in Denmark is to become a vicar, really. I was a genuinely happy one for two years. It's like the cartoon where Donald Duck runs on the bridge and has not discovered that there's no bridge. I was actually doing quite brilliantly running on that bridge until I discovered there was no bridge.

If I have to pinpoint something it was doing a funeral of a young lad who had committed suicide. It just struck me so much that the liturgy that we had is just baloney. It's just a bunch of stupid words. You could say any liturgy, any theology, would not do the job in a situation like that. There are no words. There are no nothings that can embrace that situation, can hold us. I know that, but it seemed to me that we had no solidity in the theology just to hold these things. I suppose the absence of God as well.

It's very bodyless, because all we bloody well need is our ears and our brain to process what we hear. Having had 500 years of that in Denmark, it's been completely corrosive. There's nothing left of whatever corner of Christianity that takes the body seriously. There are no praying practices, there are no nothings. It's a poverty-stricken theology or practice or liturgy.

I finally stopped after seven years and I cannot tell you the things I've done in order to try and make a living not being a vicar, which is difficult when one is a theologian in Denmark.

In Australia, Andrew faced a similar problem:

I literally woke up one morning with these thoughts going through my head, all these different little issues that I'd thought about and struggled with for a long time: biblical, philosophical, worldview issues. It was as if I'd been managing the cognitive dissonance around them for a very long time, and suddenly it was like the Jenga tower, where you pull out enough blocks and the whole thing collapses. I call it a reverse epiphany. I just couldn't believe anymore that 20, 21 million of us had some sort of monopoly on the truth and everyone else who believes they have a monopoly on truth is sadly misguided. A lot of things crumbled, and I was left with a sense of, 'Wow, so what do I believe? Who am I?' And that was really traumatic. What do you do when you stop being an Adventist, when you're so immersed in that culture, when your life is enmeshed at every turn? How do you disentangle yourself from that? What does it do to your identity? How do you then get along with your family? I worked for the Adventist Church. I was quite involved in my local congregation and all my friends were from the Adventist faith as well.

I've been putting feelers out with different groups that I wouldn't have had time to meet before. My wife and I have also had time to go out to garden nurseries and cafes and weekend markets. It's been good for us as a couple to have that extra time to spend together.

While Andrew's marriage has strengthened, others have found this is a deep source of pain for them. Ed (UK) tells me, 'Not everybody deconstructs as a couple. My wife remains a strong, conservative charismatic evangelical, and this is a journey I'm taking by myself.' I ask him how he navigates deconstruction in this context:

Quietly, with headphones. It's the unspoken in our relationship that is really harsh, to be honest. Pretty brutal. She said very clearly that if I officiate a gay marriage, she'll divorce me. I don't think she would, but it's the simplistic thinking that's being threatened. We've lost that symbiotic relationship that we used to have in terms of Bible study, praying and things.

It is more complicated because I'm ordained, and therefore people look at me with a certain amount of expectation and a certain amount of 'You will think this because you look and feel a certain way.' I had a bookcase full of books that told me what I should think. I would buy a book to reinforce that worldview or that particular position on a subject. What I'm finding now is I don't want to read them anymore. I jettison books that tell me what to think and incorporate books that allow bigger questions. I really opened myself to hearing from people that were different from me, going to those places of challenge, going to those places where it would be hard or difficult and hearing what they and, in turn, what God was saying. I rediscovered Celtic spirituality; that's now an important part of my daily life and my faith walk, and by getting more involved in Celtic spirituality, things like original sin will get challenged. But if I go down that road, it then challenges me: why do we use the liturgy that we use? So what word now, and what do we mean by 'sin'? What do we mean by the need for forgiveness or repentance?

The real question that I've been asking throughout this time is who am I? Where do I stand on certain things? What is sacred to me? I was transitioning through simplicity into complexity. Nowhere near harmony. It was all chaotic and stressful. I was really quite poorly, lots of mental health problems, lots of really bad coping mechanisms as well. As a leader in the Church, you are just on your own and it's not healthy. Feeling alone as a leader, that's probably been the number one thing.

The other side of this are the clergy spouses who deconstruct alone. Katya (UK) is one of them:

I am in an ostensibly Christian marriage with a Christian leader, and I absolutely categorically don't believe or subscribe to anything that he preaches, teaches or leads on. But I love and support him, and he loves and supports me. So we're trying to navigate this ambiguity, like a vehicle with two different wheels of different shapes and sizes that's still managing to bumble along. We've had to do that groundwork inside a marriage, to go back and sweep out a lot of stuff and make space for this new expression of what it's like to have completely polar beliefs from one another yet to still be able to hold each other in a respectful stance and to let each other be and breathe and not be co-dependent.

We're raising the children in a safe, neutral environment, so we don't do prayers at bedtime, we don't do grace, we don't do anything. There's a couple of crosses on the wall, but very rarely do we do anything as a family that puts Christianity as our primary religion. We talk about faith generally, we talk about mythology as well, and we talk about stories. My daughter loves history and ancient monuments. We talk about what those people believed and how people have always yearned to find meaning in their landscape and their environment, and to cherish that through the building of monuments and the writing of stories. I find by doing that, I'm healing myself by rebooting the narrative away from 'this is the truth, and everything else is a lie', to 'there's a multiplicity of ways of expressing the spiritual aspects of being a human'.

Sundays will never be safe for me until my husband doesn't have to go and do the thing that I had to go to for years and years, and we can do our own thing. We are in a very precarious position because of the decisions that we've made to throw our lot in with the Church. We're realizing that we need to build an escape route, but we're going to have to do it very carefully because there's right ways to leave ordained ministry as a family and then there's traumatic and devastating ways to leave it.

I think once you've deconstructed in the midst of this, you learn how to survive in really tough situations, and one thing that I have in spades is resilience.

Still others find that marriage itself triggers faith questions, particularly those impacted by purity culture and complementarianism:

For me, initially, it wasn't intellectual. It was entirely about my marriage because we really didn't have a healthy relationship. The first thing that really started to make me question things was our sex life was not working. At all. We both came from a purity culture background: you don't have sex until you're married, you don't live together till you're married. Looking back, I realize how many of the issues we had, we would probably have discovered had we lived together. When we had to talk about it, my wife said, 'Maybe some people just don't fit. Maybe it just doesn't work.' I think that was the first puzzle piece that was like, 'But if that's true, then this doctrine is actually a really bad idea.' Then my deconstruction started taking more speed when we got divorced.

Eventually I met someone that I fell madly in love with and she was not a Christian. There was just this fundamental compatibility and love there in a relationship that doesn't fit in the Christian box but was better than any other relationship I ever had, and it was everything I had ever wanted. So it was like, 'Wait, I did everything right and my marriage failed and it wasn't healthy for either of us. We had a miserable sex life. And as I've let go of that, now I have the opposite.' It just started to unravel from there, really.

I have a healthier, much more equal and down-to-earth relationship without anyone telling me what a healthy relationship has to be or can't be. (Josias, Denmark/Finland)

A phrase that came up again and again was 'cognitive dissonance': as Josias experienced, it's that itchy feeling that what we believe just isn't matching up to our lived experience. For Tessi (USA), this had real consequences for those she cared about:

I was working with kids that had been victims of abuse of all kinds, had behaviour problems and emotional problems, and God didn't fix any of that. That was the initial trigger for me.

Christine (UK) explains how it impacted her:

I got linked up with a group in London and we would worship all night and we had a lot of focus on the supernatural and the imperative to take the gospel out onto the streets. I had some intellectual doubts about the theology: what actually happens when you get redeemed? Why does it make a difference when you say this prayer and now you're 'in' and otherwise you would be 'out'? And various things that didn't make sense, like God is both loving and just and that's why he has to send people to hell. That stuff never cognitively made sense to me, but I got caught up in feeling like I was part of something. But as time went on it became harder to sustain that sense of 'there's going to be a revival and God's going to break through' and all that anticipation that you're believing for. It was intellectually unravelling because I felt that cognitive dissonance between my experience and the mantras that I was repeating and trying to hold on to.

Eventually I just said to God, 'I can't do this anymore. I'm not going to keep trying to pursue this and trying to believe. If you still want to have a relationship with me, you do something.' Three months later, I suddenly realized that nothing had happened.

In London, the reality is that people are coming and going all the time, so it's easy to slip away and people don't even really notice. That was disappointing because a lot of the talk was, 'We're a family and we're really close and we're a community.' That's all true if you're present, but if you just don't turn up, then you're just not a part of it. So actually, physically speaking, it was very easy to leave. I did have a couple of people who slightly condescendingly said, 'You'll be back, you're just having a season of doubts.'

One of the things that made it scary to leave was this idea that the world is a terrible place and everything out there is really depressing but Jesus is the one that gives us joy. So I had to learn that there is good in the world and not to be scared of the world. It's, 'People are just drowning their sorrows because they don't have God', but I realized that that sense of joy I used to experience of like, 'This is the presence of God, isn't it wonderful?' that wasn't exclusively because I had God. Even finding joy in the context of life not really having any objective purpose, being OK with things being temporary and not really knowing what life is.

Back in my charismatic days, I was either really high or really low. Fear and shame are just not really problems for me anymore. I suppose I've sacrificed the blissful highs that I did have. I thought it was always synonymous, that God is joy, so you couldn't give this up, there is nothing else. That's when I start to think of it as more like a cult because I thought, 'This has set itself up so that I cannot leave because it's given me no other option. It's told me that I'm part of a body, so I can't survive apart from the body of Christ. What is a foot if it's not attached to the body?' all those kinds of metaphors.

It was a new experience for me of feeling how my body actually feels rather than telling my body that Jesus has saved it. I struggled to talk about my emotions or even to name them. Now I feel more connected with my body and if I feel sad or stressed, I will acknowledge that and in time, it will lift, it doesn't need casting out like a demon or rebuking. It's been a journey of learning to be kinder to myself, and particularly to my body.

Sue (UK) faced several hardships which pushed her towards uncertainty:

I got to the stage where I just wanted to be able to ask questions, and I didn't want the answer: I wanted the question to be valued. Faith is about the question. It's not about the answer and being given a scripture that ties it all up in a parcel for you.

On a different continent and in a different stage of life, Hope (USA) hit a similar point:

I remember exactly where I was sitting. I was 27 years old, and I was reading John 6, when Jesus is speaking to the Pharisees saying that, 'You search the scriptures looking for life but you refuse to come to me.' I realized that the Pharisees were convinced that they were right, yet they were wrong to the point that they murdered the person that they believed that they were following. I really felt the weight of that.

I was tired of being in an echo chamber where any question that I asked, I would only ever hear the answers of why Calvinism or evangelicalism is correct. So I decided I was going to listen to the people that I've been told were heretics, because I just wanted to hear what someone who actually believes something different thought about it. I decided I was going to ask one question: what if what they're saying is actually true? How would that change the way I think about things? That pulled out the pin of 'God has to punish sin', and everything that I knew about the gospel unravelled. Allowing it to unravel and feeling safe in the midst of it unravelling is what completely transformed my relationship to certainty. I've been shocked to find that as I hold my hands open with what is true, it feels like I'm finding the love that I always believed was possible in the person of Jesus, but finding that everywhere.

How certainty and truth are seen shifts during deconstruction. Wendy (USA) explains it well:

I remember having this thought, 'What if it isn't absolutely true that Jesus is the saviour of the world?' and I consciously said, 'I cannot handle going there. That's too derailing for my entire existence.'

I saw truth and reality as like a stone wall: it's real, it's there, it's true. Then over time, I moved and realized it's like the constellations: it's actually different things littered throughout the landscape, and because of where I was standing, it looked like they were all one solid thing, like there is meaning and sense to this just because it looks like it from this one singular place where I'm standing.

I remember sitting on my couch right around Christmas 2012, and I was like, 'Thank you, Jesus, for being with me this whole time. And now I need to say goodbye because I know you're not real. I don't know how to handle the fact that I felt like you were real and I know that I had lots of moments where I felt really special and I felt like I talked to you and felt your presence. But you not being real feels more real to me than you being real, and so I need to say goodbye.' It was a relief and also devastating at the same time.

Gordon (UK) is another person who spoke to God about this:

I'd come to the conclusion that I didn't believe it anymore, so I did the obvious thing and I knelt down to pray and said, 'I'm sorry, God, I don't believe in you anymore.' And then God spoke to me and the words were, 'Don't worry about it. I don't believe in myself, either', and I realized that God's got a really wonderful sense of humour and, of course, it was my sense of humour.

What was best of all was standing up after that and looking out through the windows with the mosquito netting there. The sunshine was amazing in the tropics. The greens were amazing, the sky was blue, the birds all were singing and the monkeys making noises and the cicadas – it was just such an exciting world.

I realized that my life was mine, and if I wanted a purpose in life, it was up to me to create it. I didn't have to have a God telling me what I had to do. It was much more exciting than that. A whole load of weight fell off my shoulders. I was surprised: I didn't realize I was carrying that much weight, actually. Like breathing air for the first time.

Others do retain a faith, although much changed. When David (Ireland) sold his business, he found himself at a loose end and, in his words, 'driving people crazy'. His wife and adult children were delighted when he told them he was going off to spend six weeks walking the Camino de Santiago:

It wasn't a particularly spiritual thing for me; it was to go and think. But from day one, it was obvious that that wasn't going to happen. I could almost hear God say, 'OK, now you're alone we're going back to the basics.' And my Christian life is not working. It doesn't make sense. It's not sustainable. So I went right back to the basics and just living and breathing and being in nature every day and then suddenly realizing that God – can we still call God 'God'? I don't know, but I'm too old to change – but my image of God was completely and utterly wrong and how I managed to get to the age of 60 and not realize it was baffling, but the whole image I had of God was an unkind judge being volatile and judgemental.

In very quiet and subtle ways, when I started walking and talking to other people of all different faiths or no faiths or Hindus and Buddhists and just everybody, I thought, 'This is amazing. God has created such an amazing, diverse world and even looking at the exuberance of nature. How can I possibly have maintained that image?' Gradually over the next few weeks it began to dissolve and disappear. I've never gone back since then. It was an experience of God everywhere and in people that I met and the stories that people were willing to share.

The arrogance to think that we can put God in a box, that we have the answers, we know what God is, and that we can make the Bible do what we want it to do. We can get those verses and lock and load them and aim them and do whatever damage we want.

I suppose, like most people, I've less answers now than I ever had, and I'm very comfortable with that. I don't need answers. I'm content to leave those things to God or whoever. In various stages of the last two years, I've had these arguments in my head that I would have with my right wing fundamentalist evangelical friends and family members, but I'm not bothered, because they'll have all the weapons and be ready to aim and fire. And do I need that? I don't. And am I able to convince people? Not really. I'm not interested in evangelizing this new discovery.

The last few years, for the first time ever, I think my faith has actually transformed me properly. I can look back and say, 'Am I a kinder person than I was three years ago?' Yes, I think I am. I'm more loving. I'm more at peace. I mean, it's a journey, obviously, but if that's the fruit of the Spirit or whatever, then yes, that is a demonstration that the journey I'm on now is the right one and the journey I was on before was the wrong one.

I began to realize the sheer impossibility of a God who is supposed to be love having this narrow view of what it is to be saved and the view of spending eternity with only born-again evangelical Pentecostal Christians. On the daily walks on the Camino I felt layers of stuff piled on myself over the years just being stripped away and just getting back to me. It was a revelation to me that the way to find God is to find myself.

I'm really excited about life in a way that I never have been before. I'm enjoying every day. I'm enjoying getting up and I'm enjoying having – I wouldn't call them quiet times – but just being still and I'm actually enjoying reading the Bible again. It's quite a revelation when you read the Gospels and really hear Jesus' message in the raw state. It's very different than what we've been taught. Having got rid of a lot of the toxic stuff that was there, I've rediscovered God for me.

Kathy (USA) also found freedom and new life:

I was afraid of letting go of that certainty. I was afraid of letting go of that identity. I didn't want to be an atheist: I'd had those experiences that taught me there was something outside of myself that is real. I didn't want to suddenly find that I believed that I was just a lot of synapses. So that was really hard. Leaving the church wasn't so difficult because I was bored out of my mind and I didn't have good friends there because everything was such a surface interaction.

The first day that I didn't go to church was because my daughter invited me to go hiking with her. It was the first weekend in January and it was a stormy, rainy, windy, horrible day and we went up in the mountains and we went to the waterfalls and it was cold and wet and miserable, and it was one of the best days of my life. I thought, 'I'm skipping church and doing this instead, and I feel so alive. I never felt like that in church.' But walking in the awful cold, soaked to the skin and teeth chattering, I was exhilarated, and I thought, 'I want more of life. I want to do things that are unexpected. I want to choose for myself how I spend my thoughts and energies and not just follow a pattern that's set for me and I'm guilted and shamed into it.' My daughter took a picture of me. I was just looking up into the waterfall and feeling the mist on my face. I keep the picture on my desk to remind me this is how it feels to really be alive.

Counting the cost

No one deconstructs decades of faith, identity, belonging, church without cost. When I asked people what had been the hardest part of deconstruction, the thing mentioned most often was the isolation and loss of community, which is unsurprising when churches can be – or claim to be – such strong communities. The people who are still in church don't get you and the people who've never been in church don't get you either. As Matt (UK) put it:

> Church is so linked to community and friendship group, so when you lose faith, you don't just lose faith, you lose friendships and community. 'Belonging before you believe' is fine if you haven't made a commitment and they think they're going to fish you in. If you do it the other way, though, if you have belonged and then you ceased to believe, it's a very different experience.

Russell (USA) is a recovering addict whose poignant reflection points to the bittersweet nature of deconstruction:

> Tonight I am going back to the recovery ministry to celebrate a friend who I saw come in for the first time as an addict facing jail and losing her kids. She gets her five-year chip tonight and I am very proud of her. What sucks is I know I am going to be fighting back tears tonight. I miss the friends, the music, the hugs and laughter. I miss a sense of community and belonging. I miss the love of God and the security of knowing he would catch me when I fall. I just wish I still believed.

As I listened to story after story about people's isolation, and as I consider how some of my own friends have reacted to my own deconstruction, there is a widespread pattern of refusal to engage or listen; of simultaneously deeply well-meaning and deeply disrespectful words; of rejection and ostracism by Christians towards those who deconstruct. Steve B. (UK) tells me:

> I feel very isolated from my church. People who have never taken any interest in me whatsoever, now I've stepped back from worship and I've criticized the church, all of a sudden they've come out of the woodwork and I feel like I'm just going to be a notch on their Christian bedpost, like I add some messiah points to them or something. It doesn't feel good, because they're not really listening, they're just saying, 'Oh yes, but we're all broken and no church is perfect.'
> I was finding so many holes everywhere. I still haven't lost my faith in some kind of divine presence, but I'm just not willing to get so legalistic about it. As soon as I pulled at one thread, the whole thing came unravelled, and as soon as I started asking those questions, people became very threatened. As soon as I said, 'I don't necessarily believe that the Bible is completely accurate', that was like rolling a grenade into the centre of the community group.

I feel like I lost a massive part of myself. Sunday morning is particularly difficult for me. It feels like silent judgement that I'm not in church anymore, that I need help or I'm wayward or lost, Prodigal Son, whatever. The rhetoric that I had was like, 'Oh, you're deconstructing, you'll come back eventually.'

Laura (USA) found her ability to parent was suddenly in question (particularly harsh, given the emphasis that churches place on women as mothers):

There have been some friends in our church that, when I've said, 'I don't know what I believe, I'm experiencing a lot of difficulty. Can you still see me for who I am?' that relationship feels good despite this. But I have had some very close relationships where people have said, 'I can't trust you to be a good friend to me now, I don't want to be close to you.' Specifically, about how this has influenced our parenting and that being a bad influence on other families. It would have destroyed me a few years ago. It somehow feels manageable, but very, very hard.

I haven't felt huge anger for any specific person in the church because I understand that way of thinking. I have thought that way, I've treated other people that way. The anger for the systems at large has been there.

Perhaps churches are worried that if they give space to those who ask questions, there will be plenty more people who follow. Sharon (UK) was not the only one to realize that she was not as alone as she thought:

It's being made to feel that it's just me and there's something wrong with me that I don't toe the line. When I've voiced how I feel on a one-to-one basis, there's a lot of other people that are still in the church who feel the same way but they don't feel safe to express that.

I lost track of how many people found that their relationships with their own family were impacted by deconstruction, especially when church and family are so intertwined:

I think the hardest point was leaving the church I grew up in. Admitting that you believe something different from everyone else puts you out of the community and it felt like a banishment, like I had to pick, 'Do I accept everything and stay in and loved and I'm given opportunity, or do I strike out and leave that behind?' That was an incredibly difficult decision because I'd grown up in it and that was my family. You're essentially rejected by your own people. My family love me, but I'm not 'in' anymore. (Liz, UK)

Among people impacted this way were numbers of parents of adult children, like Malcolm (UK):

What's been really hard is both our sons are still very much in that tradition. One is an elder in a New Frontiers church and the other one is the leader, and he is a real Calvinist. He's a lovely guy, but on faith we're on a totally different page. He's doing a Master's in theology and I proof-read his last essay. It was all on violence in the Bible and I got quite twitchy. I have to recognize where I was at his age, though. He's a great guy but that's been really hard.

Some, like Neil (UK), have found that deconstruction shakes the stability of their most precious relationships:

95% of my friendships have been in this church. Even the most understanding and genuine of those friends has let me know that he's praying for me every week, and I know that's not just praying for me to be healthy and to succeed, it's also wanting a conversion. I can't help but feel the judgement in that, I guess, and the disregarding of my choice. And that's a tension.

To my wife, it feels like I've chosen to listen to a podcast that is destructive. I've chosen to look at theology that is outside of our normal, and that's what's been the problem, as opposed to my normal isn't working and I don't want to let go of God but I need something else. It's a really hard thing to communicate. And I get why, because to validate someone else's rejection of God or different opinion of God threatens your own when it's your core identity. I'm not unsympathetic to that.

Do I let my kids go to a Christian summer camp where, at some point in the week, there's going to be a time in the evening where they've had some worship and then they're going to say, 'We're going to choose someone that we know, might be a school friend or family member, and we're going to pray for them to come to know God.' Do I want my kids praying for me at that point and receiving the message and thinking, 'Dad's going to go to hell'? What does that do to our relationship? I can't even start to think about it too much.

Worry for children, and knowing how to parent when the old frameworks and models no longer apply, was a common theme:

There was that pressure, internal and external. I remember friends and family saying, 'What are you going to do about your kids?' That was really bothering me in my own mind and heart, like, am I going to lead my kids astray? (Marc, USA)

Tiffany (USA) has had to re-think all the paradigms they grew up with:

As a parent, it's been really tricky. I married into four kids and I want to parent them in a way that destigmatizes mental health and is sex positive and decolonizes, and they are white, white, white. They do not have even a toehold that I have in indigeneity. I want to be able to raise them with these consciousnesses and awarenesses, but it's hard. I don't want to do what was done to me, I don't want to shame them. I don't want to make them doubt the goodness of themselves, like: you're white and you're a cis boy and you are the problematic population that we talk about, but you specifically are 11.

Oh, and stripping away traditions: do we buy them fewer presents in order to be consistent with our concerns about the world, or are we just making our kids have less fun for our ideology? How do you raise the next generation? It's a clusterfuck, and I don't want them to have to live out my deconstruction of something that they never constructed.

Laura (UK) finds herself in similarly uncharted territory:

You've got no framework for good parenting because the parenting that's been modelled to you majors in discipline and obedience. I do feel like I'm learning parenting from scratch from Instagram and books and people who I respect and saying, 'What the heck? How do I do this in a way that was not done to me?' So that's hard, but also interesting because my kids are growing up without all this baggage. What are they going to be like? You're not going to do it perfectly, but that's OK. You're not having to produce children who need to comply with an evangelical world. You're producing individuals.

Many parents (of any age) started to deconstruct when they saw the impact of certain theologies or attitudes and practices on their children. For Romilly (UK) this had a knock-on effect on how she loves herself:

It does almost feel like there should be like a safety notice on churches, doesn't it, like the way it affects your mental health? In the same way that I will not let my children eat chocolate or I'll make them wait because I know it's not good for them, but then I'll eat some chocolate, I believe the stuff that I wouldn't let them believe. Why is it OK for me, but not for them?

It is not surprising that losing something that has been so central to life and identity prompts grief, even for those who retain some kind of faith. Neil (UK) poignantly explains his perspective:

> I see it as not the loss of God, but the death of God. It's like the death of a mum or a dad, something to grieve. If someone loses a wife and you say, 'Oh, well, you mustn't have loved them anyway', or 'You're better off without them', well, that doesn't cut it. It's a death. It's something that has been loved. I didn't fall out of love with God or Jesus or the communities around that. I didn't fall out of love with those things: they died.

Evie (Australia) echoes this, and highlights the misunderstanding we sometimes face:

> It was my whole life: what's that all about? I just felt hugely that had been a waste, so it was really depressing and very lonely and a real grief.
>
> One cousin wrote to me because he heard I'd been doing yoga and I was really interested in meditation and learning about how our brains work and our bodies respond. I found Buddhism really helpful, especially because they address suffering. And he wrote me this long letter about he's worried I've lost my salvation, he's worried about my spirituality, and it was really horrible. I had to block him.
>
> The hardest bit is that feeling of being set adrift in a vast sea in this tiny little boat, which might be exciting for some, but it was just very lonely and painful.

Her sense of waste is also common, especially for those of us who gave so much time and energy, perhaps our careers, to the Church or mission agencies. For an institution and a faith that claim to give meaning and to centre unconditional love, it's a terrible indictment that so many walk away with a sense of waste. Laura (UK) puts it in the perspective of her most important relationships:

> A lot of people who we thought were friends turned out just to be church friends and were obviously more attached to the church than they were to us. We'd been at that church for ten years. I, in particular, had given an awful lot to that church and the leadership team, the worship team and lots of other ways, spending all of that time and energy, sacrificing time with my young children, my husband, my own self. That sense of regret: you wonder what it was all for.

For me, perhaps the hardest form of regret is guilt for things I said and did in my own overzeal or under pressure from those I respected as leaders. Rachel (UK) feels this too:

> I think back to all the things I must have said to people, thinking that I was doing the right thing or leading them to Christ or helping them see where their life wasn't great. I don't think cringe is a big enough word for it. It's horror. I probably thought I was very loving because I was loving the sinner and hating the sin. It makes so much sense when that's the mindset that you're in and when you believe it's a matter of life and death and hell. I wish I could apologize to those people.

I can definitely relate to Kirsten (USA):

> For me, the biggest part was the shame. I was just ashamed and embarrassed. I was the one that stood up and had the prophecies and did the interpretive dance. I did it all and I'm so ashamed of it.

Everybody does things they regret in life, but when you slap God's name on it, there's an added layer of egregiousness. There is such a fine line between my guilt and responsibility as an adult, and knowing that I had been trained since I was a child to 'lean not on my own understanding', to obey my leaders above my own judgement and intuition and 'outsider' voices. Where am I complicit and where am I not? What does it mean to be culpable when the whole system is entwined with toxic elements?

Liberty

On good days I can see the complex mix of good and bad, opportunity and waste. Despite feeling disconnected from her family, Sally (UK) has also found positives in her experiences:

> I am genuinely grateful for the breadth of living in other cultures when I was growing up and seeing how wide and rich the world is, and the example of my parents doing amazing humanitarian work. Dad restored sight to thousands of people and that aspect was very positive.

Gary (Canada), now a playwright and atheist, has found ways to draw on his experiences in a mission organization:

I have no disdain for my time there at all. I think it was a training ground for who I am today. So many other friends who were there think they had ten wasted years. I had a masterclass in listening to that deep, quiet voice that you can create from.

I guess I don't have an emotionally scarred relationship to my Christianity. It's like a healthy relationship with my ex, and God is my ex.

For all the difficulty, grief and loss, deconstruction is, for the vast majority of people, lifegiving and liberating as well:

After the initial panic, that loss of direction, it's really freeing just to be able to live for simple happiness, care about the people you want to care about, and it's actually nice to have that smaller life without feeling that constant pressure to fulfil a purpose.

All the things that they say, you know, 'You'll never get true joy or true whatever outside of the Church': no, actually, you can have real joy just from having relationships that you're really comfortable with and doing things that make you feel happy. (Holly, UK)

The freedom shows up in a variety of ways, from greater cultural input to a wider diversity of friendships. (Malcolm (UK) mentions something echoed by a fair few others: 'One thing I have noticed – and probably shouldn't confess to – is that deconstruction made my language a lot worse. I never used to swear so much.') Nina (UK) has noticed the spread of freedom across her life:

I remember them sending us the statement of faith and saying, 'If you can't sign up to this, just admit that you're having a crisis of faith', and I remember thinking, 'No, I'm having an awakening of faith, this is no crisis. This is magical, I feel amazing. I feel so much freedom, I can see beauty in the world. This is no crisis, but you're right that I cannot sign up to this.' So then we left.

It's hard to separate deconstruction from healing and trauma recovery because what I deconstructed was abusive theologies that caused harm. The best thing about that is finding a sense of healing and freedom and a sense of peace with myself, that I'm OK.

In the last two or three years, we've been deconstructing what was handed to us in terms of what marriage is, looking at our relationship, how it formed, what are the messages we're taking on that are unhealthy relational dynamics? That's been good to learn about a healthy emotional life and healthy relationships and how to change individually and together. I feel really grateful for that.

The healing and peace Nina mentions is something I have also experienced – a loss of the striving and the sense of never being enough. Eva (USA) puts it this way:

> As quarantine hit and I couldn't go to church, I started to feel better about myself. I don't I hate myself so much, I don't feel like I'm carrying a huge backpack full of crap on my back. I realized it was probably because I wasn't going to church.

Ruth's (USA) story makes me smile, but it also points to that shift many experience – particularly for women – away from only ever caring for others:

> I never spend money on myself. If I would spend money, it would be for someone else. So because I have done so much growing over the year, my counsellor's like, 'What are you going to do to reward yourself?' and I was like, 'You know what? I want to buy the Tokyo Architecture LEGO set, and I'm going to put it together how I like, on my own.' The kids helped a little bit, but I'm like, 'I'm putting it together. You can hand me pieces.' That's just a small thing, but it's something that I was selfish about. No: it was taking care of myself and rewarding myself because I've never done that for me.

The denial of self and constant messaging that 'the heart is deceitful' are the antithesis of self-awareness and a sense of self. Part of deconstruction is developing these and learning to trust oneself: 'Having to really own your own thinking and change some of it and move away from people that you might love and respect, to hold your beliefs in a different way, it's given me a deep sense of self', Caro (Australia) says. This discovery of self has real consequences, as Anne (USA) has found:

> My parents have mental health problems and addictions, so I can see now that totally set me up to crave the message of that kind of Word of Faith, you have power, you have control over everything by the words you say or by keeping your thoughts pure. In church, they kept telling me we're not of the world, we're not bound to the laws of the natural world, which is scary. So deconstructing was really empowering. I finally felt like a strong, capable person who can think, and the world that God created is common-sense.

Mia (USA) also found strength within and around her:

> One of the things that kept me in the church the longest was this idea of
> Jesus got you through all this trauma and abuse and he's going to make
> meaning of all of this pain and use it for his glory, make something
> beautiful out of all of that happened to you. I was even told at one point
> that God allowed it to happen so that it would be used for his purpose.
> Especially for somebody who's been abused, one of the biggest things
> is feeling like you don't have control, you don't have a voice, you don't
> have agency, so to have that narrative continue as I was trying to heal –
> that it's somebody else controlling you and somebody else writing this
> for you – was not at all helpful.
>
> The place I'm at now is really cool because I'm no longer this thing
> that is being acted upon or because God had this plan. That's been a
> really empowering thing to have the narrative switch from 'God healed
> you' to 'This happened and I had no control over it and it was really
> awful, but I've been strong enough and the people around me have been
> strong enough and loved and supported me enough that I'm writing a
> different story now.'

Wendy (USA) tells me how this worked for her:

> One thing I told myself when I left missions was that I'm never going
> to do anything again out of obligation. If it's like, 'I feel like I should'
> or 'I'm going to feel guilty if I don't': no. Because that had been the
> majority of my decisions in life, especially regarding religion.
>
> I didn't have a clearly defined sense of self. I was letting the group
> form my view of myself. The downside of that is if I felt rejected by the
> group or abused by it, then it destroyed my sense of self and my sense
> of identity. I don't ever want that again, but I don't know what's a
> healthy sense of community, really. I'm still trying to figure that out, but
> having cancer has given me an opportunity to think more about who
> and where I feel a sense of community from and to notice that there is
> support for me in places that I didn't notice were there before.

The truth is, as Wendy says, that we do find community outside church,
often in surprising and disparate places. Kirsten (USA) had already started
to deconstruct with her husband when she was suddenly widowed very
young:

> My biggest fear, ironically, was somebody would die and nobody would
> take care of us. And guess what? Somebody died and everybody took

care of us, everybody. Oh, it makes me cry. The Baptists showed up, the Methodists showed up, the Humane Society where I volunteered showed up, the school where I taught, the lawyer, my dermatologist! Everybody showed up. Everybody tossing love on us and protection and care. I have never felt like there was something I couldn't handle because I know that there are all these people just waiting to help me. I was fed the lie that you only got that through church, and that is just bull. It is not true.

The positives are huge: my friendships are diverse. They weren't diverse: I only had other middle-class, white, Christian friends who were raised like me and thought like me. Now I have friends that think way different than me and have different ideas and interests, and that's liberating and beautiful and eye-opening.

A more diverse community has opened out people's view of 'the other' and the world around us, as well:

Treating my neighbour as the people that live physically next to me and being vulnerable with them, because before I had to be this Christian that was fully sorted. Just generally feeling more connected with people, full stop. (Steve A., UK)

Nick (UK) has also found a broader kinship with the world around him:

I'd like to think I'm slightly less judgemental, more open to see goodness in other people. I'm much more connected to the outside world. I'm very passionate about environmental issues because I think deconstruction opens up much more of a nature-based faith that sees creation as good, original blessing.

Joshua (UK) finds this has affected his theology:

Being able to incorporate other people's experiences into my theology has been really helpful for me because it gives you that reflective worldview where your worldview is formed by the other. It's made my faith less cerebral, less cognitive, trying to understand faith in a more embodied way. It's made me accept myself more and allowed me to take a lot of pressure off myself in terms of performative religion.

A changed approach to faith is an inevitable result of a new connection to people and the uncertainty deconstruction brings. I have found that both of these things make me pay far more attention to the world around me, which in turn makes me more present in the every day. Josias (Denmark/

Finland) says, 'The lack of absolute truth is refreshing. I know it could be a bit scary, but the other side of the coin is that freedom and mystery. It's OK that you have to go discover things yourself.' Marie (Australia) finds nuance away from black and white theology:

> I feel refreshed and excited that it's not a faith that is open and shut and has a trite answer or textbook responses to suffering and complex human experience. It feels good to throw some of that out. It never felt 100% right in the first place, for good reason.

There is an overarching sense from most people that, far from 'falling away', our understanding of the divine has broadened in ways we would never have dreamed. Veneda (USA) and her husband found that churches could not contain this expansion:

> We've been to different churches, and we've looked for God, and all the churches said was, 'You can't do that.' God had to be in the box or it wasn't good. But we both knew that God was bigger than what they were telling us, and there was more power and there's more to learn than the Bible. It was time to go.

Crystal (USA) expresses the spiritual flourishing many of us find in different ways:

> More and more I find it difficult to name God because who God is keeps expanding. Something like 'Heavenly Father' feels way too restrictive. How dare I tell God who he is? I am more interested and excited about having a genuine relationship with God now than I've ever been. I feel curious in a way that I haven't ever allowed myself to be before. Who knows where the journey will end?
>
> It also has made me really grateful for each day because when you move out of that mindset that we're only passing through this life and the real life starts when we go to heaven, then you don't take this beautiful Earth for granted, you don't take relationships for granted. I'm increasingly at peace with the idea that if this is all I have, then that's OK. So that makes life a lot more precious.

Despite the difficulties, the benefits of deconstruction widely outweigh the costs. It can take time, fear and heartache, but the freedom, community, sense of authenticity and healing are very much worth it.

Amazing Grace Revisited

It's 2021, and my pen hovers over the religion section of the Census. I don't fit any of the boxes.

> I'm just a seeker now. I have a blueprint of what I believe, but I haven't coloured in all the spaces. It's been 11 years since I've been out and I have less answers than I did when I started. (Veneda, USA)

> The closest label is 'hopeful agnostic' because I don't know if there's a God. It sure doesn't seem like it, but I hope there is. (Ruth, USA)

> My faith remains essential even though it has radically changed. (Ronnie, USA)

> I don't know what this story is going to look like at the end because I feel like I'm still in the middle of it. (Greg, USA)

So where does deconstruction leave us? What do we call ourselves now? What practices do we draw upon? The answers are as varied as those who deconstruct. I'm not sure those are even the right questions for me: I haven't 'landed' anywhere and I expect to keep evolving. Labels seem not to fit this place of uncertainty, curiosity and flourishing. Coming from a place of rigid certainties, it's tempting to try and find the certainties in deconstruction, and yet part of deconstruction is learning to be comfortable with uncertainty. Kay (UK) describes her ebb and flow:

> Sometimes I feel like I'm losing my faith. Other times it's got more of a depth to it because it's more real. I meet God very differently: I meet God in silence and without the hype, but there is more depth to it, and I feel like there is more depth to me. I'm more interested in making the world a better place for everybody, whatever their faith or culture, rather than just converting people.

Perhaps, for many of us, it becomes less about beliefs, more about coalescing around shared values and hopes in a way that is inclusive, and finding ways to live out those values. I can relate to what Helen (UK) says:

> It's a different approach to life. It doesn't matter what other people believe: it matters in terms of beliefs affect behaviours. There's not this epic battle going on. It's just that openness: people are OK, we're not all going to hell, and we can live local, normal lives and not change the world, and that's a valid way to live.

It feels like far less pressure, as does Joshua's (UK) position: 'Comfortable unknowing. I'm trying to reformulate my theology in a way that doesn't exclude any encounters of God, although when it comes to environments that could be abusive, it would have to exclude that', and Tim (Canada) says:

> I'm a lot more motivated by the overarching posture of openness and acceptance, and practices that facilitate healthy community and relationality as opposed to rigid dogmatism. I would still, with a lot of qualifications, identify as a Christian, but I don't have certainty ascribed to the ways that God is or works.

Fran (UK) has also learned a more open faith:

> Increasingly the way I feel more comfortable with my faith is to stop seeing it as one complete coherent system that has to all work, and if it doesn't work, it falls apart. Seeing it as interconnected gifts, almost, allowing the different parts of the tradition to be helpful when they're helpful and to dip into that as you need it in order to get through life and to live well when you need the insight of a tradition.

This openness is also something Liselotte (Denmark) and many others find: 'If my faith is like a river, I get fed by other rivers running into it. I can never be other than a Christian, but without Judaism I cannot be a Christian, and Buddhism has also helped me immensely.'

Those I interviewed are scattered across the gradient colour wheel in terms of faiths and practices, all shifted from where they once were. Simon (UK) describes where he's at:

> I love Jesus more now than I did when I first became Christian. I was a totally on-fire-for-Jesus convert, but I was like someone falling in love with a poster of Kim Wilde. When you fall in love, you project all your needs and wants onto that person without really knowing them.

Moving from falling in love to genuinely loving the person is, in part, a process of loss and vulnerability. God has not lived up to all the things that I wanted God to be when I was 15, as in all-powerful and trans-actional, a very magical thinking idea, but I genuinely love the Jesus that I know now, even though he always makes me uncomfortable.

Louisa (UK) is less sure:

I've got a lot more questions now than I had before, and I still can't work out where I'm going to land with faith. I want some kind of church tie, but I don't want the tie that I felt before. I want my children to have some kind of faith, but I don't want them to have the faith that I had growing up.

Amanda (USA) experiences 'A greater unity with the divine. I don't think about God as much, like I don't think about breathing.' This sense of things being more organic and integrated, less external, is very common, as Christine (USA) has found:

In meditation, I experienced a presence that was unconditionally loving. My experience was I'm held, there's nothing to fear, I can't get it wrong, I'm loved and so is everyone else. When people ask me, 'Do you believe in God?' I will say, 'I don't believe in God, I experience God.'

Sally (UK) has spent years going deeper with this:

It's a lifetime's journey to really listen, to pay attention, to get in touch with what is inside and then to trust it. As it turns out, my gut reactions, my instincts, are very reliable and good, but so often I have not paid attention. I've looked out there for the answer. God was always out there and you had to somehow bring Jesus into your life. I never recog-nized that everything I need is here right now. There isn't anywhere that God isn't. Coming home to myself and my lived experience and taking that seriously has been life changing. I never really saw that the things that I loved in my lived experience *were* the divine in me: my love of music, if I felt loved by a human being.

I don't know whether I can call myself a Christian. I value the Christian tradition a lot and I do follow Jesus: the original person Jesus and how the Church has passed on that message are two different things.

One thing we all experience is an uncertainty. John (UK) has spent decades in deconstruction:

I realize now that there will never be certainty in this life. There will never be an arrival in the sense that I had hoped for. There is a living with questions, and I am persuaded on my clearer-seeing days that there is a great love who cherishes us and loves us and speaks peace and wisdom to us.

The certainty can be hard to part with – it has been engrained and encouraged for so long. Amber (UK) tells me, 'I definitely haven't ended up anywhere yet. It's learning to sit in that place: there's the temptation to build a belief system just to have one.' Louisa (UK) admits that, 'Sometimes I've still got that evangelical nagging voice in my head, which shows how what you experience as a child or as a teenager remains incredibly influential', and Helen (UK) finds herself stuck with old patterns:

> I'm really excited by the possibility of relating to God in a different way and integrating that within myself, but I struggle to connect with God in any way at the moment. There's so much to unpick and unlearn that there isn't the space yet for a very different view of God. It does bring life and a more expansive view of God, but whenever I try and make that space, I get old worship songs in my head. When I try to talk to God, I find it hard to not use male pronouns, or to shift that image. I haven't found the new way yet.

For others, it is an understandable reluctance to lose certainty:

> I don't think I'm comfortable with how much uncertainty I still have. I survived my childhood by being a black and white thinker, right and wrong, good and bad. To lose that was so unsettling. (Phoebe, USA)

> I feel it shielded me. The black and whiteness of those beliefs helped me sail through teenage years because I had quite a difficult childhood. To embrace this theology where everything's really safe: at that time in my life, it was a huge source of comfort and we were cocooned in this little Christian world of loveliness. I don't feel damaged by it in the way other people have because I feel very grateful for the safety net of being in that little community for those formative years. I'm wistful for the past that I had because it was such a happy time, despite everything.
>
> I would summarize my faith as looking a bit like a mosaic now. I really like mosaics; I make them a lot. It's beautiful stuff that's smashed up. It doesn't fit together anymore. It's still lovely to look at, but it's not much use to anyone, practically. I still pray when I'm in difficult situations and I still feel like a very spiritual person. But it's a very private thing: it's years since I've talked about my faith. (Julie, UK)

In losing my own certainties, I spent a while wondering what to call myself now, which group to join. Some may find this necessary: to me it felt like a relief when I realized I didn't have to label myself. Maybe later, maybe not. Matt (UK) told me he doesn't find labels helpful either:

> The most honest thing is to say, 'I don't know, I'm agnostic', but that doesn't feel quite right. It's just another box that seems a bit narrow. Am I a Christian? Sort of. Am I an atheist? Sort of. There are many parts and my job is to not let any one of them win or take the mic, and to be at peace with that.

Part of this is a recognition that this is a process in flux, and that as people we learn over time. Emma (UK) is very aware of this:

> Probably last summer if you had asked me, 'Are you still a Christian? Do you still think God loves you?' I would have said no and no. 'Do you think you're going to go back to church?' No.
>
> I didn't engage with God at all last summer and autumn, apart from the odd, angry, depressed shout. It's only been since the start of this year that I feel like I can start to explore faith again, but it's in a very cautious way. I still couldn't tell you what I believe. At least now, I feel like I couldn't get rid of Christianity altogether. I do want to rediscover my faith and I do want to continue to walk with Jesus in some way. But I just know it's going to be different.

Sam (UK) has pared it back to the essentials:

> I reached the point where I say, 'The bottom line is God is love.' So if it doesn't look like love, it's not God, and you can't be unkind on God's behalf, because that doesn't look like love. That's the sum total of my theology. So much of evangelical Christianity I grew up with is about a search for certainty and satisfaction. Actually, being comfortable with uncertainty is where the freedom is. I don't feel the need to nail my colours to the mast on every issue.

For those who remain within some kind of Christian tradition, of course, the question becomes what to do about church. Emma (UK) is part of a pandemic-related pattern: 'If it hadn't been for Covid, I probably would've felt intense pressure to just find a church, because then no one can talk about you behind your back and say, "They're backsliding", or "They were never saved."' For clergy, there is little choice about attendance, and they have had to find new ways to do this. Mike B. (UK) put a prominent statement about being affirming and inclusive on the church website:

> I've felt much more confident offering my teaching, not imposing, being playful. So many people have left, and I got to that place slowly where I had to let go of worrying about people leaving. When you do it's so freeing.
>
> I have tried to lead the church on deconstruction. When I first came here, we got loads of people from other churches wanting to join and they were a nightmare, on the whole. They tried to take over and we would get, 'You need to pray for Israel', and, 'We need a healing ministry.' Now, we rarely get people because they see our website and they think we're part of the devil, but it's kept a lot of people away for their own sake as well.

Elise (UK) tries to balance the needs of her congregation:

> I've tried to preach into a space that allows repressed things to be thought about. I don't want to burn people's houses down because it's not kind. If that is the space that somebody needs to be in for their faith to continue to serve them, I'm not going to cause harm to that. But equally, if people are in that place where they're pushing against the boundaries, trying to work out how much slack there is, I'm trying to encourage them to ask those questions and to not have it all sewn up.

Ed (UK) finds that an alternative to church brings greater leeway:

> What I like about chaplaincy is it's a level playing field and everything's open. People that I minister to, by and large, are of no faith or have had a faith experience, usually a painful one. I'm not trying to establish a church. I'm ministering into a community of which I am a small part, and there's very few expectations.

Then there are the deconstructed pastors who pick up the pieces that other churches have damaged, like Simon (UK):

> We were going to take Leeds for Jesus and all of that, but the salvation mission of Revive has turned into saving people from losing their faith because of the harmful side effects of primarily evangelical charismatic churches. A lot of my time as a pastor is spent with people going through this exhausting process of trying to find out whether there's even a baby in the bath water that they're throwing out. A lot of these

churches have such a self-enclosed theology of, 'If you don't do it this way, you're not really a Christian', and there's no sense of, 'We can see that this church is not healthy for you right now. Maybe this other group would be good for you to grow', so people come to us with the sense of betraying their community and their faith.

Ronnie (USA) is concerned about not becoming what he has experienced:

We were so fundamentalist that I wanted to be Southern Baptist because they were so liberal! Having been subjected to severe pastoral abuse, I don't want to muzzle anybody and abuse my own position. I think I have more former church staff persons in my congregation than any other congregation for 200 miles. It's a safe place for them.

Of those surveyed, only 20% were still in the church in which their deconstruction began. Those who find a new church have tended to find a more flexible expression, often more traditional, as James (UK) and Nathan (USA) explain:

I tried to go back to my old church a couple of times, but I felt really anxious walking in the doors, so I started going to this Anglican church down the road. They seemed more open on theology. When I turned up, the rector said, 'One of the things I love about the Church of England is you can be sitting next to somebody on the pew who's got a very different theology from you', and I was like, 'Yeah, this will do for now.'

Part of the reason why I like the Episcopal church we go to is because there's not a whole lot of expectations. It's not like an evangelical church where you're constantly getting beat over the head about how you need to be involved in all kinds of different things. It's just like, well, if you show up every now and again, they're happy, but they're not trying to force you into doing things. The church we go to is involved in a lot of social things, but even then, it's not like everything has to be done through the church.

I like the pastor and I like the service. I still want my kids to have a sense of sacredness. One of the things I like about Common Prayer is that people all over the world are reading the same thing, so you have a connection to something that is much bigger than you.

Evan (UK) looks at what church should be:

I'm part of a small church community that is not affiliated with anything. It doesn't matter what stage you're at: you can believe what you want. Surely this is more what church is supposed to be: just a community that looks out for each other? It does social justice things in the community, and there's no judgement or anything. And a lot of what we do is based around food.

Sam's (UK) point is one that churches will have to grapple with, with or without deconstruction:

Church used to be where I got all my teaching, whereas over the last ten years, there's so many excellent podcasts and stuff on YouTube, and the Church as a resource for learning has played such a small part in my spiritual growth. With the pandemic, no one's been to church for a couple of years now, and I miss hanging out with the people, but I haven't missed the rest of it.

The key thing is a greater sense of ease and permission, as Laura (USA) has granted herself:

We are part of an Anglican church, and I don't know what will happen there or what will not happen there. I decided that I will go on days that that feels like a safe thing. Maybe I'll never feel that way again. I don't know, but I haven't made any big decisions, and I feel OK with not doing that now.

Where church trauma or disillusionment is too deep to return to church, there is solace in experiencing the divine elsewhere, as KP (USA) has found:

There is a Quaker meeting near here, and I have my eye on them. We'll see where things go in the future.

Last year, I just went hiking all the time and the gratuitousness in nature makes me remember the gratuitousness of the divine. If I did nothing for the rest of my life except notice that and remind other people that that exists, that would be a faith practice. I wouldn't need to step foot in church, I'd just be like, 'Corn is a thing that exists and we get to consume it, and that means God's amazing.'

This more nature-based faith is a strong theme among those who deconstruct. I'm with Evie (Australia) on seeing the divine in my dogs:

I love nature and animals and the clouds and birds. That's where I meet with God. My husband has found a lot of joy and comfort in the liturgy and in learning about the classic mystics. I'm interested, but I walk my dog at the beach and I have a beautifully overwhelming sense of God and the wholeness of it all. I find loving my little rescue dog, watching the waves, and I've got a tree that I lean against and listen to birds, and I find God more in that situation now. I probably always did but I didn't think that was OK.

The practices around faith have to change, too. Adam (UK) has re-thought how he prays:

I find myself still pursuing the notion that there is a God, but how we as humans interact with God, I'm uncertain, having unpicked the idea of a shopping-list prayer or the interventionist God. I struggle with prayer in the terms that I once thought of it, but value much more times of silence and solitude. I don't approach that as being as transactional as I once did. It's less of a liturgy to get right and more a springboard into how we perceive the world, yourself, life, God.

Bill (USA) takes a more relaxed approach than he once did: 'I gotta say, it's very freeing not to have to think "Did you pray today? Did you follow this step today?" Just living your life and doing it in the most loving way possible is really all that's being asked.'

Many people remarked on how their practices now are more embodied or tactile. Matt (Australia) has chosen something plenty of us find helpful: 'Doing yoga and finding God in those embodied processes, I've had deeper experiences of the Spirit than previously, when I could be singing worship songs and that felt like a very external process, like God being put onto you.'

Plenty of those who deconstruct, of course, no longer identify with Christianity. David (Puerto Rico/Netherlands) tells me about his reaction to leaving Christianity:

I took a bit of an aggressive atheist approach, but I think that was my reaction to it after being inside: I had to fight back in my head. So, like telling people that it didn't make sense and just being annoying. Now, I have some appreciation for religions. I think they have a place in society, although I think they present a lot of dangers, but I met people that are just good people doing good things.

I'm an optimist nihilist, in the sense that I don't think we have a big purpose in life. We are just a blink in space and time. But that's the beauty about it: every single moment is precious and you hopefully enjoy it and can do things without harming others. And that's enough.

Many retain some sense of spirituality but explore paths that feel more true to them. There are quite a few pagans, among other related practices. Kit (UK/Thailand) experiences the Holy Spirit through reiki, and Eva (USA) also found that church was not the only path:

> I started exploring different things, and what I found is that the spirit I could feel sometimes when I was praying or in church, I could feel in shaman meditations and Buddhist ceremonies and out in the middle of nowhere by myself. The Church is trying to hold something that they don't really own or hold.

Katie (USA) set out to find what worked for her:

> I hadn't been to church in years, but something was missing and I thought, 'Well, shit, I'm not going back to church ever again. I will go for a wedding and a funeral, and they better not be mine.' I started going down the religion section in the library – here's Judaism, here's Islam, Buddhism, Ba'hai, and here's the witchcraft, and it was those witchcraft books that felt like coming home. 2015 or 16, I did my first ritual, which was a home blessing, and I never went back. It's so different from Christianity, because the focus switches from this ethereal, temperamental being onto you are responsible for yourself, you bear the consequences. It's an exercise in independent thinking and judgement, but also creativity.

The nature and creativity theme comes in strongly here too, as Laura (UK) has experienced:

> I would consider my worldview to be fairly animist. I maybe describe myself as coming from a Christian tradition, but I wouldn't describe myself as Christian because it's just too much baggage with that label.
> I do a lot of craft-knitting, crochet, weaving, spinning, and I've come to see those almost like a spiritual practice, because I'm participating in the creative force that underpins everything by working with natural materials and creating something, and it feels very much like meditation and connection. Connection is how I see spirituality at the moment.
> Being in nature is the other aspect of that, recognizing myself as part of a larger whole. That's where the animism comes in. When I left church, I felt like I was leaving behind domesticated, agricultural religion and going back to the rewilding, foraging, hunter-gatherer religion where it's a bit wilder and less prescribed.

Jemma (UK) had written on her survey that she identifies with 'post-Christian, neo-pagan spirituality'. I'm intrigued, and ask her more when we speak:

I do not identify as a Christian anymore, but it's a recognition that that is a huge part of my background and the faith I've come from. It feels important to me to recognize that. And then the other part of it is a bit of playfulness. I know it will get evangelicals' backs up, which is quite naughty but fun.

Whatever form my faith has come in has been grounded in my experience of the outdoors, of nature, of feeling a connection with the Earth, and previously I interpreted that within Christianity and sacramental theology. I suppose I've always felt connected to paganism, in a sense, partly growing up in the countryside where there's a lot of remnants of pre-Christian beliefs physically in the landscape and in customs and cultures and rituals, Neolithic sites and stone circles. Deconstructing Christianity and moving into a space where I could be more curious and creative, I started reading more. I wouldn't describe myself as hardcore pagan; it's more the ability to have that connection with the Earth for the Earth's sake, rather than it being interpreted through a male God. So that's where the paganism side of it comes from, and neo-, recognizing that we do not know what they believed and worshipped back then.

In many ways I feel that my spirituality has flourished since coming out of the Church, because it is fully my own, fully connected with me and my body rather than having to conform to a particular way of doing things or seeing myself or seeing the Earth. It's been really liberating to live in that nuanced, fuzzy place, recognizing that you don't have to be decided either way on things and that you can hold different truths and ideas together, even if they contradict each other. It doesn't matter if it's not logical. Being able to find creativity in that has been hugely fulfilling and just fun.

For some, deconstruction has taken their career in a new direction: Lynn (Canada/Ireland) is an ordinand who is finishing her theology PhD; Tessi (USA) is coaching and studying for a PhD on purity culture, and MJ (USA) says:

I run a coaching business where I help women who have suffered under purity culture find comfort in their own skin and improve their relationship with sex. It's crazy to me that I am a person who is no longer a believer. I thought I would be leading Bible studies or preaching. But it's rewarding and fulfilling, and I'm making a difference for people.

Sometimes I think about Amazing Grace, just the inverse of it. I was so frigging lost inside of Christianity. I was a worse person, way poorer judgement calls in the name of Christianity versus outside of it, and so Amazing Grace; I take it to mean I was blind inside of Christianity. I was blind to the needs of the world, to humanity. Now I feel free, now I feel saved.

Whatever path deconstruction takes us on, the fact remains that many of us have lost community, or find relationships changed in some way:

> Most of our friends from the last 25 years have been from evangelical church circles, and I find myself with a sense of distance, not quite wanting to tell them where I'm at now. How much energy do I want to put into maintaining or rebuilding some of those friendships? Or do we just maintain loose links and look for new, deeper friendships else-where with people for whom where we're at is not such an issue? No one's been nasty to us, but it's just that feeling of, 'I don't have much in common here now.' (Heather, UK)

It's one of the biggest questions and one of the biggest things that stop people from leaving churches, especially when we have experienced real, deep friendships. There are plenty of online platforms to connect to others deconstructing, but virtual friendships and single-interest groups will only get you so far (although it's great to find others who understand where you are at): at some point we need real-life community. One of the messages that came through strongly from everyone is that we do find friendships and community outside, even if it is different, and probably more scattered across groups. Certainly my own friendships have become far more diverse in the last few years – there's the friends I swim with; the online book group where I feel safe; the unexpected connections I've found, including through writing this book. They are all sustaining in their own way. Julie (UK) tells me how she felt when she left church:

> I felt like I was letting down a community, but nobody contacted me and it was really eye-opening. So I left church and I joined an advocacy group for refugees and an environmental group. I suddenly felt liber-ated because I can join in the causes that I care about. I met a load of people through that who were strongly humanitarian.

Fran (UK) also joined something they cared about, and their experience points to the insight that deconstruction can potentially bring:

> I was sincere in wanting to get involved in these causes, but a part of it was looking to fill the hole of what had previously given me a sense of mission and purpose. What I find interesting is how often I see similarities between political and progressive causes and church. I joined the Labour Party a few years ago. I went to my first meeting and I got so many church flashbacks. They even handed round a donation basket, and I was like, 'How have I managed to find myself in the exact same organization again?' There's a lot of the same problems of people getting run over from the mission, people burning out because they don't know how to keep going in the long run and people letting their convictions turn into iron-hard doctrines. Actually, through the process of deconstruction, you can have a good perspective that can help you avoid some of that stuff.

For others, coalescing around something they just enjoy can be life-giving – perhaps especially when coming from backgrounds where 'fun' had to be church-based:

> I just get involved in whatever I enjoy doing, like being outside or painting or doing community service, and meet people that way. I have the social energy now that I'm not in church. Not being in church makes me feel like my community is the world. (Eva, USA)

Jemma (UK) has found that the old line that no community can ever match what church provides is simply not true: 'Joining a cycling club, the sense of inclusion and belonging I've gained from being part of that community is so much stronger and more fulfilling than any community I had in church.' Others find themselves taking initiative, as KP (USA) explains:

> What I've been thinking is should I just create the community that I want to have? Anytime I find anybody else who also wants to ask questions about what it means to show up as a human in the world and understand there's something bigger than us, then I find hope. I need to bring more of the threads together in my own life and figure out some way to bring people and ideas together.

Liselotte (Denmark) has helped create a space that works for those involved:

We're about 12, 14 people, never more than that. We're a bunch of Baptists and Catholics and then me and others representing the Lutheran Church, and we do Lectio Divina. I go to church when I go there. It's messy, it's noisy, it's participatory. That's my key word: we all participate. No one is doing more than others. I get to hear how the text that day hits that body. It's so dear to me, even though it is a bit odd and unruly, or perhaps because it's odd and unruly.

With two other Lutheran vicars, I've been doing women's rituals once every year. We have dancing, we have shouting, we have ugliness. We use tactile things: we use water and tear the bread and try to use our bodies doing things that do not resemble the liturgy.

Whereas Josh (USA) has created community out of those who were hurt alongside him:

Four of us co-led a virtual group for graduates from our Bible college that needed to work through spiritual trauma. We have about 100 people, and over two or three years, we were able to create a safe space for people to talk about their embodied stress and anxiety, to share their stories of what they went through, either in Bible college or missionary work and church planting.

The school was particularly harsh on women. We've raised funds three times to help women that were stuck in abusive relationships in other countries where their husbands had control of the email and the bank accounts, and they couldn't get out with their kids. We were able to route funds through their family members to buy plane tickets and set up retainers for attorneys for them when they got out. It's something I would have never imagined doing in another season of my life.

Every so often there is a wonderful surprise. Charles (USA) re-connected with old mission friends and was cautious about explaining where he was at:

Basically it clicked that we were running down the same path, and it was like a floodgate in both directions. I had this feeling that I've been out walking in the wilderness, in the dark, and all of a sudden the sun starts to come up and I realize, 'Oh my gosh, I'm not alone. There's somebody here next to me, that is so exciting.' Then the sun comes up a little more and I recognize who it is and it's not just somebody: it's somebody I know. It's an old friend. It was so healing and comforting that we've had this friend here all along.

Matt (UK) looks to the future for communities once centred around church:

> The thought of getting together with people in the same place runs the risk of recreating some sort of institution that ends up being a different version of what something was before. I don't think I'll ever be part of that sort of organized religion again, but I'm fascinated by questions around faith.
>
> It feels like there is a changing consciousness at the moment; a slow awakening or emergence of a corporate consciousness outside Church. The climate emergency and Covid are causing some people to stop and think about their lives. Traditional churches, and certainly the evangelical churches, are behind on that conversation. They risk not even being part of the conversation. But people of faith or people who've had faith and are on this journey are leading or provoking or encouraging different conversations.

It's a thought echoed by others in and out of church. Deconstruction feels like a part of that bigger thing. As Mike A. (UK) puts it, 'We may be on a journey to a more authentic, loving kind of faith that could be more inclusive and more realistic to our world.'

Bittersweet Hope

It's last weekend, and I've walked with friends to a lake on top of a mountain. The view is spectacular, no one else is there, and the water is warm. I stand on top of a rock, arms outstretched, wind in my hair, wearing nothing but red nail polish. Then I throw myself into the water and feel to my core that life is good.

I know that I'm not alone, that there is a worldwide significant movement of people with lots of different backgrounds who are deconstructing. There is a whole community of hope out there, and it's accessible. (Ed, UK)

I laugh about how 17-year-old me would be horrified by the life that I live now. I am married to a woman, I live with a bunch of atheists, I drink, I like to smoke weed once in a while and I haven't touched the Bible in a year. I would be literally horrified but I'm honestly so happy. (Mia, Costa Rica/USA)

I followed God all the way out of my faith. I never left him; I just got to the end of the path and kept on walking. I believe the God I loved at the end is still smiling at me for leaving her behind and becoming fully myself. (Tiffany, USA)

The stories I listened to for this book were full of tears and laughter. They form a tiny part of a much broader movement of people deconstructing their faith and finding their own way forward. I hope that they provide solidarity, ideas of how to move forward, and courage for the journey, whatever point you are at.

There is no single way to deconstruct, no manual: that's kind of the point. It's a taking back of agency and personal authority; a renewed discovery of self. Anyone who tells you how to deconstruct probably has an idea of where they think you should land and is defining the space for you. While you may see yourself in elements of others' journeys, yours is unique.

You may run into obstacles: the all-encompassing nature of faith and church culture, and what happens when your entire worldview and identity shift and belonging is taken away, means that some turmoil is almost inevitable. You may also encounter trauma: increasingly, the term 'religious trauma syndrome' (Winell, 2006) is being acknowledged. Whether church-based or from theological concepts that stay embedded well after we stop intellectually assenting to them, this is not unusual. Like all trauma, it sits deep in the body, bypassing conscious attempts to overcome it (and not helped by often having denied it for years or decades in church). Liselotte (Denmark) lives with lasting consequences:

> It's been 15 years since I left as an active vicar, and I have bodily reactions when I have to take part. I try to talk to myself and say, 'Come on, you're being ridiculous. Don't react like that.' I know it might sound a bit too high strung and dramatic, but it's been traumatizing: I have reactions that are way too violent really, way too deep, and I think that that was those years of having to bloody well smile and be cheerful delivering the goods.

For some it's hearing a worship song or evangelical jargon; for others it's trying to do what they were taught was right. Eva (USA) has discovered her own road to healing:

> I actually bought myself a new Bible. I was like, 'Maybe this will make me want to read it.' I found when I try to read it, it's like my body rejects it, like, 'No, we're not doing that.' I don't know if it's because I read it so much or if it's because I can't read it without hearing the interpretation that I've always been given that I think is complete crap. So maybe I can do a hard reset for a long time and come back to it after I have explored a lot of things and I can read it on a different level.

People mentioned a variety of things they had found helpful for healing: embodied practices like yoga, drumming and tactile crafts; spending time in nature and connecting with others who understand what you have been through. Podcasts were mentioned by well over half, and authors who would once have been 'dodgy' have been a source of validation and learning to many of us (see Further Resources). The great thing about deconstruction, for those of us who have had proscribed lists of books and media, is that you have your own mind back: you can explore what you want, find healing where it lies for you.

Many people mentioned therapy and spiritual direction, and I know from personal experience that therapy has been vital. However, while awareness of religious trauma is growing, especially in the USA, it can be hard to find a therapist who understands or is willing to learn about your experience. Many people echoed Kay's (UK) words:

> It was hard trying to find a counsellor that got it, because Christian counsellors just wanted to get you back to church. I found a counsellor who wasn't a Christian, but he was just like, 'Why don't you just ditch the whole thing? Why would you carry on putting yourself in that stupid situation?' so then I felt silly. To find somebody that understands that your faith is precious to you but that you don't want all the rubbish that goes with the dogma and church: it's hard to find someone that gets both those things.

Evie (Australia) faced similar misunderstanding: 'I was trying to explain to the therapist and she was like, 'Oh hooray, thank goodness you're rid of all of that.' I don't think she understands the enormity of it, really, the pain of the process.'

If you have been in a coercive environment, it's worth explaining this to a therapist, and asking that they think of it akin to someone leaving a coercively controlling relationship or a cult. And if a therapeutic relationship isn't working for you, move on and find one that does. Even if you haven't faced religious trauma, deconstruction is a huge upheaval and reassessment, and, if accessible, therapy can be useful. As Heather (UK) puts it: 'For the last six months, I've done some therapy-type stuff, and it's interesting how much your psychological stuff is very tied up with a whole load of the faith stuff.'

Amber (UK), whose story we heard at the beginning, continues to work hard to see a slower, deeper healing than the 'breakthrough' kind she once believed in:

> I can tell you all the different evangelical interpretations of the wall of Jericho falling, but I can't tell you who's in the charts. So not only do I feel disconnected and a bit lost around other people, but I don't understand what people are talking about most of the time.
>
> Who am I? Where do I fit? I'm trying not to define myself against where I've been, so I refuse to call myself an exvangelical because that's defining myself by what I've left behind. I'm trying to look forward to who I'm becoming, but it's like starting from scratch. I'm having to dig so very deep to try and find a sense of self. My therapist is a lifesaver.
>
> The fact things worked out with my husband is amazing, and it's beginning to become a safe place to me. It's taking a lot of work. He was always my safe place when we were teenagers, before he got involved

with the church, and we're becoming that very slowly for each other again as trust builds. We're no longer up-and-coming ministry success extraordinaire. We are just us, trying to figure this shit out.

It's exciting, but still, I miss the security of it: I've burned my whole life down. I still have my house, my cats and my husband, but that's all. I have lost my career as well. I'm still not well enough to work properly and I'm literally sat at the bottom with debris around me, trying to sort through it, like, what of this was actually me? Where was I in all of this?

I feel mostly empathy for the people who hurt me, because I see how they were just a product of the system. But I'm learning how to extend that empathy to myself. It's very messy, very complicated. It's going to take quite a long time, I think.

What she says about empathy for those who hurt her challenges me. Anger is valid – even bitterness! But I also have to ask myself how much of my anger at others is justly directed at them, how much of their behaviour or worldview is their enmeshment in a system that gives them few options, and how much is actually my anger at myself and what I was both entangled and complicit in?

Trauma plus a lifetime of certainties are a set-up for continued rigidity of thought: those patterns are set fast in our minds. Online deconstruction platforms and social media accounts, such as those that coalesce around podcasts, can be life-giving and validating – Marie (Australia) says, 'Listening to people in other spaces is so encouraging. I don't know where I would be if I hadn't found some of those spaces and had some of my questions normalized.' I know that I, too, have found healing in some of those communities. However, some can also be robust spaces where black-and-white, them-and-us perspectives continue. As Ronnie (USA) puts it, 'Fundamentalism and the desire for certainty is one heck of a drug, and you can be a fundamentalist along the parameters of whatever paradigm you're dealing with.' Sam (UK) expresses a caution we could perhaps all use:

I'm quite selective over the extent to which I engage in discussions about deconstruction because I've noticed an unhealthy tribalism in the post-evangelical subcultures out there, which I find equally problematic. Any level of fundamentalism in any form misses the complexity and the nuance that is in everybody.

Exchanging one rigid mode of thinking for another dismisses our diverse journeys and risks excluding those who have already been hurt. Simon (UK) pastors those deconstructing, often dealing with church-inflicted damage:

The thing I don't enjoy is the kind of trolling of, 'Well, you're not deconstructed enough.' It's that victim-revenge of, 'The Church has hurt me, and you work for the Church, so I'm entitled to punish you.' You don't know my story and you don't know why I'm still here. You don't know what I'm trying to change from the inside. From a psychological point of view, it's perfectly understandable that there is so much othering among people who have deconstructed, but it's not a good look.

George (Australia/UK) tells me about a negative interaction with a congregant who projected her experience of an abusive youth leader onto him: 'I wear the face of other people's abusers, and that's a really difficult dynamic.' He has been reading liberation theology written in contexts of terrible oppression, and describes what he has learned:

How do you teach people to recognize and ultimately undo oppression? The danger is you teach them to win the oppression game, which flips the oppression, rather than undermining the actual construct – it makes the oppressor the new oppressed. You're not going to heal this by reversing the tables. You've got to take the table away.

Why replicate the patterns we worked so hard to escape? It is up to all of us to be kind to others and to ourselves as we make our way through deconstruction.

It may seem odd to include trauma and new fundamentalisms in a chapter about hope, but true hope and healing do not lie in denial of pain and damage. Nor do they lie in simply forgetting where we have come from and what we learned. Jude (Australia) grapples with holding old and new together:

What do you call yourself when you don't want to identify as a Christian? And yet, that's not really the truth about me. If I push it all away, then I'm not integrating a dorky church kid and a pastor and a stereotypical church family. That's what we were, and now I'm a heretic.

The key word she uses is integration. Nick (UK) had to write a 'spiritual autobiography' as part of a spiritual direction course:

I wrote it as a dialogue between my now self and my previous self at the peak of my evangelical powers. I expected it to be a bit one-directional, looking at myself back then with a bit of pity and embarrassment, but the more I wrote the story, the more I realized there was actually a huge amount that was really positive. I don't remember having as much fun with people. I don't remember laughing as much. There was all the stuff that's the baggage that we've talked about, then there was a huge amount of goodness and life and vibrancy and freedom.

So there's something about needing to integrate with your own self in the past, but it is integration, not looking back at it as, 'That's all bad.' That's just playing the conversion game again: 'I converted from a non-Christian to a Christian and now I've converted to be a deconstructed Christian.' It's not that: it's some sense of being more at peace with yourself in the past.

To me, integration is also a better word than reconstruction. When people talk about reconstruction, they often presume (or impose) a fixed idea of reconstructing to a particular place – usually wherever they themselves are at. When the term is co-opted by those who have not deconstructed, it generally comes with a 'coming back to the fold' meaning. The boundaries are still decided for you: it rarely means 'find your own place of thriving, wherever that may be'.

Reconstruction also implies a journey with an end, a place to land, rather than one of lifelong curiosity and openness and changing as we learn and become more aware. This is a journey of recovering; forgiving and trusting oneself; of re-embodiment; of finding external community and inner voice, and agency within both. Integration feels more inclusive of all of that.

Integration and healing point to hope, too. I asked people where they found hope and thriving now. Mike B. (UK) is one of many who find it in the younger generation who are unafraid to ask questions, seek change, listen to the vulnerable: 'I find hope that the younger generation is so much less racist, homophobic and everything. There's the Church saying, "We're bowing to the way of the younger generation", and I'm thinking, "No, the Spirit's at work in them."' Despite hardship, Ed (UK) says:

I see signs of hope everywhere. If I'm perfectly honest, more so outside the Church than inside the Church. I see signs of hope in the young people who are getting hold of life and asking big questions of themselves. Who am I? What is this world and what do I want to do in it? What good can I bring to it? My son is growing up in an entirely different world to what I grew up in, and I see real hope in him and his generation because they are not bound by the things that I was bound by. But I also see signs of hope in older pilgrims who've done the hard work and blazed a trail for us to follow and are writing books, sharing experiences, leaving signs of hope for us to pick up like confetti along a trail.

Margaret (Canada) echoes this sense of collective change:

> I find hope in the fact that some parts of Christendom are falling apart, because we've become a system rather than a community, and I think if there is a God, God would prefer us to be a community and not a system.
>
> I hope with some of the young adults I know who still have a spirituality, still even identify as Christian, but are doing it in a whole different way than what I and my peers did: community-building, both faith and non-faith, and social justice. I find a lot of hope in that.
>
> With the breakdown of some of these bigger systems, I hope we're doing more sitting around the table, breaking bread together and seeing each other's humanity first and not each other's ideologies or politics. I see signs of that even as I see other horrible stuff.

Sophie (UK) is in her early 20s, a perfect example of this:

> I find a lot of hope in life and the miracle that we exist and how much there is to discover and how there's always going to be more things to learn about. The connectedness of humanity: the fact that we can create social movements and we have the power to change how things are, think about things and critique them and come together and take action and have effects on the world. Especially since Covid: we were able to overnight change everything. That gives me hope that we can do that for things like climate change and dismantling the patriarchy and white supremacy and all these other issues.
>
> I do also find hope in faith and the spiritual, when I think about love and suffering and how they unite us, and the story of Jesus and resurrection. Even the death of plants and stars creates more life, and I would like to believe that's the same for our lives too. I'm still willing to risk being wrong about the story of Jesus and Christianity because I think there's so much beauty in that regard.

Yet the younger generation are not the only ones changing things. Robert (USA) has been doing this for decades: 'Where do I find my hope and thriving? I would say in the progressive movement, of which the gay community is part. I'm very activist oriented. I wish I could be more. Old age is catching up with me.'

Gordon (UK) is one of many who find hope in those close to home:

> We're in contact with all five of our children, all eight of our grandchildren, and we have a loving relationship with all of them, so I get a

lot of my upness from them. My wife is ill, so I'm expecting her to die somewhat sooner than we would like, but we spend most of our time laughing when we're together.

We've just celebrated our fifty-first wedding anniversary and, being very romantic, we bought each other funerals. Actually, I'm surprisingly optimistic. I made one of those PowerPoint presentations that people play at funerals where you have scrolling photographs. I did one for my wife and it was just a wonderful celebration of life: there were pictures of her as a little girl, and when we were getting married, then when we had our first adopted son and there with the son that was born to us, and it went on and on and it was just, aren't we lucky to be alive on the Little Blue Dot? What we've got is unbelievably precious: aren't we lucky to have lived it and to have seen it and be part of this beautiful, amazing place?

There is definitely a sense of hope in coming together and creating something new, as Adam (UK) expresses:

Where I'm seeing hope is in how communities interrelate and how friendships can form. The reflection that lockdown has facilitated: significant portions of the Church are thinking, 'Right, how do we get back on with stuff again?' and I'm thinking, 'Not at all.' It looks very different. It feels quite hopeful to see kindred spirits who are also thinking, 'But what is life about now? What does human flourishing look like?'

Phoebe (USA) also feels part of bigger change:

There are people who have been struggling longer than I have. There are people who are just starting to struggle now and wondering how they're going to come out of this, or will they come out or will they constantly struggle? What has been helpful is to hear other people, not that it happens a lot in person: mostly, it's through podcasts. But it is very helpful to know that maybe God is up to something bigger through so many people going through deconstruction. Maybe this isn't a horrible thing, and maybe we aren't all falling away. Maybe we're onto something that is more loving, more Christlike. Maybe it's time for an enormous upheaval.

Alongside this wider change is the hope that is found in personal change, often hard-won. Amber (UK) herself gives me hope:

What gives me hope is the fact that I have survived all of this, and that in itself is an achievement. I'm still here, I'm still alive and I'm sentient. Some of the kindness I've experienced from people, even just in little moments or in big ways: I see such kindness and goodness in a way that I've never experienced before, just being held in that place of utter brokenness.

I find hope in the fact that life has continued around me. It all sounds a bit existential, but that's the point I'm at. I have no grand narrative anymore. I have no sense of overarching purpose for my life. The most I've got is the idea that perhaps I will come through this stronger, with more to bring to the world, whatever that looks like, but that's a lot less than I used to have in terms of destiny, calling, purpose, mission.

I'm very proud of myself; that gives me hope, that sustains me. I'm proud of my journey, I'm proud of how far I've come. I'm proud of what I survived. I'm proud of my husband and what we've walked through. I'm proud of the decisions I've made at various points, and I'm forgiving myself for others. I've lived a lot of life for someone my age, and it gives me hope that if I can live through this, maybe I can take the rest of life.

So it's not very tangible, it's all tiny little straws of hope here, there and everywhere in the midst of a lot of pain. But it's enough. Yeah, it's enough.

For me, it's a mixture of these: a younger generation who challenge in ways I wouldn't have dared; the old friends I've kept and the new communities I'm part of; enjoying the day-to-day without a sense of the epic; the freedom and flourishing I feel. For all the bitter of the bittersweet, I wouldn't go back to where I was before.

The deconstruction has cost everything and showed me that there's nothing actually to lose because everything that is real is here and is available. For myself I would use the word awakening, and, like in most fairy tales, it's a rude awakening. And yet, why would you want to go back to sleep? (Jude, Australia)

I find hope that, through deconstruction, we discover the things that the faith of our past once promised us.

References

On Fire

Blake, A., 2021, 'The rapid decline of white evangelical America?', *The Washington Post*, 28 July, at: https://www.washingtonpost.com/politics/2021/07/08/rapid-decline-white-evangelical-america/ (accessed 8.11.22).

Butler, J., 2021, '4 Causes of Deconstruction', *The Gospel Coalition*, 9 November, at: https://www.thegospelcoalition.org/article/4-causes-deconstruction/ (accessed 8.11.22).

Watts, A., 2012, *The Wisdom of Insecurity: A Message for an Age of Anxiety*, 4th edn, London: Ebury Digital.

Money, Sex and Power

Cosper, M., 2021, 'The Rise and Fall of Mars Hill', *Christianity Today*, at: https://www.christianitytoday.com/ct/podcasts/rise-and-fall-of-mars-hill/ (accessed 8.11.22).

Lewis, A., 2013, 'Child "training" book triggers backlash', *BBC News*, 11 December, at: https://www.bbc.co.uk/news/magazine-25268343 (accessed 8.11.22).

Lifton, R., 1961, *Thought Reform and the Psychology of Totalism*, New York: Norton.

Linda, H., 2010, 'Quotes from *To Train Up A Child*', *Why Not Train A Child?*, 20 April, at: https://whynottrainachild.com/2010/04/20/quotes-from-ttuac/ (accessed 8.11.22).

He/Him/God

Johnson, E., 1991, *She Who Is*, New York: Crossroad.

Chewed Gum

Brenner, A., n.d., 'Gender and class in the Song of Songs', *Bible Odyssey*, at: https://www.bibleodyssey.org/passages/related-articles/gender-and-class-in-the-song-of-songs (accessed 8.11.22).

Focus on the Family, 2011, 'What it means to be "unequally yoked"', *Focus on the Family*, at: https://www.focusonthefamily.com/family-qa/what-it-means-to-be-unequally-yoked/ (accessed 8.11.22).

Gregoire, S., 2021, 'Is the evangelical view of sex at the root of our sex scandals?', *Religion News Service*, 18 February, at: https://religionnews.com/2021/02/18/ravi-zacharias-carl-lentz-is-the-evangelical-view-of-sex-at-the-root-of-our-sex-scandals/ (accessed 8.11.22).

Gregoire, S., Lindenbach, R. and Sawatsky, J., 2021, *The Great Sex Rescue*, Ada: Baker Books.

Gregoire, S., n.d., *The Bare Marriage Podcast*, at: https://baremarriage.com (accessed 8.11.22).

Happel-Parkins, A., Azim, K. and Moses, A., 2020, '"I just beared through it": Southern US Christian women's experiences of chronic dyspareunia', *Journal of Women's Health Physical Therapy*, 44(2), pp. 72–86.

Harris, J., 2018, 'Read Joshua Harris' full statement on "I Kissed Dating Goodbye"', *ChurchLeaders*, 23 October, at: https://churchleaders.com/news/336098-joshua-harris-statement-i-kissed-dating-goodbye.html (accessed 8.11.22).

Heise, L. and Kotsadam, A., 2015, 'Cross-national and multilevel correlates of partner violence: an analysis of data from population-based surveys', *The Lancet Global Health*, 3(6), pp. e332–e340, at: https://www.thelancet.com/journals/langlo/article/PIIS2214-109X(15)00013-3/fulltext (accessed 8.11.22).

LaHaye, T. and B., 1998, *The Act of Marriage*, 2nd edn, Grand Rapids: Zondervan.

Weems, R., 2004, 'The passionate woman who wrote "Song of Songs"', *Beliefnet*, at: https://www.beliefnet.com/faiths/2004/06/the-passionate-woman-who-wrote-song-of-songs.aspx (accessed 8.11.22).

Perfect Design

Klein, L., 2018, *Pure*, New York: Atria.

Heretic

Bell, R., 2012, *Love Wins*, New York: HarperCollins.

Metcalfe, M., 2020, 'How do words to and for the divine influence our behaviour to each other? Can these words be changed to contribute to the flourishing of all humankind?', PhD thesis, University of Winchester, at: https://cris.winchester.ac.uk/ws/portalfiles/portal/10474737/Thesis.pdf (accessed 18.12.22).

Bittersweet Hope

Winell, M., 2006, *Leaving the Fold*, Berkeley: Apocryphile Press.

Further Resources

In addition to resources and authors mentioned in the References section, there are plenty of other resources that people have found helpful. It would be impossible to list them all, so this is a list of authors and podcasts that were mentioned frequently by contributors:

Authors

Austin Channing Brown
Barbara Brown Taylor
Brad Jersak
Brian McLaren
Christena Cleveland
Cole Arthur Riley
David P. Gushee
James Cone

Kristin Kobes du Mez
Nadia Bolz Weber
Rachel Held Evans
Richard Rohr
Sarah Bessey
Steve Chalke
Sue Monk Kidd

Podcasts

Exvangelical/Powers and Principalities
Evolving Faith
Heaven Bent
In The Shift
Nomad
Straight White American Jesus
The Bible for Normal People
Unchurchable